Parallel Computing: Concepts and Applications

Parallel Computing: Concepts and Applications

Edited by
Sean Brisley

www.willfordpress.com

Published by Willford Press,
118-35 Queens Blvd., Suite 400,
Forest Hills, NY 11375, USA

ISBN: 978-1-68285-479-2

Cataloging-in-Publication Data

Parallel computing : concepts and applications / edited by Sean Brisley.
    p. cm.
Includes bibliographical references and index.
ISBN 978-1-68285-479-2
1. Parallel computers. 2. Parallel processing (Electronic computers).
3. Parallel programming (Computer science). I. Brisley, Sean.
QA76.58 .P37 2018
004.35--dc23

For information on all Willford Press publications
visit our website at www.willfordpress.com

Contents

Preface VII

Chapter 1   **A Brief Introduction of Parallel Algorithms** 1
     i.   Parallel Computers... 1
     ii.   Parallel Algorithm.. 3
     iii.   Models of Parallel Algorithm... 12
     iv.   Algorithm... 15

Chapter 2   **Dense and Space Matrix Algorithms** 100
     i.   Introduction to Processor Arrays.. 100
     ii.   Mesh Network.. 114
     iii.   Hypercube Network.. 124
     iv.   Block Matrix... 127

Chapter 3   **Processing Techniques of Parallel Algorithms**... 133
     i.   Parallel Query.. 133
     ii.   15 Puzzle Problem.. 136
     iii.   Discrete Event Simulation.. 140
     iv.   Dither... 143
     v.   Evaluation... 154

Chapter 4   **Sorting Algorithm: An Integrated Study** 177
     i.   Enumeration... 177
     ii.   Enumeration Sort... 183
     iii.   Odd–even Sort.. 184
     iv.   Merge Sort... 190

Chapter 5   **Search and Selection Algorithm: An Essential Aspect**................................ 202
     i.   Search Algorithm... 202
     ii.   Selection Algorithm... 206

Permissions

Index

Preface

As an important part of computer science and technology, parallel computing refers to the art of performing multiple different computations and calculations simultaneously. Parallel computing has many sub-fields namely task parallelism, bit-level parallelism, data parallelism and instruction-level parallelism. In the present day scenario, parallel computing is being implemented in fields like sequence analysis, mathematical finance, protein folding, etc. This book attempts to understand the multiple branches that fall under the discipline of parallel computing and how such concepts have practical applications. For someone with an interest and eye for detail, this textbook covers the most significant topics in the field of parallel computing.

A short introduction to every chapter is written below to provide an overview of the content of the book:

Chapter 1 - The first personal computers used were uniprocessor systems. These processors could handle just a single task at a time. This limitation led to the development of parallel systems, which could simultaneously process many data and multitask as well. It is a much faster and simpler alternative to the uniprocessor system. The section briefly discusses models of parallel algorithms, its characteristics and benefits. This chapter will provide an integrated understanding of parallel algorithms; **Chapter 2** - Data decomposition is important in parallel computing algorithms. Matrices and vectors are used to divide tasks. Processor arrays are storage spaces that contain elements required for data processing. The chapter strategically encompasses and incorporates the major components and key concepts of dense and space matrix algorithms, providing a complete understanding; **Chapter 3** - A significant amount of time is consumed in a single processing system if a query, which is decomposed into segments, is processed. Therefore, it is easier and time-saving to process a query in a parallel processing system. The section explores the 15 puzzle problem, discrete event simulation and dither as well. Parallel computing is best understood in confluence with the major topics listed in the following chapter; **Chapter 4** - Sorting enables the processing of data in a precise order. Enumeration, odd-even sort and merge sort are discussed in this chapter. Through enumeration, the position of an element can be found by ordering a list. Another technique for sorting is odd-even sort, which compares adjacent odd/ even indexed pair and if a pair is wrongly sequenced, it is switched. The following chapter elucidates the various tools and techniques that are related to sorting; **Chapter 5** - Searching for something in a database is a basic function that a computer performs. People search the Internet for content everyday. A search algorithm performs the required function by finding data in a database. The process takes place in sorted, unsorted and random sequences. The section closely examines the key concepts of searching and selection by algorithm to provide an extensive understanding of the subject.

Finally, I would like to thank my fellow scholars who gave constructive feedback and my family members who supported me at every step.

Editor

A Brief Introduction of Parallel Algorithms

The first personal computers used were uniprocessor systems. These processors could handle just a single task at a time. This limitation led to the development of parallel systems, which could simultaneously process many data and multitask as well. It is a much faster and simpler alternative to the uniprocessor system. The section briefly discusses models of parallel algorithms, its characteristics and benefits. This chapter will provide an integrated understanding of parallel algorithms.

Parallel Computers

The computer era has a very long history

- 1642 – Blaise Pascal's Calculating machine

- 1812-1832 Charles Babbage's difference engine

- 1853-1871 Analytical engine

- 1930-1940 Electro mechanical computers

- 1940- First electronic computer

- 1950s -compact systems

- 1986- till date - Parallel and distributed systems

Uniprocessor Systems

First Personal computers were introduced. These computers were compact,but only could execute one instruction at a time, since there is only one processor. It is a single user system and it is dedicated system. In a single processor system there will never be more than one running process as shown in figure where the tasks task1,task2,task3 and task4 are executed in sequence. If there are more processes, the rest will have to wait until the CPU is free. Further if the currently executing process is waiting for the I/O then there can be a context switch to the waiting process. Multiprocessing can occur in some operating systems. If it is a personal computer then the processes have to run one after the other.

Disadvantages of Uniprocessor System

Sufficient time is wasted when the process waits for i/o. If the system crashes then there is none to replace it. The uniprocessor system provides slow performance. Further the hard drive is small and we can feed only small input data. The same hard drive is used for all the processes and there is a chance that the hard drive easily crashes and the data is lost. There is a limitation to the RAM that can be supported by a PC. One cannot work on imaging and gaming applications with PC. Even if it is executed there will be a lot of struggle. The motherboard of the PC can easily get crashed. This is yet another problem. Next issue is on the power supply. We have to build a reliable power supply. Most PCs are to be supported by the SMPS which again adds to the cost. With PC, database applications cannot be run efficiently. There are limitations to both virtual memory and hard disk. Hence we migrate to parallel systems.

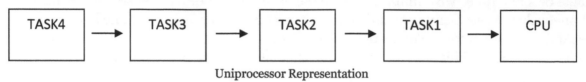

Uniprocessor Representation

Parallel Systems

Parallel processing is much faster than sequential processing when it comes to doing repetitive calculations on vast amount of data. This is because a parallel processor is capable of multi-threading on a large scale, and can therefore simultaneously process several streams of data. The one advantage of parallel processing is that it is much faster for simple, repetitive calculations on vast amounts of similar data. If a difficult computational problem needs to be attacked, where the execution time of program code must be reduced, parallel processing may be useful, which is as shown in figure. Some (not all) problems may be subdivided into pieces. If so, the pieces may be simultaneously processed by multiple processing units. Examples of such divisible problems include graphics, graphs, mathematical problems like sets and signal processing. The advantage is the processing time is reduced, possibly by up to 1/n (for n processors). Another advantage is the power consumption. As the electrical power used by a processor generally increases by the square of its switching speed, power-sensitive applications can reduce power use by compensating for reduced switching speed with additional computing units. For example, halving the switching speed and doubling the processing elements results in half the power use for about the same computing ability. Generally, parallel processing refers to the division of a single computation problem into pieces for simultaneous work, where using multiple computation units for multiple unrelated problems is just multiprocessing. Although parallel processing is often done in a single machine with multiple processors, it can also be done among multiple computers connected with a network. Although most current PCs with 2 or more cores are capable of running parallel processing programs, complex problems, like weather forecast or climate simulation, are often run on specialized computers with many CPUs (possibly thousands). In recent years cluster technology, such as linux "beowulf" clusters, has enabled connecting generic PCs for parallel processing, an inexpensive alternative to expensive special-purpose equipment. In software, the use of threads is a common way of enabling the user program to make use of the computer's parallel processing abilities. A process is a single running program on computer, consisting of a memory space in the computer inhabited by a thread. Modern computer operating systems allow the user to write programs to create multiple threads to achieve the desired goal. It is up to the programmer to create and organize these threads, assure they will not step on each other's toes, and will receive, process, and deliver their assigned work.

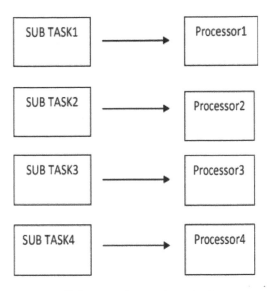

Parallel Processing Representation

Parallel Algorithm

In computer science, a parallel algorithm, as opposed to a traditional serial algorithm, is an algorithm which can be executed a piece at a time on many different processing devices, and then combined together again at the end to get the correct result.

Many parallel algorithms are executed concurrently – though in general concurrent algorithms are a distinct concept – and thus these concepts are often conflated, with which aspect of an algorithm is parallel and which is concurrent not being clearly distinguished. Further, non-parallel, non-concurrent algorithms are often referred to as "sequential algorithms", by contrast with concurrent algorithms.

Parallelizability

Algorithms vary significantly in how parallelizable they are, ranging from easily parallelizable to completely unparallelizable. Further, a given problem may accommodate different algorithms, which may be more or less parallelizable.

Some problems are easy to divide up into pieces in this way – these are called *embarrassingly parallel problems*. For example, splitting up the job of checking all of the numbers from one to a hundred thousand to see which are primes could be done by assigning a subset of the numbers to each available processor, and then putting the list of positive results back together. Algorithms are also used for things such as solving Rubik's Cubes and for hash decryption.

Some problems cannot be split up into parallel portions, as they require the results from a preceding step to effectively carry on with the next step – these are called inherently serial problems. Examples include iterative numerical methods, such as Newton's method, iterative solutions to the three-body problem, and most of the available algorithms to compute pi (π).

Motivation

Parallel algorithms on individual devices have become more common since the early 2000s because of substantial improvements in multiprocessing systems and the rise of multi-core processors. Up until the end of 2004, single-core processor performance rapidly increased via frequency scaling, and thus it was easier to construct a computer with a single fast core than one with many slower cores with the same throughput, so multicore systems were of more limited use. Since 2004 however, frequency scaling hit a wall, and thus multicore systems have become more widespread, making parallel algorithms of more general use.

Issues

Communication

The cost or complexity of serial algorithms is estimated in terms of the space (memory) and time (processor cycles) that they take. Parallel algorithms need to optimize one more resource, the communication between different processors. There are two ways parallel processors communicate, shared memory or message passing.

Shared memory processing needs additional locking for the data, imposes the overhead of additional processor and bus cycles, and also serializes some portion of the algorithm.

Message passing processing uses channels and message boxes but this communication adds transfer overhead on the bus, additional memory need for queues and message boxes and latency in the messages. Designs of parallel processors use special buses like crossbar so that the communication overhead will be small but it is the parallel algorithm that decides the volume of the traffic.

If the communication overhead of additional processors outweighs the benefit of adding another processor, one encounters parallel slowdown.

Load Balancing

Another problem with parallel algorithms is ensuring that they are suitably load balanced, by ensuring that *load* (overall work) is balanced, rather than input size being balanced. For example, checking all numbers from one to a hundred thousand for primality is easy to split amongst processors; however, if the numbers are simply divided out evenly (1–1,000, 1,001–2,000, etc.), the amount of work will be unbalanced, as smaller numbers are easier to process by this algorithm (easier to test for primality), and thus some processors will get more work to do than the others, which will sit idle until the loaded processors complete.

Distributed Algorithms

A subtype of parallel algorithms, *distributed algorithms* are algorithms designed to work in cluster computing and distributed computing environments, where additional concerns beyond the scope of "classical" parallel algorithms need to be addressed.

Analysis of Parallel Algorithms

This article discusses the analysis of parallel algorithms. Like in the analysis of "ordinary", sequential, algorithms, one is typically interested in asymptotic bounds on the resource consumption (mainly time spent computing), but the analysis is performed in the presence of multiple processor units that cooperate to perform computations. Thus, one can determine not only how many "steps" a computation takes, but also how much faster it becomes as the number of processors goes up.

Overview

Suppose computations are executed on a machine that has p processors. Let T_p denote the time that expires between the start of the computation and its end. Analysis of the computation's running time focuses on the following notions:

- The *work* of a computation executed by p processors is the total number of primitive operations that the processors perform. Ignoring communication overhead from synchronizing the processors, this is equal to the time used to run the computation on a single processor, denoted T_1.

- The *span* is the length of the longest series of operations that have to be performed sequentially due to data dependencies (the *critical path*). The span may also be called the *critical path length* or the *depth* of the computation. Minimizing the span is important in designing parallel algorithms, because the span determines the shortest possible execution time. Alternatively, the span can be defined as the time T_∞ spent computing using an idealized machine with an infinite number of processors.

- The *cost* of the computation is the quantity pT_p. This expresses the total time spent, by all processors, in both computing and waiting.

Several useful results follow from the definitions of work, span and cost:

- *Work law*. The cost is always at least the work: $pT_p \geq T_1$. This follows from the fact that p processors can perform at most p operations in parallel.

- *Span law*. A finite number p of processors cannot outperform an infinite number, so that $T_p \geq T_\infty$.

Using these definitions and laws, the following measures of performance can be given:

- *Speedup* is the gain in speed made by parallel execution compared to sequential execution: $S_p = T_1 / T_p$. When the speedup is $\Omega(n)$ for input size n (using big O notation), the speedup is linear, which is optimal in simple models of computation because the work law implies that $T_1 / T_p \leq p$ (super-linear speedup can occur in practice due to memory hierarchy effects). The situation $T_1 / T_p = p$ is called perfect linear speedup. An algorithm that exhibits linear speedup is said to be scalable.

- *Efficiency* is the speedup per processor, S_p / p.

- *Parallelism* is the ratio T_1 / T_∞. It represents the maximum possible speedup on any number of processors. By the span law, the parallelism bounds the speedup: if $p > T_1 / T_\infty$, then $T_1 / T_p \leq T_1 / T_\infty < p$.

- The *slackness* is $T_1 / (pT_\infty)$. A slackness less than one implies (by the span law) that perfect linear speedup is impossible on p processors.

Execution on a Limited Number of Processors

Analysis of parallel algorithms is usually carried out under the assumption that an unbounded number of processors is available. This is unrealistic, but not a problem, since any computation that can run in parallel on N processors can be executed on $p < N$ processors by letting each processor execute multiple units of work. A result called *Brent's law* states that one can perform such a "simulation" in time T_p, bounded by

$$T_p \leq T_N + \frac{T_1 - T_N}{p},$$

or, less precisely,

$$T_p = O\left(T_N + \frac{T_1}{p}\right).$$

An alternative statement of the law bounds T_p above and below by

$$\frac{T_1}{p} \leq T_p < \frac{T_1}{p} + T_\infty.$$

showing that the span (depth) T_∞ and the work T_1 together provide reasonable bounds on the computation time.

Load Balancing (Computing)

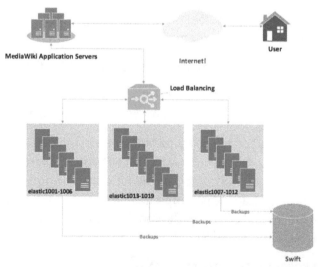

User requests to the Wikimedia Elasticsearch server cluster are routed via load balancing

In computing, load balancing improves the distribution of workloads across multiple computing resources, such as computers, a computer cluster, network links, central processing units, or disk drives. Load balancing aims to optimize resource use, maximize throughput, minimize response time, and avoid overload of any single resource. Using multiple components with load balancing instead of a single component may increase reliability and availability through redundancy. Load balancing usually involves dedicated software or hardware, such as a multilayer switch or a Domain Name System server process.

Load balancing differs from channel bonding in that load balancing divides traffic between network interfaces on a network socket (OSI model layer 4) basis, while channel bonding implies a division of traffic between physical interfaces at a lower level, either per packet (OSI model Layer 3) or on a data link (OSI model Layer 2) basis with a protocol like shortest path bridging.

Internet-based Services

One of the most commonly used applications of load balancing is to provide a single Internet service from multiple servers, sometimes known as a server farm. Commonly load-balanced systems include popular web sites, large Internet Relay Chat networks, high-bandwidth File Transfer Protocol sites, Network News Transfer Protocol (NNTP) servers, Domain Name System (DNS) servers, and databases.

Round-robin DNS

An alternate method of load balancing, which does not require a dedicated software or hardware node, is called *round robin DNS*. In this technique, multiple IP addresses are associated with a single domain name; clients are given ip in round robin fashion. Ip is assigned to clients for a time quantum.

DNS Delegation

Another more effective technique for load-balancing using DNS is to delegate www.example.org as a sub-domain whose zone is served by each of the same servers that are serving the web site. This technique works particularly well where individual servers are spread geographically on the Internet. For example:

```
one.example.org A 192.0.2.1

two.example.org A 203.0.113.2

www.example.org NS one.example.org

www.example.org NS two.example.org
```

However, the zone file for www.example.org on each server is different such that each server resolves its own IP Address as the A-record. On server *one* the zone file for www.example.org reports:

```
@ in a 192.0.2.1
```

On server *two* the same zone file contains:

```
@ in a 203.0.113.2
```

This way, when a server is down, its DNS will not respond and the web service does not receive any traffic. If the line to one server is congested, the unreliability of DNS ensures less HTTP traffic reaches that server. Furthermore, the quickest DNS response to the resolver is nearly always the one from the network's closest server, ensuring geo-sensitive load-balancing. A short TTL on the A-record helps to ensure traffic is quickly diverted when a server goes down. Consideration must be given the possibility that this technique may cause individual clients to switch between individual servers in mid-session.

Client-side Random Load Balancing

Another approach to load balancing is to deliver a list of server IPs to the client, and then to have client randomly select the IP from the list on each connection. This essentially relies on all clients generating similar loads, and the Law of Large Numbers to achieve a reasonably flat load distribution across servers. It has been claimed that client-side random load balancing tends to provide better load distribution than round-robin DNS; this has been attributed to caching issues with round-robin DNS, that in case of large DNS caching servers, tend to skew the distribution for round-robin DNS, while client-side random selection remains unaffected regardless of DNS caching.

With this approach, the method of delivery of list of IPs to the client can vary, and may be implemented as a DNS list (delivered to all the clients without any round-robin), or via hardcoding it to the list. If a "smart client" is used, detecting that randomly selected server is down and connecting randomly again, it also provides fault tolerance.

Server-side Load Balancers

For Internet services, server-side load balancer is usually a software program that is listening on the port where external clients connect to access services. The load balancer forwards requests to one of the "backend" servers, which usually replies to the load balancer. This allows the load balancer to reply to the client without the client ever knowing about the internal separation of functions. It also prevents clients from contacting back-end servers directly, which may have security benefits by hiding the structure of the internal network and preventing attacks on the kernel's network stack or unrelated services running on other ports.

Some load balancers provide a mechanism for doing something special in the event that all backend servers are unavailable. This might include forwarding to a backup load balancer, or displaying a message regarding the outage.

It is also important that the load balancer itself does not become a single point of failure. Usually load balancers are implemented in high-availability pairs which may also replicate session persistence data if required by the specific application.

Scheduling Algorithms

Numerous scheduling algorithms, also called load-balancing methods, are used by load balancers to determine which back-end server to send a request to. Simple algorithms include random choice or round robin. More sophisticated load balancers may take additional factors into account, such as a server's reported load, least response times, up/down status (determined by a monitoring poll of some kind), number of active connections, geographic location, capabilities, or how much traffic it has recently been assigned.

Persistence

An important issue when operating a load-balanced service is how to handle information that must be kept across the multiple requests in a user's session. If this information is stored locally on one backend server, then subsequent requests going to different backend servers would not be able to find it. This might be cached information that can be recomputed, in which case load-balancing a request to a different backend server just introduces a performance issue.

Ideally the cluster of servers behind the load balancer should be session-aware, so that if a client connects to any backend server at any time the user experience is unaffected. This is usually achieved with a shared database or an in-memory session database, for example Memcached.

One basic solution to the session data issue is to send all requests in a user session consistently to the same backend server. This is known as *persistence* or *stickiness*. A significant downside to this technique is its lack of automatic failover: if a backend server goes down, its per-session information becomes inaccessible, and any sessions depending on it are lost. The same problem is usually relevant to central database servers; even if web servers are "stateless" and not "sticky", the central database is.

Assignment to a particular server might be based on a username, client IP address, or be random. Because of changes of the client's perceived address resulting from DHCP, network address translation, and web proxies this method may be unreliable. Random assignments must be remembered by the load balancer, which creates a burden on storage. If the load balancer is replaced or fails, this information may be lost, and assignments may need to be deleted after a timeout period or during periods of high load to avoid exceeding the space available for the assignment table. The random assignment method also requires that clients maintain some state, which can be a problem, for example when a web browser has disabled storage of cookies. Sophisticated load balancers use multiple persistence techniques to avoid some of the shortcomings of any one method.

Another solution is to keep the per-session data in a database. Generally this is bad for performance because it increases the load on the database: the database is best used to store information less transient than per-session data. To prevent a database from becoming a single point of failure, and to improve scalability, the database is often replicated across multiple machines, and load balancing is used to spread the query load across those replicas. Microsoft's ASP.net State Server technology is an example of a session database. All servers in a web farm store their session data on State Server and any server in the farm can retrieve the data.

In the very common case where the client is a web browser, a simple but efficient approach is to store the per-session data in the browser itself. One way to achieve this is to use a browser cookie, suitably time-stamped and encrypted. Another is URL rewriting. Storing session data on the client is generally the preferred solution: then the load balancer is free to pick any backend server to handle a request. However, this method of state-data handling is poorly suited to some complex business logic scenarios, where session state payload is big and recomputing it with every request on a server is not feasible. URL rewriting has major security issues, because the end-user can easily alter the submitted URL and thus change session streams.

Yet another solution to storing persistent data is to associate a name with each block of data, and use a distributed hash table to pseudo-randomly assign that name to one of the available servers, and then store that block of data in the assigned server.

Load Balancer Features

Hardware and software load balancers may have a variety of special features. The fundamental feature of a load balancer is to be able to distribute incoming requests over a number of backend servers in the cluster according to a scheduling algorithm. Most of the following features are vendor specific:

- *Asymmetric load:* A ratio can be manually assigned to cause some backend servers to get a greater share of the workload than others. This is sometimes used as a crude way to account for some servers having more capacity than others and may not always work as desired.

- *Priority activation:* When the number of available servers drops below a certain number, or load gets too high, standby servers can be brought online.

- *SSL Offload and Acceleration:* Depending on the workload, processing the encryption and authentication requirements of an SSL request can become a major part of the demand on the Web Server's CPU; as the demand increases, users will see slower response times, as the SSL overhead is distributed among Web servers. To remove this demand on Web servers, a balancer can terminate SSL connections, passing HTTPS requests as HTTP requests to the Web servers. If the balancer itself is not overloaded, this does not noticeably degrade the performance perceived by end users. The downside of this approach is that all of the SSL processing is concentrated on a single device (the balancer) which can become a new bottleneck. Some load balancer appliances include specialized hardware to process SSL. Instead of upgrading the load balancer, which is quite expensive dedicated hardware, it may be cheaper to forgo SSL offload and add a few Web servers. Also, some server vendors such as Oracle/Sun now incorporate cryptographic acceleration hardware into their CPUs such as the T2000. F5 Networks incorporates a dedicated SSL acceleration hardware card in their local traffic manager (LTM) which is used for encrypting and decrypting SSL traffic. One clear benefit to SSL offloading in the balancer is that it enables it to do balancing or content switching based on data in the HTTPS request.

- *Distributed Denial of Service (DDoS) attack protection:* load balancers can provide features such as SYN cookies and delayed-binding (the back-end servers don't see the client until it finishes its TCP handshake) to mitigate SYN flood attacks and generally offload work from the servers to a more efficient platform.

- *HTTP compression:* reduces amount of data to be transferred for HTTP objects by utilizing gzip compression available in all modern web browsers. The larger the response and the further away the client is, the more this feature can improve response times. The tradeoff is that this feature puts additional CPU demand on the load balancer and could be done by web servers instead.

- *TCP offload:* different vendors use different terms for this, but the idea is that normally each HTTP request from each client is a different TCP connection. This feature utilizes HTTP/1.1 to consolidate multiple HTTP requests from multiple clients into a single TCP socket to the back-end servers.

- *TCP buffering:* the load balancer can buffer responses from the server and spoon-feed the data out to slow clients, allowing the web server to free a thread for other tasks faster than it would if it had to send the entire request to the client directly.

- *Direct Server Return:* an option for asymmetrical load distribution, where request and reply have different network paths.

- *Health checking:* the balancer polls servers for application layer health and removes failed servers from the pool.

- *HTTP caching:* the balancer stores static content so that some requests can be handled without contacting the servers.

- *Content filtering:* some balancers can arbitrarily modify traffic on the way through.

- *HTTP security:* some balancers can hide HTTP error pages, remove server identification headers from HTTP responses, and encrypt cookies so that end users cannot manipulate them.

- *Priority queuing:* also known as rate shaping, the ability to give different priority to different traffic.

- *Content-aware switching:* most load balancers can send requests to different servers based on the URL being requested, assuming the request is not encrypted (HTTP) or if it is encrypted (via HTTPS) that the HTTPS request is terminated (decrypted) at the load balancer.

- *Client authentication:* authenticate users against a variety of authentication sources before allowing them access to a website.

- *Programmatic traffic manipulation:* at least one balancer allows the use of a scripting language to allow custom balancing methods, arbitrary traffic manipulations, and more.

- *Firewall:* direct connections to backend servers are prevented, for network security reasons Firewall is a set of rules that decide whether the traffic may pass through an interface or not.

- *Intrusion prevention system:* offer application layer security in addition to network/transport layer offered by firewall security.

Use in Telecommunications

Load balancing can be useful in applications with redundant communications links. For example, a company may have multiple Internet connections ensuring network access if one of the connections fails. A failover arrangement would mean that one link is designated for normal use, while the second link is used only if the primary link fails.

Using load balancing, both links can be in use all the time. A device or program monitors the availability of all links and selects the path for sending packets. The use of multiple links simultaneously increases the available bandwidth.

Shortest Path Bridging

The IEEE approved the IEEE 802.1aq standard May 2012, also known and documented in most books as Shortest Path Bridging (SPB). SPB allows all links to be active through multiple equal cost paths, provides faster convergence times to reduce down time, and simplifies the use of load balancing in mesh network topologies (partially connected and/or fully connected) by allowing traffic to load share across all paths of a network. SPB is designed to virtually eliminate human error during configuration and preserves the plug-and-play nature that established Ethernet as the de facto protocol at Layer 2.

Routing

Many telecommunications companies have multiple routes through their networks or to external networks. They use sophisticated load balancing to shift traffic from one path to another to avoid network congestion on any particular link, and sometimes to minimize the cost of transit across external networks or improve network reliability.

Another way of using load balancing is in network monitoring activities. Load balancers can be used to split huge data flows into several sub-flows and use several network analyzers, each reading a part of the original data. This is very useful for monitoring fast networks like 10GbE or STM64, where complex processing of the data may not be possible at wire speed.

Relationship to Failovers

Load balancing is often used to implement failover—the continuation of a service after the failure of one or more of its components. The components are monitored continually (e.g., web servers may be monitored by fetching known pages), and when one becomes non-responsive, the load balancer is informed and no longer sends traffic to it. When a component comes back online, the load balancer begins to route traffic to it again. For this to work, there must be at least one component in excess of the service's capacity (N+1 redundancy). This can be much less expensive and more flexible than failover approaches where each single live component is paired with a single backup component that takes over in the event of a failure (dual modular redundancy). Some types of RAID systems can also utilize hot spare for a similar effect.

Models of Parallel Algorithm

The Data-Parallel Model

In this model, the tasks arestatically or semi-statically attached onto processes and each task performs identical operationson a variety of data. This type of parallelism that is a result of single operations being appliedon multiple data items is called data parallelism. The task may be executed inphases and the data operated upon in different phases may be different. Typically, data-parallel computation phases are interspersed with interactions to synchronize the tasks or to get freshdata to the tasks. Since all tasks perform same computations, the decomposition of theproblem into tasks is usually based on data partitioning because a uniform partitioning of datafollowed by a static mapping is sufficient to guarantee load balance.Data-parallel algorithms can be implemented in both shared-address-space and message-passing paradigms. However, the partitioned address- space in a message-passing paradigmmay allow better control of placement, and thus may offer a better handle on locality. On theother hand, shared-address space can ease the programming effort, especially if the distribution of data is different in different phases of the algorithm. Interaction overheads in the data-parallel model can be minimized by choosing a locality preserving decomposition and, if applicable, by overlapping computation and interaction and byusing optimized collective interaction routines. A key characteristic of data-parallel problems is that for most problems, the degree of data parallelism increases with the size of the problem, making it possible to use more processes to effectively solve larger problems. An example of a data-parallel algorithm is dense matrix multiplication problem.

The Task Graph Model

The computations in any parallel algorithm can be viewed as a taskgraph. The task graph may be either trivial or nontrivial. The type of parallelism that is expressed by the task graph is called task parallelism. In certain parallel algorithms, the taskgraph is explicitly used in establishing relationship between various tasks. In the task graph model, the interrelationshipsamong the tasks are utilized to promote locality or to reduce interaction costs. This model isapplied to solve problems in which the amount of data associated with the tasks ishuge relative to the amount of computation associated with them. The tasks are mapped statically to help optimize the cost of data movement among tasks. Some times a decentralized dynamic mapping may be used. This mapping uses the information concerning thetask-dependency graph structure and the interaction pattern of tasks to minimize interaction overhead. Work is more easily shared in paradigms with globally addressable space, but mechanisms are available to share work in disjoint address space.Typical interaction-reducing techniques applicable to this model include reducing the volumeand frequency of interaction by promoting locality while mapping the tasks based on the interaction pattern of tasks, and using asynchronous interaction methods to overlap the interaction with computation. Examples of algorithms based on the task graph model include parallel quicksort, sparse matrix factorization, and many parallel algorithms derived via divide-and-conquerapproach.

The Work Pool Model

The work pool or the task poolmodel is characterized by a dynamic mapping of tasks onto processes for load balancing in which any task may potentially be executed by any process. There is no desired pre-mapping of tasks onto processes. The mapping may be centralized or decentralized. Pointers to the tasks may be stored in a physically shared list, priority queue, hash table, or tree, or they could be stored in a physically distributed data structure. The workmay be statically available in the beginning, or could be dynamically generated; i.e., the processes may generate work and add it to the global (possibly distributed) work pool. If thework is generated dynamically and a decentralized mapping is used, then termination detection algorithm would be required so that all processes can actually detectthe completion of the entire program (i.e., exhaustion of all potential tasks) and stop looking for more work. In the message-passing paradigm, the work pool model is typically used when the amount ofdata associated with tasks is relatively small compared to the computation associated with the tasks. As a result, tasks can be readily moved around without causing too much data interaction overhead. The granularity of the tasks can be adjusted to attain the desired level of trade off between load-imbalance and the overhead of accessing the work pool for adding and extracting tasks.Parallelization of loops by chunk scheduling or related methods is an example ofthe use of the work pool model with centralized mapping when the tasks are statically available. Parallel tree search where the work is represented by a centralized or distributed data structure is an example of the use of the work pool model where the tasks are generated dynamically.

The Master-Slave Model

In the master-slave or the manager-workermodel, one or more master processes generatework and allocate it to slave processes. The tasks may be allocated a priori if the managercan estimate the size of the tasks or if a random mapping can do an adequate job of load balancing. In another scenario, workers are assigned smaller pieces of work at different times. The latter scheme is preferred if it is time consuming for the master to generate work andhence it is not desirable to make all workers wait until the master has generated all workpieces. In some cases, work may need to be performed in phases, and work in each phase must finish before work in the next phases can be generated. In this case, the manager may cause all workers to synchronize after each phase. Usually, there is no desired pre-mapping of work to processes, and any worker can do any job assigned to it. The manager-worker model can be generalized to the hierarchical or multi-level manager-worker model in which the toplevel manager feeds large chunks of tasks to second-level managers, who further subdivide thet asks among their own workers and may perform part of the work them selves. This model is generally equally suitable to shared-address-space or message-passing paradigms since the interaction is naturally two-way; i.e., the manager knows that it needs to give out work and workers know that they need to get work from the manager. While using the master-slave model, care should be taken to ensure that the master does not become a bottleneck, which may happen if the tasks are too small (or the workers are relatively fast). The granularity of tasks should be chosen such that the cost of doing work dominates the cost of communication and the cost of synchronization. Asynchronousinteraction may help overlap interaction and the computation associated with work generationby the master. It may also reduce waiting times if the nature of requests from workers is nondeterministic.

The Pipeline or Producer-Consumer Model

In the pipeline model, a stream of data is passed on through a succession of processes, each of which performs some task on it. This simultaneous execution of different programs on a data stream is called stream parallelism. With the exception of the process initiating the pipeline, the arrival of new data triggers the execution of a new task by a process in the pipeline. The processes could form such pipelines in the shape of linear or multidimensional arrays, trees, orgeneral graphs with or without cycles. A pipeline is a chain of producers and consumers. Eachprocess in the pipeline can be viewed as a consumer of a sequence of data items for the process preceding it in the pipeline and as a producer of data for the process following it in the pipeline. The pipeline does not need to be a linear chain; it can be a directed graph. The pipeline model usually involves a static mapping of tasks onto processes. Load balancing is a function of task granularity. The larger the granularity, the longer it takes to fill up the pipeline, i.e. for the trigger produced by the first process in the chain to propagate to the last process, there by keeping some of the processes waiting. However, too fine agranularity may increase interaction overheads because processes will need to interact toreceive fresh data after smaller pieces of computation. The most common interaction reduction technique applicable to this model is overlapping interaction with computation. An example of a two-dimensional pipeline is the parallel LU factorization algorithm.

Hybrid Models

In some cases, more than one model may be applicable to the problem at hand, resulting in ahybrid algorithm model. A hybrid model may be composed either of multiple models applied hierarchically or multiple models applied sequentially to different phases of a parallel algorithm. In some cases, an algorithm formulation may have characteristics of more than one algorithm model. For instance, data may flow in a pipelined manner in a pattern guided by a taskgraph. In another scenario, the major computation may be described by a taskgraph, but each node of the graph may represent a supertask comprising multiple subtasks that may be suitable for data-parallel or pipelined parallelism. Parallel quicksort is one of the applications for which a hybrid model is ideally suited.

Algorithm

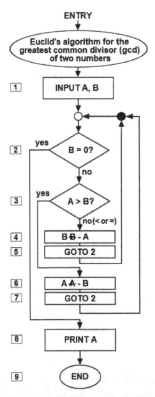

Flow chart of an algorithm (Euclid's algorithm) for calculating the greatest common divisor (g.c.d.) of two numbers a and b in locations named A and B. The algorithm proceeds by successive subtractions in two loops: IF the test B ≥ A yields "yes" (or true) (more accurately the *number b* in location B is greater than or equal to the *number a* in location A) THEN, the algorithm specifies B ← B – A (meaning the number $b - a$ replaces the old b). Similarly, IF A > B, THEN A ← A – B. The process terminates when (the contents of) B is 0, yielding the g.c.d. in A. (Algorithm derived from Scott 2009:13; symbols and drawing style from Tausworthe 1977).

In mathematics and computer science, an algorithm is a self-contained sequence of actions to be performed. Algorithms can perform calculation, data processing and automated reasoning tasks.

An algorithm is an effective method that can be expressed within a finite amount of space and time and in a well-defined formal language for calculating a function. Starting from an initial state and initial input (perhaps empty), the instructions describe a computation that, when executed, proceeds through a finite number of well-defined successive states, eventually producing "output" and terminating at a final ending state. The transition from one state to the next is not necessarily deterministic; some algorithms, known as randomized algorithms, incorporate random input.

The concept of *algorithm* has existed for centuries; however, a partial formalization of what would become the modern *algorithm* began with attempts to solve the Entscheidungsproblem (the "decision problem") posed by David Hilbert in 1928. Subsequent formalizations were framed as attempts to define "effective calculability" or "effective method"; those formalizations included the Gödel–Herbrand–Kleene recursive functions of 1930, 1934 and 1935, Alonzo Church's lambda calculus of 1936, Emil Post's "Formulation 1" of 1936, and Alan Turing's Turing machines of 1936–7 and 1939. Giving a formal definition of algorithms, corresponding to the intuitive notion, remains a challenging problem.

Historical Background

Etymologically, the word 'algorithm' is a combination of the Latin word *algorismus*, named after Al-Khwarizmi, a 9th-century Persian mathematician, and the Greek word *arithmos*, i.e., meaning "number". In English, it was first used in about 1230 and then by Chaucer in 1391. English adopted the French term, but it wasn't until the late 19th century that "algorithm" took on the meaning that it has in modern English.

Another early use of the word is from 1240, in a manual titled *Carmen de Algorismo* composed by Alexandre de Villedieu. It begins thus:

Haec algorismus ars praesens dicitur, in qua / Talibus Indorum fruimur bis quinque figuris.

which translates as:

Algorism is the art by which at present we use those Indian figures, which number two times five.

The poem is a few hundred lines long and summarizes the art of calculating with the new style of Indian dice, or Talibus Indorum, or Hindu numerals.

Informal Definition

An informal definition could be "a set of rules that precisely defines a sequence of operations." which would include all computer programs, including programs that do not perform numeric calculations. Generally, a program is only an algorithm if it stops eventually.

A prototypical example of an algorithm is the Euclidean algorithm to determine the maximum common divisor of two integers; an example (there are others) is described by the flow chart above and as an example in a later section.

Boolos & Jeffrey (1974, 1999) offer an informal meaning of the word in the following quotation:

No human being can write fast enough, or long enough, or small enough† (†"smaller and smaller without limit ...you'd be trying to write on molecules, on atoms, on electrons") to list all members of an enumerably infinite set by writing out their names, one after another, in some notation. But humans can do something equally useful, in the case of certain enumerably infinite sets: They can give *explicit instructions for determining the **n**th member of the set*, for arbitrary finite n. Such instructions are to be given quite explicitly, in a form in which *they could be followed by a computing machine*, or by a *human who is capable of carrying out only very elementary operations on symbols.*

An "enumerably infinite set" is one whose elements can be put into one-to-one correspondence with the integers. Thus, Boolos and Jeffrey are saying that an algorithm implies instructions for a process that "creates" output integers from an *arbitrary* "input" integer or integers that, in theory, can be arbitrarily large. Thus an algorithm can be an algebraic equation such as $y = m + n$ — two arbitrary "input variables" m and n that produce an output y. But various authors' attempts to define the notion indicate that the word implies much more than this, something on the order of (for the addition example):

> Precise instructions (in language understood by "the computer") for a fast, efficient, "good" process that specifies the "moves" of "the computer" (machine or human, equipped with the necessary internally contained information and capabilities) to find, decode, and then process arbitrary input integers/symbols m and n, symbols + and = ... and "effectively" produce, in a "reasonable" time, output-integer y at a specified place and in a specified format.

The concept of *algorithm* is also used to define the notion of decidability. That notion is central for explaining how formal systems come into being starting from a small set of axioms and rules. In logic, the time that an algorithm requires to complete cannot be measured, as it is not apparently related with our customary physical dimension. From such uncertainties, that characterize ongoing work, stems the unavailability of a definition of *algorithm* that suits both concrete (in some sense) and abstract usage of the term.

Formalization

Algorithms are essential to the way computers process data. Many computer programs contain algorithms that detail the specific instructions a computer should perform (in a specific order) to carry out a specified task, such as calculating employees' paychecks or printing students' report cards. Thus, an algorithm can be considered to be any sequence of operations that can be simulated by a Turing-complete system. Authors who assert this thesis include Minsky (1967), Savage (1987) and Gurevich (2000):

Minsky: "But we will also maintain, with Turing . . . that any procedure which could "naturally" be called effective, can in fact be realized by a (simple) machine. Although this may seem extreme, the arguments . . . in its favor are hard to refute".

Gurevich: "...Turing's informal argument in favor of his thesis justifies a stronger thesis: every algorithm can be simulated by a Turing machine ... according to Savage [1987], an algorithm is a computational process defined by a Turing machine".

Typically, when an algorithm is associated with processing information, data can be read from an input source, written to an output device and stored for further processing. Stored data are regarded as part of the internal state of the entity performing the algorithm. In practice, the state is stored in one or more data structures.

For some such computational process, the algorithm must be rigorously defined: specified in the way it applies in all possible circumstances that could arise. That is, any conditional steps must be systematically dealt with, case-by-case; the criteria for each case must be clear (and computable).

Because an algorithm is a precise list of precise steps, the order of computation is always crucial to the functioning of the algorithm. Instructions are usually assumed to be listed explicitly, and are described as starting "from the top" and going "down to the bottom", an idea that is described more formally by *flow of control*.

So far, this discussion of the formalization of an algorithm has assumed the premises of imperative programming. This is the most common conception, and it attempts to describe a task in discrete, "mechanical" means. Unique to this conception of formalized algorithms is the assignment operation, setting the value of a variable. It derives from the intuition of "memory" as a scratchpad. There is an example below of such an assignment.

For some alternate conceptions of what constitutes an algorithm see functional programming and logic programming.

Expressing Algorithms

Algorithms can be expressed in many kinds of notation, including natural languages, pseudocode, flowcharts, drakon-charts, programming languages or control tables (processed by interpreters). Natural language expressions of algorithms tend to be verbose and ambiguous, and are rarely used for complex or technical algorithms. Pseudocode, flowcharts, drakon-charts and control tables are structured ways to express algorithms that avoid many of the ambiguities common in natural language statements. Programming languages are primarily intended for expressing algorithms in a form that can be executed by a computer, but are often used as a way to define or document algorithms.

There is a wide variety of representations possible and one can express a given Turing machine program as a sequence of machine tables, as flowcharts and drakon-charts, or as a form of rudimentary machine code or assembly code called "sets of quadruples".

Representations of algorithms can be classed into three accepted levels of Turing machine description:

1. High-level description

> "...prose to describe an algorithm, ignoring the implementation details. At this level we do not need to mention how the machine manages its tape or head."

2. Implementation description

> "...prose used to define the way the Turing machine uses its head and the way that it stores

data on its tape. At this level we do not give details of states or transition function."

3. Formal description

Most detailed, "lowest level", gives the Turing machine's "state table".

For an example of the simple algorithm "Add m+n" described in all three levels, see Algorithm#Examples.

Implementation

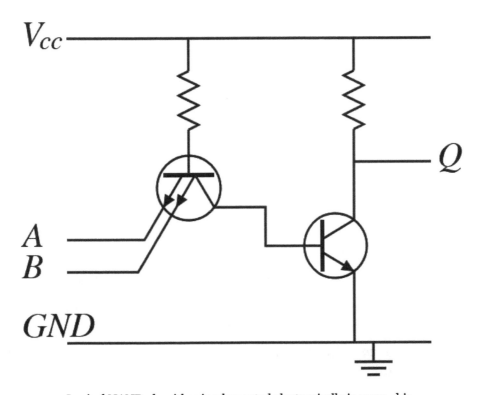

Logical NAND algorithm implemented electronically in 7400 chip

Most algorithms are intended to be implemented as computer programs. However, algorithms are also implemented by other means, such as in a biological neural network (for example, the human brain implementing arithmetic or an insect looking for food), in an electrical circuit, or in a mechanical device.

Computer Algorithms

In computer systems, an algorithm is basically an instance of logic written in software by software developers to be effective for the intended "target" computer(s) to produce *output* from given (perhaps null) *input*. An optimal algorithm, even running in old hardware, would produce faster results than a non-optimal (higher time complexity) algorithm for the same purpose, running in more efficient hardware; that is why algorithms, like computer hardware, are considered technology.

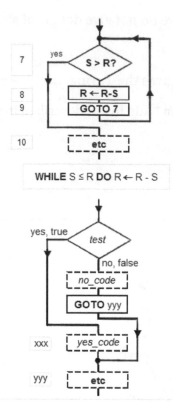

Flowchart examples of the canonical Böhm-Jacopini structures: the SEQUENCE (rectangles descending the page), the WHILE-DO and the IF-THEN-ELSE. The three structures are made of the primitive conditional GOTO (IF `test`=true THEN GOTO step xxx) (a diamond), the unconditional GOTO (rectangle), various assignment operators (rectangle), and HALT (rectangle). Nesting of these structures inside assignment-blocks result in complex diagrams (cf Tausworthe 1977:100,114).

"Elegant" (compact) programs, "good" (fast) programs : The notion of "simplicity and elegance" appears informally in Knuth and precisely in Chaitin:

> Knuth: ". . .we want *good* algorithms in some loosely defined aesthetic sense. One criterion . . . is the length of time taken to perform the algorithm . . .. Other criteria are adaptability of the algorithm to computers, its simplicity and elegance, etc"

> Chaitin: " . . . a program is 'elegant,' by which I mean that it's the smallest possible program for producing the output that it does"

Chaitin prefaces his definition with: "I'll show you can't prove that a program is 'elegant'"—such a proof would solve the Halting problem (ibid).

Algorithm versus function computable by an algorithm: For a given function multiple algorithms may exist. This is true, even without expanding the available instruction set available to the programmer. Rogers observes that "It is . . . important to distinguish between the notion of *algorithm*, i.e. procedure and the notion of *function computable by algorithm*, i.e. mapping yielded by procedure. The same function may have several different algorithms".

Unfortunately there may be a tradeoff between goodness (speed) and elegance (compactness)—an elegant program may take more steps to complete a computation than one less elegant. An example that uses Euclid's algorithm appears below.

Computers (and computors), models of computation: A computer (or human "computor") is a restricted type of machine, a "discrete deterministic mechanical device" that blindly follows its instructions. Melzak's and Lambek's primitive models reduced this notion to four elements: (i) discrete, distinguishable *locations*, (ii) discrete, indistinguishable *counters* (iii) an agent, and (iv) a list of instructions that are *effective* relative to the capability of the agent.

Minsky describes a more congenial variation of Lambek's "abacus" model in his "Very Simple Bases for Computability". Minsky's machine proceeds sequentially through its five (or six, depending on how one counts) instructions, unless either a conditional IF–THEN GOTO or an unconditional GOTO changes program flow out of sequence. Besides HALT, Minsky's machine includes three *assignment* (replacement, substitution) operations: ZERO (e.g. the contents of location replaced by 0: $L \leftarrow 0$), SUCCESSOR (e.g. $L \leftarrow L+1$), and DECREMENT (e.g. $L \leftarrow L-1$). Rarely must a programmer write "code" with such a limited instruction set. But Minsky shows (as do Melzak and Lambek) that his machine is Turing complete with only four general *types* of instructions: conditional GOTO, unconditional GOTO, assignment/replacement/substitution, and HALT.

Simulation of an algorithm: computer (computor) language: Knuth advises the reader that "the best way to learn an algorithm is to try it . . . immediately take pen and paper and work through an example". But what about a simulation or execution of the real thing? The programmer must translate the algorithm into a language that the simulator/computer/computor can *effectively* execute. Stone gives an example of this: when computing the roots of a quadratic equation the computor must know how to take a square root. If they don't, then the algorithm, to be effective, must provide a set of rules for extracting a square root.

This means that the programmer must know a "language" that is effective relative to the target computing agent (computer/computor).

But what model should be used for the simulation? Van Emde Boas observes "even if we base complexity theory on abstract instead of concrete machines, arbitrariness of the choice of a model remains. It is at this point that the notion of *simulation* enters". When speed is being measured, the instruction set matters. For example, the subprogram in Euclid's algorithm to compute the remainder would execute much faster if the programmer had a "modulus" instruction available rather than just subtraction (or worse: just Minsky's "decrement").

Structured programming, canonical structures: Per the Church–Turing thesis, any algorithm can be computed by a model known to be Turing complete, and per Minsky's demonstrations, Turing completeness requires only four instruction types—conditional GOTO, unconditional GOTO, assignment, HALT. Kemeny and Kurtz observe that, while "undisciplined" use of unconditional GOTOs and conditional IF-THEN GOTOs can result in "spaghetti code", a programmer can write structured programs using only these instructions; on the other hand "it is also possible, and not too hard, to write badly structured programs in a structured language". Tausworthe augments the three Böhm-Jacopini canonical structures: SEQUENCE, IF-THEN-ELSE, and WHILE-DO, with two more: DO-WHILE and CASE. An additional benefit of a structured program is that it lends itself to proofs of correctness using mathematical induction.

Canonical flowchart symbols: The graphical aide called a flowchart offers a way to describe and document an algorithm (and a computer program of one). Like program flow of a Minsky machine, a flowchart always starts at the top of a page and proceeds down. Its primary symbols are only four: the directed arrow showing program flow, the rectangle (SEQUENCE, GOTO), the diamond (IF-THEN-ELSE), and the dot (OR-tie). The Böhm–Jacopini canonical structures are made of these primitive shapes. Sub-structures can "nest" in rectangles, but only if a single exit occurs from the superstructure. The symbols, and their use to build the canonical structures, are shown in the diagram.

Algorithm Example

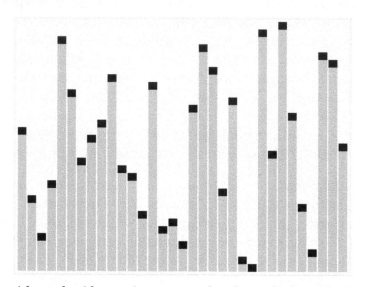

The quicksort algorithm sorting an array of randomized values. The element
farthest to the right hand side is chosen as the pivot.

One of the simplest algorithms is to find the largest number in a list of numbers of random order. Finding the solution requires looking at every number in the list. From this follows a simple algorithm, which can be stated in a high-level description English prose, as:

High-level description:

1. If there are no numbers in the set then there is no highest number.

2. Assume the first number in the set is the largest number in the set.

3. For each remaining number in the set: if this number is larger than the current largest number, consider this number to be the largest number in the set.

4. When there are no numbers left in the set to iterate over, consider the current largest number to be the largest number of the set.

(Quasi-)formal description: Written in prose but much closer to the high-level language of a computer program, the following is the more formal coding of the algorithm in pseudocode or pidgin code:

```
Algorithm LargestNumber

  Input: A list of numbers L.

  Output: The largest number in the list L.
```

```
if L.size = 0 return null

largest ← L

for each item in L, do

   if item > largest, then

      largest ← item

return largest
```

- "←" is a shorthand for "changes to". For instance, "*largest ← item*" means that the value of *largest* changes to the value of *item*.

- "return" terminates the algorithm and outputs the value that follows.

Euclid's Algorithm

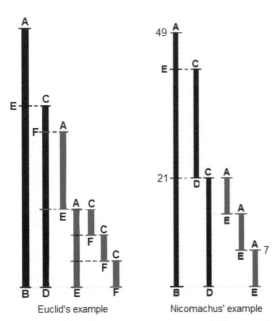

Euclid's example   Nicomachus' example

The example-diagram of Euclid's algorithm from T.L. Heath (1908), with more detail added. Euclid does not go beyond a third measuring, and gives no numerical examples. Nicomachus gives the example of 49 and 21: "I subtract the less from the greater; 28 is left; then again I subtract from this the same 21 (for this is possible); 7 is left; I subtract this from 21, 14 is left; from which I again subtract 7 (for this is possible); 7 is left, but 7 cannot be subtracted from 7." Heath comments that, "The last phrase is curious, but the meaning of it is obvious enough, as also the meaning of the phrase about ending 'at one and the same number'."(Heath 1908:300).

Euclid's algorithm to compute the greatest common divisor (GCD) to two numbers appears as Proposition II in Book VII ("Elementary Number Theory") of his *Elements*. Euclid poses the problem thus: "Given two numbers not prime to one another, to find their greatest common measure". He defines "A number [to be] a multitude composed of units": a counting number, a positive integer not including zero. To "measure" is to place a shorter measuring length s successively (q times) along longer length l until the remaining portion r is less than the shorter length s. In modern words, remainder $r = l - q \times s$, q being the quotient, or remainder r is the "modulus", the integer-fractional part left over after the division.

For Euclid's method to succeed, the starting lengths must satisfy two requirements: (i) the lengths must not be zero, AND (ii) the subtraction must be "proper"; i.e., a test must guarantee that the smaller of the two numbers is subtracted from the larger (alternately, the two can be equal so their subtraction yields zero).

Euclid's original proof adds a third requirement: the two lengths must not be prime to one another. Euclid stipulated this so that he could construct a reductio ad absurdum proof that the two numbers' common measure is in fact the *greatest*. While Nicomachus' algorithm is the same as Euclid's, when the numbers are prime to one another, it yields the number "1" for their common measure. So, to be precise, the following is really Nicomachus' algorithm.

Computer Language for Euclid's Algorithm

Only a few instruction *types* are required to execute Euclid's algorithm—some logical tests (conditional GOTO), unconditional GOTO, assignment (replacement), and subtraction.

- A *location* is symbolized by upper case letter(s), e.g. S, A, etc.

- The varying quantity (number) in a location is written in lower case letter(s) and (usually) associated with the location's name. For example, location L at the start might contain the number $l = 3009$.

An Inelegant Program for Euclid's Algorithm

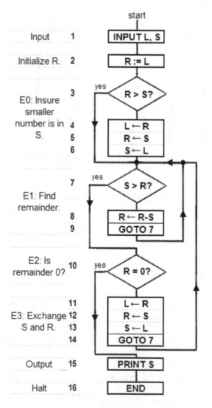

"Inelegant"

"Inelegant" is a translation of Knuth's version of the algorithm with a subtraction-based remainder-loop replacing his use of division (or a "modulus" instruction). Derived from Knuth 1973:2–4. Depending on the two numbers "Inelegant" may compute the g.c.d. in fewer steps than "Elegant".

The following algorithm is framed as Knuth's four-step version of Euclid's and Nicomachus', but, rather than using division to find the remainder, it uses successive subtractions of the shorter length s from the remaining length r until r is less than s. The high-level description, shown in boldface, is adapted from Knuth 1973:2–4:

Input

1 [Into two locations L and S put the numbers l and s that represent the two lengths]:

 INPUT L, S

2 [Initialize R: make the remaining length r equal to the starting/initial/input length l]:

 R ← L

E0: [Ensure $r \geq s$.]

```
3 [Ensure the smaller of the two numbers is in S and the larger in R]:

  IF R > S THEN

    the contents of L is the larger number so skip over the exchange-steps 4, 5 and 6:

    GOTO step 6

  ELSE
```

 swap the contents of R and S.

4 L ← R (this first step is redundant, but is useful for later discussion).

5 R ← S

6 S ← L

E1: [Find remainder]: Until the remaining length r in R is less than the shorter length s in S, repeatedly subtract the measuring number s in S from the remaining length r in R.

7 IF S > R THEN

 done measuring so

 GOTO 10

 ELSE

  measure again,

8 R ← R − S

9 [Remainder-loop]:

 GOTO 7.

E2: [Is the remainder zero?]: EITHER (i) the last measure was exact, the remainder in R is zero, and the program can halt, OR (ii) the algorithm must continue: the last measure left a remainder in R less than measuring number in S.

```
10 IF R = 0 THEN

    done so

    GOTO step 15
```

```
ELSE
   CONTINUE TO step 11,
```

E3: [Interchange *s* and *r*]: The nut of Euclid's algorithm. Use remainder *r* to measure what was previously smaller number *s*; L serves as a temporary location.

11 $L \leftarrow R$

12 $R \leftarrow S$

13 $S \leftarrow L$

```
14  [Repeat the measuring process]:
   GOTO 7
```

OUTPUT

```
15 [Done. S contains the greatest common divisor]:
   PRINT S
```

DONE

```
16 HALT, END, STOP.
```

An Elegant Program for Euclid's Algorithm

The following version of Euclid's algorithm requires only six core instructions to do what thirteen are required to do by "Inelegant"; worse, "Inelegant" requires more *types* of instructions. The flowchart of "Elegant" can be found at the top of this article. In the (unstructured) Basic language, the steps are numbered, and the instruction LET [] = [] is the assignment instruction symbolized by $\leftarrow$.

```
 5 REM Euclid's algorithm for greatest common divisor
 6 PRINT "Type two integers greater than 0"
10 INPUT A,B
20 IF B=0 THEN GOTO 80
30 IF A > B THEN GOTO 60
40 LET B=B-A
50 GOTO 20
60 LET A=A-B
70 GOTO 20
80 PRINT A
90 END
```

The following version can be used with Object Oriented languages:

```
// Euclid's algorithm for greatest common divisor
```

```
integer euclidAlgorithm (int A, int B){

    A=Math.abs(A);

    B=Math.abs(B);

    while (B!=0){

        if (A>B) A=A-B;

        else B=B-A;

    }

    return A;

}
```

How "Elegant" works: In place of an outer "Euclid loop", "Elegant" shifts back and forth between two "co-loops", an A > B loop that computes A ← A – B, and a B ≤ A loop that computes B ← B – A. This works because, when at last the minuend M is less than or equal to the subtrahend S (Difference = Minuend – Subtrahend), the minuend can become *s* (the new measuring length) and the subtrahend can become the new *r* (the length to be measured); in other words the "sense" of the subtraction reverses.

Testing the Euclid Algorithms

Does an algorithm do what its author wants it to do? A few test cases usually suffice to confirm core functionality. One source uses 3009 and 884. Knuth suggested 40902, 24140. Another interesting case is the two relatively prime numbers 14157 and 5950.

But exceptional cases must be identified and tested. Will "Inelegant" perform properly when R > S, S > R, R = S? Ditto for "Elegant": B > A, A > B, A = B? (Yes to all). What happens when one number is zero, both numbers are zero? ("Inelegant" computes forever in all cases; "Elegant" computes forever when A = 0.) What happens if *negative* numbers are entered? Fractional numbers? If the input numbers, i.e. the domain of the function computed by the algorithm/ program, is to include only positive integers including zero, then the failures at zero indicate that the algorithm (and the program that instantiates it) is a partial function rather than a total function. A notable failure due to exceptions is the Ariane 5 Flight 501 rocket failure (4 June 1996).

Proof of program correctness by use of mathematical induction: Knuth demonstrates the application of mathematical induction to an "extended" version of Euclid's algorithm, and he proposes "a general method applicable to proving the validity of any algorithm". Tausworthe proposes that a measure of the complexity of a program be the length of its correctness proof.

Measuring and Improving the Euclid Algorithms

Elegance (compactness) versus goodness (speed): With only six core instructions, "Elegant" is the clear winner, compared to "Inelegant" at thirteen instructions. However, "Inelegant" is *faster* (it arrives at HALT in fewer steps). Algorithm analysis indicates why this is the case: "Elegant" does *two* conditional tests in every subtraction loop, whereas "Inelegant" only does one. As the algorithm (usually) requires many loop-throughs, *on average* much time is wasted doing a "B = 0?" test that is needed only after the remainder is computed.

Can the algorithms be improved?: Once the programmer judges a program "fit" and "effective"—that is, it computes the function intended by its author—then the question becomes, can it be improved?

The compactness of "Inelegant" can be improved by the elimination of five steps. But Chaitin proved that compacting an algorithm cannot be automated by a generalized algorithm; rather, it can only be done heuristically; i.e., by exhaustive search (examples to be found at Busy beaver), trial and error, cleverness, insight, application of inductive reasoning, etc. Observe that steps 4, 5 and 6 are repeated in steps 11, 12 and 13. Comparison with "Elegant" provides a hint that these steps, together with steps 2 and 3, can be eliminated. This reduces the number of core instructions from thirteen to eight, which makes it "more elegant" than "Elegant", at nine steps.

The speed of "Elegant" can be improved by moving the "B=0?" test outside of the two subtraction loops. This change calls for the addition of three instructions (B = 0?, A = 0?, GOTO). Now "Elegant" computes the example-numbers faster; whether this is always the case for any given A, B and R, S would require a detailed analysis.

Algorithmic Analysis

It is frequently important to know how much of a particular resource (such as time or storage) is theoretically required for a given algorithm. Methods have been developed for the analysis of algorithms to obtain such quantitative answers (estimates); for example, the sorting algorithm above has a time requirement of $O(n)$, using the big O notation with n as the length of the list. At all times the algorithm only needs to remember two values: the largest number found so far, and its current position in the input list. Therefore, it is said to have a space requirement of *O(1)*, if the space required to store the input numbers is not counted, or $O(n)$ if it is counted.

Different algorithms may complete the same task with a different set of instructions in less or more time, space, or 'effort' than others. For example, a binary search algorithm (with cost O(log n)) outperforms a sequential search (cost O(n)) when used for table lookups on sorted lists or arrays.

Formal Versus Empirical

The analysis and study of algorithms is a discipline of computer science, and is often practiced abstractly without the use of a specific programming language or implementation. In this sense, algorithm analysis resembles other mathematical disciplines in that it focuses on the underlying properties of the algorithm and not on the specifics of any particular implementation. Usually pseudocode is used for analysis as it is the simplest and most general representation. However, ultimately, most algorithms are usually implemented on particular hardware / software platforms and their algorithmic efficiency is eventually put to the test using real code. For the solution of a "one off" problem, the efficiency of a particular algorithm may not have significant consequences (unless n is extremely large) but for algorithms designed for fast interactive, commercial or long life scientific usage it may be critical. Scaling from small n to large n frequently exposes inefficient algorithms that are otherwise benign.

Empirical testing is useful because it may uncover unexpected interactions that affect performance. Benchmarks may be used to compare before/after potential improvements to an algorithm after program optimization.

Execution Efficiency

To illustrate the potential improvements possible even in well established algorithms, a recent significant innovation, relating to FFT algorithms (used heavily in the field of image processing), can decrease processing time up to 1,000 times for applications like medical imaging. In general, speed improvements depend on special properties of the problem, which are very common in practical applications. Speedups of this magnitude enable computing devices that make extensive use of image processing (like digital cameras and medical equipment) to consume less power.

Classification

There are various ways to classify algorithms, each with its own merits.

By Implementation

One way to classify algorithms is by implementation means.

Recursion

> A recursive algorithm is one that invokes (makes reference to) itself repeatedly until a certain condition (also known as termination condition) matches, which is a method common to functional programming. Iterative algorithms use repetitive constructs like loops and sometimes additional data structures like stacks to solve the given problems. Some problems are naturally suited for one implementation or the other. For example, towers of Hanoi is well understood using recursive implementation. Every recursive version has an equivalent (but possibly more or less complex) iterative version, and vice versa.

Logical

> An algorithm may be viewed as controlled logical deduction. This notion may be expressed as: *Algorithm = logic + control*. The logic component expresses the axioms that may be used in the computation and the control component determines the way in which deduction is applied to the axioms. This is the basis for the logic programming paradigm. In pure logic programming languages the control component is fixed and algorithms are specified by supplying only the logic component. The appeal of this approach is the elegant semantics: a change in the axioms has a well-defined change in the algorithm.

Serial, parallel or distributed

> Algorithms are usually discussed with the assumption that computers execute one instruction of an algorithm at a time. Those computers are sometimes called serial computers. An algorithm designed for such an environment is called a serial algorithm, as opposed to parallel algorithms or distributed algorithms. Parallel algorithms take advantage of computer architectures where several processors can work on a problem

at the same time, whereas distributed algorithms utilize multiple machines connected with a network. Parallel or distributed algorithms divide the problem into more symmetrical or asymmetrical subproblems and collect the results back together. The resource consumption in such algorithms is not only processor cycles on each processor but also the communication overhead between the processors. Some sorting algorithms can be parallelized efficiently, but their communication overhead is expensive. Iterative algorithms are generally parallelizable. Some problems have no parallel algorithms, and are called inherently serial problems.

Deterministic or non-deterministic

Deterministic algorithms solve the problem with exact decision at every step of the algorithm whereas non-deterministic algorithms solve problems via guessing although typical guesses are made more accurate through the use of heuristics.

Exact or approximate

While many algorithms reach an exact solution, approximation algorithms seek an approximation that is close to the true solution. Approximation may use either a deterministic or a random strategy. Such algorithms have practical value for many hard problems.

Quantum algorithm

They run on a realistic model of quantum computation. The term is usually used for those algorithms which seem inherently quantum, or use some essential feature of quantum computation such as quantum superposition or quantum entanglement.

By Design Paradigm

Another way of classifying algorithms is by their design methodology or paradigm. There is a certain number of paradigms, each different from the other. Furthermore, each of these categories include many different types of algorithms. Some common paradigms are:

Brute-force or exhaustive search

This is the naive method of trying every possible solution to see which is best.

Divide and conquer

A divide and conquer algorithm repeatedly reduces an instance of a problem to one or more smaller instances of the same problem (usually recursively) until the instances are small enough to solve easily. One such example of divide and conquer is merge sorting. Sorting can be done on each segment of data after dividing data into segments and sorting of entire data can be obtained in the conquer phase by merging the segments. A simpler variant of divide and conquer is called a *decrease and conquer algorithm*, that solves an identical subproblem and uses the solution of this subproblem to solve the bigger problem. Divide and conquer divides the problem into multiple subproblems and so the conquer stage is more complex than decrease and conquer algorithms. An example of decrease and conquer algorithm is the binary search algorithm.

Search and enumeration

Many problems (such as playing chess) can be modeled as problems on graphs. A graph exploration algorithm specifies rules for moving around a graph and is useful for such problems. This category also includes search algorithms, branch and bound enumeration and backtracking.

Randomized algorithm

Such algorithms make some choices randomly (or pseudo-randomly). They can be very useful in finding approximate solutions for problems where finding exact solutions can be impractical. For some of these problems, it is known that the fastest approximations must involve some randomness. Whether randomized algorithms with polynomial time complexity can be the fastest algorithms for some problems is an open question known as the P versus NP problem. There are two large classes of such algorithms:

1. Monte Carlo algorithms return a correct answer with high-probability. E.g. RP is the subclass of these that run in polynomial time.

2. Las Vegas algorithms always return the correct answer, but their running time is only probabilistically bound, e.g. ZPP.

Reduction of complexity

This technique involves solving a difficult problem by transforming it into a better known problem for which we have (hopefully) asymptotically optimal algorithms. The goal is to find a reducing algorithm whose complexity is not dominated by the resulting reduced algorithm's. For example, one selection algorithm for finding the median in an unsorted list involves first sorting the list (the expensive portion) and then pulling out the middle element in the sorted list (the cheap portion). This technique is also known as *transform and conquer*.

Optimization Problems

For optimization problems there is a more specific classification of algorithms; an algorithm for such problems may fall into one or more of the general categories described above as well as into one of the following:

Linear programming

When searching for optimal solutions to a linear function bound to linear equality and inequality constraints, the constraints of the problem can be used directly in producing the optimal solutions. There are algorithms that can solve any problem in this category, such as the popular simplex algorithm. Problems that can be solved with linear programming include the maximum flow problem for directed graphs. If a problem additionally requires that one or more of the unknowns must be an integer then it is classified in integer programming. A linear programming algorithm can solve such a problem if it can be proved that all restrictions for integer values are superficial, i.e., the solutions satisfy these restrictions anyway. In the general case, a specialized algorithm or an algorithm that finds approximate solutions is used, depending on the difficulty of the problem.

Dynamic programming

When a problem shows optimal substructures — meaning the optimal solution to a problem can be constructed from optimal solutions to subproblems — and overlapping subproblems, meaning the same subproblems are used to solve many different problem instances, a quicker approach called *dynamic programming* avoids recomputing solutions that have already been computed. For example, Floyd–Warshall algorithm, the shortest path to a goal from a vertex in a weighted graph can be found by using the shortest path to the goal from all adjacent vertices. Dynamic programming and memoization go together. The main difference between dynamic programming and divide and conquer is that subproblems are more or less independent in divide and conquer, whereas subproblems overlap in dynamic programming. The difference between dynamic programming and straightforward recursion is in caching or memoization of recursive calls. When subproblems are independent and there is no repetition, memoization does not help; hence dynamic programming is not a solution for all complex problems. By using memoization or maintaining a table of subproblems already solved, dynamic programming reduces the exponential nature of many problems to polynomial complexity.

The greedy method

A greedy algorithm is similar to a dynamic programming algorithm in that it works by examining substructures, in this case not of the problem but of a given solution. Such algorithms start with some solution, which may be given or have been constructed in some way, and improve it by making small modifications. For some problems they can find the optimal solution while for others they stop at local optima, that is, at solutions that cannot be improved by the algorithm but are not optimum. The most popular use of greedy algorithms is for finding the minimal spanning tree where finding the optimal solution is possible with this method. Huffman Tree, Kruskal, Prim, Sollin are greedy algorithms that can solve this optimization problem.

The heuristic method

In optimization problems, heuristic algorithms can be used to find a solution close to the optimal solution in cases where finding the optimal solution is impractical. These algorithms work by getting closer and closer to the optimal solution as they progress. In principle, if run for an infinite amount of time, they will find the optimal solution. Their merit is that they can find a solution very close to the optimal solution in a relatively short time. Such algorithms include local search, tabu search, simulated annealing, and genetic algorithms. Some of them, like simulated annealing, are non-deterministic algorithms while others, like tabu search, are deterministic. When a bound on the error of the non-optimal solution is known, the algorithm is further categorized as an approximation algorithm.

By Field of Study

Every field of science has its own problems and needs efficient algorithms. Related problems in one field are often studied together. Some example classes are search algorithms, sorting algorithms, merge algorithms, numerical algorithms, graph algorithms, string algorithms, computational geometric algorithms, combinatorial algorithms, medical algorithms, machine learning, cryptography, data compression algorithms and parsing techniques.

Fields tend to overlap with each other, and algorithm advances in one field may improve those of other, sometimes completely unrelated, fields. For example, dynamic programming was invented for optimization of resource consumption in industry, but is now used in solving a broad range of problems in many fields.

By Complexity

Algorithms can be classified by the amount of time they need to complete compared to their input size:

- Constant time: if the time needed by the algorithm is the same, regardless of the input size. E.g. an access to an array element.

- Linear time: if the time is proportional to the input size. E.g. the traverse of a list.

- Logarithmic time: if the time is a logarithmic function of the input size. E.g. binary search algorithm.

- Polynomial time: if the time is a power of the input size. E.g. the bubble sort algorithm has quadratic time complexity.

- Exponential time: if the time is an exponential function of the input size. E.g. Brute-force search.

Some problems may have multiple algorithms of differing complexity, while other problems might have no algorithms or no known efficient algorithms. There are also mappings from some problems to other problems. Owing to this, it was found to be more suitable to classify the problems themselves instead of the algorithms into equivalence classes based on the complexity of the best possible algorithms for them.

Continuous Algorithms

The adjective "continuous" when applied to the word "algorithm" can mean:

- An algorithm operating on data that represents continuous quantities, even though this data is represented by discrete approximations—such algorithms are studied in numerical analysis; or

- An algorithm in the form of a differential equation that operates continuously on the data, running on an analog computer.

Legal Issues

Algorithms, by themselves, are not usually patentable. In the United States, a claim consisting solely of simple manipulations of abstract concepts, numbers, or signals does not constitute "processes" (USPTO 2006), and hence algorithms are not patentable (as in Gottschalk v. Benson). However, practical applications of algorithms are sometimes patentable. For example, in Diamond v. Diehr, the application of a simple feedback algorithm to aid in the curing of synthetic rubber was deemed patentable. The patenting of software is highly controversial, and there are highly criticized patents involving algorithms, especially data compression algorithms, such as Unisys' LZW patent.

Additionally, some cryptographic algorithms have export restrictions.

Etymology

The words 'algorithm' and 'algorism' come from the name al-Khwārizmī. Al-Khwārizmī was a Persian mathematician, astronomer, geographer, and scholar in the House of Wisdom in Baghdad, whose name means 'the native of Khwarezm', a region that was part of Greater Iran and is now in Uzbekistan. About 825, he wrote a treatise in the Arabic language, which was translated into Latin in the 12th century under the title *Algoritmi de numero Indorum*. This title means "Algoritmi on the numbers of the Indians", where "Algoritmi" was the translator's Latinization of Al-Khwarizmi's name. Al-Khwarizmi was the most widely read mathematician in Europe in the late Middle Ages, primarily through his other book, the Algebra. In late medieval Latin, *algorismus*, English 'algorism', the corruption of his name, simply meant the "decimal number system". In the 15th century, under the influence of the Greek word 'number' (*cf.* 'arithmetic'), the Latin word was altered to *algorithmus*, and the corresponding English term 'algorithm' is first attested in the 17th century; the modern sense was introduced in the 19th century.

History: Development of the Notion of "Algorithm"

Ancient Near East

Algorithms were used in ancient Greece. Two examples are the Sieve of Eratosthenes, which was described in Introduction to Arithmetic by Nicomachus, and the Euclidean algorithm, which was first described in Euclid's Elements (c. 300 BC). Babylonian clay tablets describe and employ algorithmic procedures to compute the time and place of significant astronomical events.

Discrete and Distinguishable Symbols

Tally-marks: To keep track of their flocks, their sacks of grain and their money the ancients used tallying: accumulating stones or marks scratched on sticks, or making discrete symbols in clay. Through the Babylonian and Egyptian use of marks and symbols, eventually Roman numerals and the abacus evolved (Dilson, p. 16–41). Tally marks appear prominently in unary numeral system arithmetic used in Turing machine and Post–Turing machine computations.

Manipulation of Symbols as "Place Holders" for Numbers: Algebra

The work of the ancient Greek geometers (Euclidean algorithm), the Indian mathematician Brahmagupta, and the Islamic mathematics Al-Khwarizmi (from whose name the terms "algorism" and "algorithm" are derived), and Western European mathematicians culminated in Leibniz's notion of the calculus ratiocinator (ca 1680):

A good century and a half ahead of his time, Leibniz proposed an algebra of logic, an algebra that would specify the rules for manipulating logical concepts in the manner that ordinary algebra specifies the rules for manipulating numbers.

Mechanical Contrivances with Discrete States

The clock: Bolter credits the invention of the weight-driven clock as "The key invention [of Europe in the Middle Ages]", in particular the verge escapement that provides us with the tick and tock of a mechanical clock. "The accurate automatic machine" led immediately to "mechanical automata" beginning in the 13th century and finally to "computational machines"—the difference engine and analytical engines of Charles Babbage and Countess Ada Lovelace, mid-19th century. Lovelace is credited with the first creation of an algorithm intended for processing on a computer – Babbage's analytical engine, the first device considered a real Turing-complete computer instead of just a calculator – and is sometimes called "history's first programmer" as a result, though a full implementation of Babbage's second device would not be realized until decades after her lifetime.

Logical machines 1870—Stanley Jevons' "logical abacus" and "logical machine": The technical problem was to reduce Boolean equations when presented in a form similar to what are now known as Karnaugh maps. Jevons (1880) describes first a simple "abacus" of "slips of wood furnished with pins, contrived so that any part or class of the [logical] combinations can be picked out mechanically . . . More recently however I have reduced the system to a completely mechanical form, and have thus embodied the whole of the indirect process of inference in what may be called a *Logical Machine*" His machine came equipped with "certain moveable wooden rods" and "at the foot are 21 keys like those of a piano [etc] . . .". With this machine he could analyze a "syllogism or any other simple logical argument".

This machine he displayed in 1870 before the Fellows of the Royal Society. Another logician John Venn, however, in his 1881 *Symbolic Logic*, turned a jaundiced eye to this effort: "I have no high estimate myself of the interest or importance of what are sometimes called logical machines ... it does not seem to me that any contrivances at present known or likely to be discovered really deserve the name of logical machines". But not to be outdone he too presented "a plan somewhat analogous, I apprehend, to Prof. Jevon's *abacus* ... [And] [a]gain, corresponding to Prof. Jevons's logical machine, the following contrivance may be described. I prefer to call it merely a logical-diagram machine ... but I suppose that it could do very completely all that can be rationally expected of any logical machine".

Jacquard loom, Hollerith punch cards, telegraphy and telephony—the electromechanical relay: Bell and Newell (1971) indicate that the Jacquard loom (1801), precursor to Hollerith cards (punch cards, 1887), and "telephone switching technologies" were the roots of a tree leading to the development of the first computers. By the mid-19th century the telegraph, the precursor of the telephone, was in use throughout the world, its discrete and distinguishable encoding of letters as "dots and dashes" a common sound. By the late 19th century the ticker tape (ca 1870s) was in use, as was the use of Hollerith cards in the 1890 U.S. census. Then came the teleprinter (ca. 1910) with its punched-paper use of Baudot code on tape.

Telephone-switching networks of electromechanical relays (invented 1835) was behind the work of George Stibitz (1937), the inventor of the digital adding device. As he worked in Bell Laboratories, he observed the "burdensome' use of mechanical calculators with gears. "He went home one evening in 1937 intending to test his idea... When the tinkering was over, Stibitz had constructed a binary adding device".

Davis (2000) observes the particular importance of the electromechanical relay (with its two "binary states" *open* and *closed*):

> "It was only with the development, beginning in the 1930s, of electromechanical calculators using electrical relays, that machines were built having the scope Babbage had envisioned."

Mathematics During the 19th Century up to the Mid-20th Century

Symbols and rules: In rapid succession the mathematics of George Boole (1847, 1854), Gottlob Frege (1879), and Giuseppe Peano (1888–1889) reduced arithmetic to a sequence of symbols manipulated by rules. Peano's *The principles of arithmetic, presented by a new method* (1888) was "the first attempt at an axiomatization of mathematics in a symbolic language".

But Heijenoort gives Frege (1879) this kudos: Frege's is "perhaps the most important single work ever written in logic. ... in which we see a " 'formula language', that is a *lingua characterica*, a language written with special symbols, "for pure thought", that is, free from rhetorical embellishments ... constructed from specific symbols that are manipulated according to definite rules". The work of Frege was further simplified and amplified by Alfred North Whitehead and Bertrand Russell in their Principia Mathematica (1910–1913).

The paradoxes: At the same time a number of disturbing paradoxes appeared in the literature, in particular the Burali-Forti paradox (1897), the Russell paradox (1902–03), and the Richard Paradox. The resultant considerations led to Kurt Gödel's paper (1931)—he specifically cites the paradox of the liar—that completely reduces rules of recursion to numbers.

Effective calculability: In an effort to solve the Entscheidungsproblem defined precisely by Hilbert in 1928, mathematicians first set about to define what was meant by an "effective method" or "effective calculation" or "effective calculability" (i.e., a calculation that would succeed). In rapid succession the following appeared: Alonzo Church, Stephen Kleene and J.B. Rosser's λ-calculus a finely honed definition of "general recursion" from the work of Gödel acting on suggestions of Jacques Herbrand (cf. Gödel's Princeton lectures of 1934) and subsequent simplifications by Kleene. Church's proof that the Entscheidungsproblem was unsolvable, Emil Post's definition of effective calculability as a worker mindlessly following a list of instructions to move left or right through a sequence of rooms and while there either mark or erase a paper or observe the paper and make a yes-no decision about the next instruction. Alan Turing's proof of that the Entscheidungsproblem was unsolvable by use of his "a- [automatic-] machine"—in effect almost identical to Post's "formulation", J. Barkley Rosser's definition of "effective method" in terms of "a machine". S. C. Kleene's proposal of a precursor to "Church thesis" that he called "Thesis I", and a few years later Kleene's renaming his Thesis "Church's Thesis" and proposing "Turing's Thesis".

Emil Post (1936) and Alan Turing (1936–37, 1939)

Here is a remarkable coincidence of two men not knowing each other but describing a process of men-as-computers working on computations—and they yield virtually identical definitions.

Emil Post (1936) described the actions of a "computer" (human being) as follows:

> "...two concepts are involved: that of a *symbol space* in which the work leading from problem to answer is to be carried out, and a fixed unalterable *set of directions*."

His symbol space would be

> "a two way infinite sequence of spaces or boxes... The problem solver or worker is to move and work in this symbol space, being capable of being in, and operating in but one box at a time.... a box is to admit of but two possible conditions, i.e., being empty or unmarked, and having a single mark in it, say a vertical stroke."

> "One box is to be singled out and called the starting point. ...a specific problem is to be given in symbolic form by a finite number of boxes [i.e., INPUT] being marked with a stroke. Likewise the answer [i.e., OUTPUT] is to be given in symbolic form by such a configuration of marked boxes...."

> "A set of directions applicable to a general problem sets up a deterministic process when applied to each specific problem. This process terminates only when it comes to the direction of type (C) [i.e., STOP]".

Alan Turing's statue at Bletchley Park

Alan Turing's work preceded that of Stibitz (1937); it is unknown whether Stibitz knew of the work of Turing. Turing's biographer believed that Turing's use of a typewriter-like model derived from a youthful interest: "Alan had dreamt of inventing typewriters as a boy; Mrs. Turing had a typewriter; and he could well have begun by asking himself what was meant by calling a typewriter 'mechanical'". Given the prevalence of Morse code and telegraphy, ticker tape machines, and teletypewriters we might conjecture that all were influences.

Turing—his model of computation is now called a Turing machine—begins, as did Post, with an analysis of a human computer that he whittles down to a simple set of basic motions and "states of mind". But he continues a step further and creates a machine as a model of computation of numbers.

"Computing is normally done by writing certain symbols on paper. We may suppose this paper is divided into squares like a child's arithmetic book....I assume then that the computation is carried out on one-dimensional paper, i.e., on a tape divided into squares. I shall also suppose that the number of symbols which may be printed is finite...."

"The behaviour of the computer at any moment is determined by the symbols which he is observing, and his "state of mind" at that moment. We may suppose that there is a bound B to the number of symbols or squares which the computer can observe at one moment. If he wishes to observe more, he must use successive observations. We will also suppose that the number of states of mind which need be taken into account is finite..."

"Let us imagine that the operations performed by the computer to be split up into 'simple operations' which are so elementary that it is not easy to imagine them further divided."

Turing's reduction yields the following:

The simple operations must therefore include:

(a) Changes of the symbol on one of the observed squares

(b) Changes of one of the squares observed to another square within L squares of one of the previously observed squares.

"It may be that some of these change necessarily invoke a change of state of mind. The most general single operation must therefore be taken to be one of the following:

(A) A possible change (a) of symbol together with a possible change of state of mind.

(B) A possible change (b) of observed squares, together with a possible change of state of mind"

"We may now construct a machine to do the work of this computer."

A few years later, Turing expanded his analysis (thesis, definition) with this forceful expression of it:

"A function is said to be "effectively calculable" if its values can be found by some purely mechanical process. Though it is fairly easy to get an intuitive grasp of this idea, it is nevertheless desirable to have some more definite, mathematical expressible definition . . . [he discusses the history of the definition pretty much as presented above with respect to Gödel, Herbrand, Kleene, Church, Turing and Post] . . . We may take this statement literally, understanding by a purely mechanical process one which could be carried out by a machine. It is possible to give a mathematical description, in a certain normal form, of the structures of these machines. The development of these ideas leads to the author's definition of a computable function, and to an identification of computability † with effective calculability . . . .

"† We shall use the expression "computable function" to mean a function calculable by a machine, and we let "effectively calculable" refer to the intuitive idea without particular identification with any one of these definitions".

J. B. Rosser (1939) and S. C. Kleene (1943)

J. Barkley Rosser defined an 'effective mathematical method' in the following manner (italicization added):

> "'Effective method' is used here in the rather special sense of a method each step of which is precisely determined and which is certain to produce the answer in a finite number of steps. With this special meaning, three different precise definitions have been given to date. The simplest of these to state (due to Post and Turing) says essentially that *an effective method of solving certain sets of problems exists if one can build a machine which will then solve any problem of the set with no human intervention beyond inserting the question and (later) reading the answer.* All three definitions are equivalent, so it doesn't matter which one is used. Moreover, the fact that all three are equivalent is a very strong argument for the correctness of any one." (Rosser 1939:225–6)

Rosser's footnote #5 references the work of (1) Church and Kleene and their definition of λ-definability, in particular Church's use of it in his *An Unsolvable Problem of Elementary Number Theory* (1936); (2) Herbrand and Gödel and their use of recursion in particular Gödel's use in his famous paper *On Formally Undecidable Propositions of Principia Mathematica and Related Systems I* (1931); and (3) Post (1936) and Turing (1936–7) in their mechanism-models of computation.

Stephen C. Kleene defined as his now-famous "Thesis I" known as the Church–Turing thesis. But he did this in the following context:

> "*Algorithmic theories...* In setting up a complete algorithmic theory, what we do is to describe a procedure, performable for each set of values of the independent variables, which procedure necessarily terminates and in such manner that from the outcome we can read a definite answer, "yes" or "no," to the question, "is the predicate value true?"" (Kleene 1943:273)

History After 1950

A number of efforts have been directed toward further refinement of the definition of "algorithm", and activity is on-going because of issues surrounding, in particular, foundations of mathematics (especially the Church–Turing thesis) and philosophy of mind (especially arguments about artificial intelligence).

Algorithms in Today's Society

Algorithms are complex codes which are instructions for solving a problem or completing a task. They are often considered as an automated process in which mathematical equations compute data to achieve an end result. Algorithms have been shaped by many technological advances which help extend their use and functionality in society. The internet today relies on algorithms and all online searching tools are accomplished through them. Our electronic devices, such as phones, cameras, and laptops, rely on algorithmic codes to help process numbers and calculations.

The Use of Algorithms in Popular Technology

Google's Search Engine

Google's goals as a search engine tool is to "organize the world's information and make it universally accessible and useful". Its search engine relies on the use of algorithms to help deliver its search results while collecting information from its visitors to help improve its search results. When a user inputs a keyword, the algorithmic code works by searching through millions of online web pages that match the keywords used to search. Its search engine also assigns a rank to each page, including how many times the keywords appear within a web page. Web pages that are categorized as having a high rank typically appear on the top, showing only the links closely relating to the keyword search.

Facebook's News Feed

Facebook is a social networking site that makes it easy for people to connect and keep in touch online. In 2006, Facebook introduced the "News Feed" tool which shows a personalized list of news stories which are influenced by your connections and activity on Facebook. The company relies on a system of metrics which monitors user engagement with content, which users provide unintentionally through online metrics. This information is then used to better serve the Facebook user with the help of algorithms embedded into its online platform, which are continuously developed and modified by engineers at Facebook.

Controversy Surrounding the Use of Algorithms

Facebook

In 2014, Facebook was criticized for experimenting on its users. A paper in the "Proceedings of the National Academy of Sciences" revealed that Facebook manipulated the newsfeeds of 689,000 users in order to study their emotions through social networks. The academic paper, titled "Experimental evidence of massive-scale emotional contagion through social network's" concluded that the emotions experienced by users online were influenced by the posts they read, which may have also lead to a behavioral change in their real life.

A spokeswoman from Facebook responded that the study was carried out "to improve our services and to make the content people see on Facebook as relevant and engaging as possible" and that "a big part of this is understanding how people respond to different types of content, whether it's positive or negative in tone, news from friends, or information from pages they follow."

In 2016, a former journalist who worked at Facebook revealed that the employees who were responsible on curating news suppressed conservative news stories. According to Gizmodo, the employees were tasked to promote different news stories on the trending news section, even though the conservative news was highly trending.

Google

In 2016, Google faced public criticism after receiving a number of complaints over the autocomplete suggestions in its search engine which suggested anti-semitic and other hateful recommendations in the search. Google has since then altered its algorithm to deter any hateful suggestions from appearing.

2016 U.S. Election Period

During the 2016 U.S. presidential election, the promulgation of fake news stories gained much attention in headlines by news outlets. Issues in the automated process of algorithms helped spread fake news across various online websites such as Google news and Facebook. Researchers from news outlets criticized that misleading headlines, news content, and pictures deceived people into believing these stories were substantially true. The issue at hand was not just with fake news, it seemed that algorithms played an important role in delivering fake news to people's newsfeed. It seemed like that the algorithms had a flaw when detecting the truthfulness between real news and fake news. Companies such as Facebook and Google were criticized for being at forefront of the problem, and began to address that their algorithms required revision, and publicly admitted to the fault in their algorithms.

Legal Concerns

Researcher, Andrew Tutt, argues that algorithms should be FDA regulated. His academic work emphasizes that the rise of increasingly complex algorithms calls for the need to think about the effects of algorithms today. Due to the nature and complexity of algorithms, it will prove to be difficult to hold algorithms accountable under criminal law. Tutt recognizes that while some algorithms will be beneficial to help meet technological demand, others should not be used or sold if they fail to meet safety requirements. Thus, for Tutt, algorithms will require "closer forms of federal uniformity, expert judgment, political independence, and pre-market review to prevent the introduction of unacceptably dangerous algorithms into the market."

Data Parallelism

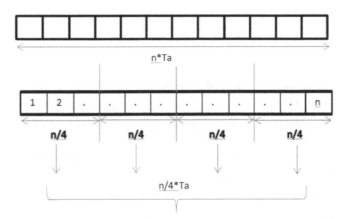

Sequential vs. Data Parallel job execution

Data parallelism is a form of parallelization across multiple processors in parallel computing environments. It focuses on distributing the data across different nodes, which operate on the data in parallel. It can be applied on regular data structures like arrays and matrices by working on each element in parallel. It contrasts to task parallelism as another form of parallelism.

A data parallel job on an array of 'n' elements can be divided equally among all the processors. Let us assume we want to sum all the elements of the given array and the time for a single addition operation is Ta time units. In the case of sequential execution, the time taken by the process will be n*Ta time units as it sums up all the elements of an array. On the other hand, if we execute this job as a data parallel job on 4 processors the time taken would reduce to (n/4)*Ta + Merging overhead time units. Parallel execution results in a speedup of 4 over sequential execution. One important thing to note is that the locality of data references plays an important part in evaluating the performance of a data parallel programming model. Locality of data depends on the memory accesses performed by the program as well as the size of the cache.

History

Exploitation of the concept of Data Parallelism started in 1960s with the development of Solomon machine. Solomon machine, also called a vector processor wanted to expedite the math performance by working on a large data array(operating on multiple data in consecutive time steps). Concurrency of data was also exploited by operating on multiple data points at the same time using a single instruction. These generation of processors were called Array Processors. Today, data parallelism is best exemplified in graphics processing units(GPUs) which use both the techniques of operating on multiple data points in space and time using a single instruction.

Description

In a multiprocessor system executing a single set of instructions (SIMD), data parallelism is achieved when each processor performs the same task on different pieces of distributed data. In some situations, a single execution thread controls operations on all pieces of data. In others, different threads control the operation, but they execute the same code.

For instance, consider matrix multiplication and addition in a sequential manner as discussed in the example.

Example

Below is the sequential pseudo-code for multiplication and addition of two matrices where the result is stored in the matrix C. The pseudo-code for multiplication calculates the dot product of two matrices A, B and stores the result into the output matrix C.

If the following programs were executed sequentially, the time taken to calculate the result would be of the $O(n^3)$ (assuming row lengths and column lengths of both matrices are n) and $O(n)$ for multiplication and addition respectively.

```
//Matrix Multiplication

for(i=0; i<row_length_A; i++)

{

        for (k=0; k<column_length_B; k++)

        {

                sum = 0;

                for (j=0; j<column_length_A; j++)

                {
```

```
                    sum += A[i][j]*B[j][k];
            }
            C[i][k]=sum;
        }
}
//Array addition
for(i=0;i<n;i++) {
    c[i]=a[i]+b[i];
    }
```

We can exploit data parallelism in the preceding codes to execute it faster as the arithmetic is loop independent. Parallelization of the matrix multiplication code is achieved by using OpenMP. An OpenMP directive, "omp parallel for" instructs the compiler to execute the code in the for loop in parallel. For multiplication, we can divide matrix A and B into blocks along rows and columns respectively. This allows us to calculate every element in matrix C individually thereby making the task parallel. For example: *A[m x n] dot B [n x k]* can be finished in $O(n)$ instead of $O(m*n*k)$ when executed in parallel using $m*k$ processors.

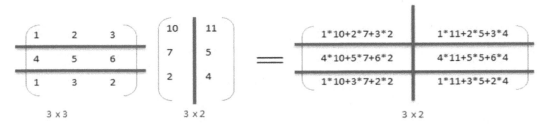

Data Parallelism in matrix multiplication

```
//Matrix multiplication in parallel
#pragma omp parallel for schedule(dynamic,1) collapse(2)
for(i=0; i<row_length_A; i++){
        for (k=0; k<column_length_B; k++){
                sum = 0;
                for (j=0; j<column_length_A; j++){
                        sum += A[i][j]*B[j][k];
                }
                C[i][k]=sum;
        }
}
```

It can be observed from the example that a lot of processors will be required as the matrix sizes keep on increasing. Keeping the execution time low is the priority but as the matrix size increases, we are faced with other constraints like complexity of such a system and its associated costs.

Therefore, constraining the number of processors in the system, we can still apply the same principle and divide the data into bigger chunks to calculate the product of two matrices.

For addition of arrays in a data parallel implementation, let's assume a more modest system with two Central Processing Units (CPU) A and B, CPU A could add all elements from the top half of the arrays, while CPU B could add all elements from the bottom half of the arrays. Since the two processors work in parallel, the job of performing array addition would take one half the time of performing the same operation in serial using one CPU alone.

The program expressed in pseudocode below—which applies some arbitrary operation, foo, on every element in the array d—illustrates data parallelism:

```
if CPU = "a"

    lower_limit := 1

    upper_limit := round(d.length/2)

else if CPU = "b"

    lower_limit := round(d.length/2) + 1

    upper_limit := d.length

for i from lower_limit to upper_limit by 1

    foo(d[i])
```

In an SPMD system executed on 2 processor system, both CPUs will execute the code.

Data parallelism emphasizes the distributed (parallel) nature of the data, as opposed to the processing (task parallelism). Most real programs fall somewhere on a continuum between task parallelism and data parallelism.

Steps to Parallelization

The process of parallelizing a sequential program can be broken down into four discrete steps.

Type	Description
Decomposition	The program is broken down into tasks, the smallest exploitable unit of concurrency.
Assignment	Tasks are assigned to processes.
Orchestration	Data access, communication, and synchronization of processes.
Mapping	Processes are bound to processors.

Data Parallelism vs. Task Parallelism

Data Parallelism	Task Parallelism
Same operations are performed on different subsets of same data.	Different operations are performed on the same or different data.
Synchronous computation	Asynchronous computation

Speedup is more as there is only one execution thread operating on all sets of data.	Speedup is less as each processor will execute a different thread or process on the same or different set of data.
Amount of parallelization is proportional to the input data size.	Amount of parallelization is proportional to the number of independent tasks to be performed.
Designed for optimum load balance on multi processor system.	Load balancing depends on the availability of the hardware and scheduling algorithms like static and dynamic scheduling.

Data Parallelism vs. Model Parallelism

Data Parallelism	Model Parallelism
Same model is used for every thread but the data given to each of them is divided and shared.	Same data is used for every thread, and model is split among threads.
It is fast for small networks but very slow for large networks since large amounts of data needs to be transferred between processors all at once.	It is slow for small networks and fast for large networks.
Data parallelism is ideally used in array and matrix computations and convolutional neural networks	Model parallelism finds its applications in deep learning

Mixed Data and Task Parallelism

Data and task parallelism, can be simultaneously implemented by combining them together for the same application. This is called Mixed data and task parallelism. Mixed parallelism requires sophisticated scheduling algorithms and software support. It is the best kind of parallelism when communication is slow and number of processors is large.

Mixed data and task parallelism has many applications. It is particularly used in the following applications:

1. Mixed data and task parallelism finds applications in the global climate modeling. Large data parallel computations are performed by creating grids of data representing earth's atmosphere and oceans and task parallelism is employed for simulating the function and model of the physical processes.

2. In timing based circuit simulation. The data is divided among different sub-circuits and parallelism is achieved with orchestration from the tasks.

Data Parallel Programming Environments

A variety of data parallel programming environments are available today, most widely used of which are:

1. Message Passing Interface: It is a cross-platform message passing programming interface for parallel computers. It defines the semantics of library functions to allow users to write portable message passing programs in C, C++ and Fortran.

2. Open Multi Processing (Open MP): It's an Application Programming Interface (API) which supports shared memory programming models on multiple platforms of multiprocessor systems .

3. CUDA and OpenACC: CUDA and OpenACC (respectively) are parallel computing API plat-

forms designed to allow a software engineer to utilize GPU's computational units for general purpose processing.

4. Threading Building Blocks and RaftLib: Both open source programming environments that enable mixed data/task parallelism in C/C++ environments across heterogeneous resources.

Applications

Data Parallelism finds its applications in a variety of fields ranging from physics, chemistry, biology, material sciences to signal processing. Sciences imply data parallelism for simulating models like molecular dynamics, sequence analysis of genome data and other physical phenomenon. Driving forces in signal processing for data parallelism are video encoding, image and graphics processing, wireless communications to name a few.

Task Parallelism

Task parallelism (also known as function parallelism and control parallelism) is a form of parallelization of computer code across multiple processors in parallel computing environments. Task parallelism focuses on distributing tasks—concurrently performed by processes or threads—across different processors. It contrasts to data parallelism as another form of parallelism.

Description

In a multiprocessor system, task parallelism is achieved when each processor executes a different thread (or process) on the same or different data. The threads may execute the same or different code. In the general case, different execution threads communicate with one another as they work. Communication usually takes place by passing data from one thread to the next as part of a workflow.

As a simple example, if a system is running code on a 2-processor system (CPUs "a" & "b") in a parallel environment and we wish to do tasks "A" and "B", it is possible to tell CPU "a" to do task "A" and CPU "b" to do task "B" simultaneously, thereby reducing the run time of the execution. The tasks can be assigned using conditional statements as described below.

Task parallelism emphasizes the distributed (parallelized) nature of the processing (i.e. threads), as opposed to the data (data parallelism). Most real programs fall somewhere on a continuum between task parallelism and data parallelism.

Thread-level parallelism (TLP) is the parallelism inherent in an application that runs multiple threads at once. This type of parallelism is found largely in applications written for commercial servers such as databases. By running many threads at once, these applications are able to tolerate the high amounts of I/O and memory system latency their workloads can incur - while one thread is delayed waiting for a memory or disk access, other threads can do useful work.

The exploitation of thread-level parallelism has also begun to make inroads into the desktop market with the advent of multi-core microprocessors. This has occurred because, for various reasons, it has become increasingly impractical to increase either the clock speed or instructions per clock of a single core. If this trend continues, new applications will have to be designed to utilize multiple threads in order to benefit from the increase in potential computing power. This contrasts with previous microprocessor innovations in which existing code was automatically sped up by running it on a newer/faster computer.

Example

The pseudocode below illustrates task parallelism:

```
program:
...
if CPU="a" then
    do task "A"
else if CPU="b" then
    do task "B"
end if
...
end program
```

The goal of the program is to do some net total task ("A+B"). If we write the code as above and launch it on a 2-processor system, then the runtime environment will execute it as follows.

- In an SPMD system, both CPUs will execute the code.

- In a parallel environment, both will have access to the same data.

- The "if" clause differentiates between the CPUs. CPU "a" will read true on the "if" and CPU "b" will read true on the "else if", thus having their own task.

- Now, both CPU's execute separate code blocks simultaneously, performing different tasks simultaneously.

Code executed by CPU "a":

```
program:
...
do task "A"
...
end program
```

Code executed by CPU "b":

```
program:
...
do task "B"
...
```

```
end program
```

This concept can now be generalized to any number of processors.

Task-parallel Languages

Examples of (fine-grained) task-parallel languages can be found in the realm of Hardware Description Languages like Verilog and VHDL, which can also be considered as representing a "code static" software paradigm where the program has a static structure and the data is changing - as against a "data static" model where the data is not changing (or changing slowly) and the processing (applied methods) change (e.g. database search).

Master/Slave (Technology)

Master/slave is a model of communication where one device or process has unidirectional control over one or more other devices. In some systems a master is selected from a group of eligible devices, with the other devices acting in the role of slaves.

In other words, "The master/slave configuration is basically used for load sharing purposes when two identical motors connected to two different drives are coupled to a common load". One drive is defined as the master and is configured for running in the speed-control mode whereas the other defined as slave is configured for running in torque-control mode.

Examples

- In database replication, the master database is regarded as the authoritative source, and the slave databases are synchronized to it.

- Hydraulic and pneumatic systems may use a master cylinder to control one or several slave cylinders.

- Peripherals connected to a bus in a computer system.

- Railway locomotives operating in multiple (for example: to pull loads too heavy for a single locomotive) can be referred to as a master/slave configuration - with the operation of all locomotives in the train slaved to the controls of the first locomotive.

- Duplication is often done with several cassette tape or compact disc recorders linked together. Operating the controls on the master triggers the same commands on the slaves, so that recording is done in parallel.

- In parallel ATA hard drive arrangements, the terms master and slave are used but neither drive has control over the other. The terms also do not indicate precedence of one drive over the other in most situations. "Master" is merely another term for device 0 and "slave" indicates device 1.

- Rmpi package in R is a standard master/slaves programming model.

- On the Macintosh platform, rebooting into Target Disk Mode allows one computer to operate as a dumb disk enclosure presenting its storage devices to another via SCSI, FireWire, or Thunderbolt, essentially a slave mode bridge.

- A master clock that provides time signals used to synchronize one or more slave clocks as part of a clock network.

Appropriateness of Usage

In 2003, the County of Los Angeles in California asked that manufacturers, suppliers and contractors to stop using "master" and "slave" terminology on its products; the county made this request "based on the cultural diversity and sensitivity of Los Angeles County". Following outcries about the request, the County of Los Angeles issued a statement saying that the decision was "nothing more than a request". Due to the controversy, the term was selected as the most politically incorrect word in 2004 by Global Language Monitor.

In May 2014, GitHub user fcurella submitted a pull request to the GitHub repository for the Python framework Django, initially changing it to "leader/follower" and finally to "primary/replica". This triggered an active discussion of the appropriateness of the master/slave terminology as well as the appropriateness of the change.

In June 2014, Drupal 8 did the same as Django did, citing that the word "replica" is already in use by IBM, Microsoft, Engine Yard, Amazon Web Services, and ACM.

In September 2016, Deprecated instances of the terms "slave" in preference of "replica".

Producer–consumer Problem

In computing, the producer–consumer problem (also known as the bounded-buffer problem) is a classic example of a multi-process synchronization problem. The problem describes two processes, the producer and the consumer, who share a common, fixed-size buffer used as a queue. The producer's job is to generate data, put it into the buffer, and start again. At the same time, the consumer is consuming the data (i.e., removing it from the buffer), one piece at a time. The problem is to make sure that the producer won't try to add data into the buffer if it's full and that the consumer won't try to remove data from an empty buffer.

The solution for the producer is to either go to sleep or discard data if the buffer is full. The next time the consumer removes an item from the buffer, it notifies the producer, who starts to fill the buffer again. In the same way, the consumer can go to sleep if it finds the buffer to be empty. The next time the producer puts data into the buffer, it wakes up the sleeping consumer. The solution can be reached by means of inter-process communication, typically using semaphores. An inadequate solution could result in a deadlock where both processes are waiting to be awakened. The problem can also be generalized to have multiple producers and consumers.

Inadequate Implementation

To solve the problem, a less experienced programmer might come up with a solution shown below. In the solution two library routines are used, sleep and wakeup. When sleep is called, the caller is blocked until another process wakes it up by using the wakeup routine. The global variable itemCount holds the number of items in the buffer.

```
int itemCount = 0;

Procedure Producer() {
```

```
    while (true) {

        item = produceItem();

        if (itemCount == BUFFER_SIZE) {

            sleep();

        }

        putItemIntoBuffer(item);

        itemCount = itemCount + 1;

        if (itemCount == 1) {

            wakeup(consumer);

        }

    }

}

procedure consumer() {

    while (true) {

        if (itemCount == 0) {

            sleep();

        }

        item = removeItemFromBuffer();

        itemCount = itemCount - 1;

        if (itemCount == BUFFER_SIZE - 1) {

            wakeup(producer);

        }

        consumeItem(item);

    }

}
```

The problem with this solution is that it contains a race condition that can lead to a deadlock. Consider the following scenario:

1. The consumer has just read the variable itemCount, noticed it's zero and is just about to move inside the if block.

2. Just before calling sleep, the consumer is interrupted and the producer is resumed.

3. The producer creates an item, puts it into the buffer, and increases itemCount.

4. Because the buffer was empty prior to the last addition, the producer tries to wake up the consumer.

5. Unfortunately the consumer wasn't yet sleeping, and the wakeup call is lost. When the consumer resumes, it goes to sleep and will never be awakened again. This is because the

consumer is only awakened by the producer when itemCount is equal to 1.

6. The producer will loop until the buffer is full, after which it will also go to sleep.

Since both processes will sleep forever, we have run into a deadlock. This solution therefore is unsatisfactory.

An alternative analysis is that if the programming language does not define the semantics of concurrent accesses to shared variables (in this case itemCount) without use of synchronization, then the solution is unsatisfactory for that reason, without needing to explicitly demonstrate a race condition.

Using Semaphores

Semaphores solve the problem of lost wakeup calls. In the solution below we use two semaphores, fillCount and emptyCount, to solve the problem. fillCount is the number of items already in the buffer and available to be read, while emptyCount is the number of available spaces in the buffer where items could be written. fillCount is incremented and emptyCount decremented when a new item is put into the buffer. If the producer tries to decrement emptyCount when its value is zero, the producer is put to sleep. The next time an item is consumed, emptyCount is incremented and the producer wakes up. The consumer works analogously.

```
semaphore fillCount = 0; // items produced

semaphore emptyCount = BUFFER_SIZE; // remaining space

procedure producer() {

    while (true) {

        item = produceItem();

        down(emptyCount);

        putItemIntoBuffer(item);

        up(fillCount);

    }

}

procedure consumer() {

    while (true) {

        down(fillCount);

        item = removeItemFromBuffer();

        up(emptyCount);

        consumeItem(item);

    }

}
```

The solution above works fine when there is only one producer and consumer. With multiple producers sharing the same memory space for the item buffer, or multiple consumers sharing the same memory space, this solution contains a serious race condition that could result in two or more processes reading or writing into the same slot at the same time. To understand how this is possible, imagine how the procedure putItemIntoBuffer() can be implemented. It could contain two actions, one determining the next available slot and the other writing into it. If the procedure can be executed concurrently by multiple producers, then the following scenario is possible:

1. Two producers decrement emptyCount

2. One of the producers determines the next empty slot in the buffer

3. Second producer determines the next empty slot and gets the same result as the first producer

4. Both producers write into the same slot

To overcome this problem, we need a way to make sure that only one producer is executing putItemIntoBuffer() at a time. In other words, we need a way to execute a critical section with mutual exclusion. The solution for multiple producers and consumers is shown below.

```
mutex buffer_mutex; // similar to "semaphore buffer_mutex = 1", but different

semaphore fillCount = 0;

semaphore emptyCount = BUFFER_SIZE;

procedure producer() {

    while (true) {

        item = produceItem();

        down(emptyCount);

            down(buffer_mutex);

                putItemIntoBuffer(item);

            up(buffer_mutex);

        up(fillCount);

    }

}

procedure consumer() {

    while (true) {

        down(fillCount);

            down(buffer_mutex);

                item = removeItemFromBuffer();

            up(buffer_mutex);

        up(emptyCount);

        consumeItem(item);

    }
```

```
}
```

Notice that the order in which different semaphores are incremented or decremented is essential: changing the order might result in a deadlock. It is important to note here that though mutex seems to work as a semaphore with value of 1 (binary semaphore), but there is difference in the fact that mutex has ownership concept. Ownership means that mutex can only be "incremented" back (set to 1) by the same process that "decremented" it (set to 0), and all others tasks wait until mutex is available for decrement (effectively meaning that resource is available), which ensures mutual exclusivity and avoids deadlock. Thus using mutexes improperly can stall many processes when exclusive access is not required, but mutex is used instead of semaphore.

Using Monitors

The following pseudo code shows a solution to the producer–consumer problem using monitors. Since mutual exclusion is implicit with monitors, no extra effort is necessary to protect the critical section. In other words, the solution shown below works with any number of producers and consumers without any modifications. It is also noteworthy that using monitors makes race conditions much less likely than when using semaphores.

```
monitor ProducerConsumer {

    int itemCount;

    condition full;

    condition empty;

    procedure add(item) {

        while (itemCount == BUFFER_SIZE) {

            wait(full);

        }

        putItemIntoBuffer(item);

        itemCount = itemCount + 1;

        if (itemCount == 1) {

            notify(empty);

        }

    }

    procedure remove() {

        while (itemCount == 0) {

            wait(empty);

        }

        item = removeItemFromBuffer();

        itemCount = itemCount - 1;

        if (itemCount == BUFFER_SIZE - 1) {

            notify(full);
```

```
        }
        return item;
    }
}
procedure producer() {
    while (true) {
        item = produceItem();
        ProducerConsumer.add(item);
    }
}
procedure consumer() {
    while (true) {
        item = ProducerConsumer.remove();
        consumeItem(item);
    }
}
```

Note the use of while statements in the above code, both when testing if the buffer is full or empty. With multiple consumers, there is a race condition where one consumer gets notified that an item has been put into the buffer but another consumer is already waiting on the monitor so removes it from the buffer instead. If the while was instead an if, too many items might be put into the buffer or a remove might be attempted on an empty buffer.

Without Semaphores or Monitors

The producer–consumer problem, particularly in the case of a single producer and single consumer, strongly relates to implementing a FIFO or a channel. The producer–consumer pattern can provide highly efficient data communication without relying on semaphores, mutexes, or monitors *for data transfer*. Use of those primitives can give performance issues as they are expensive to implement. Channels and FIFOs are popular just because they avoid the need for end-to-end atomic synchronization. A basic example coded in C is shown below. Note that:

- Atomic read-modify-write access to shared variables is avoided, as each of the two Count variables is updated only by a single thread. Also, these variables stay incremented all the time; the relation remains correct when their values wrap around on an integer overflow.

- This example does not put threads to sleep, which may be acceptable depending on the system context. The sched_yield() is there just to behave nicely and could be removed. Thread libraries typically require semaphores or condition variables to control the sleep/wakeup of threads. In a multi-processor environment, thread sleep/wakeup would occur much less frequently than passing of data tokens, so avoiding atomic operations on data passing is beneficial.

- This example does not work for multiple producers and/or consumers because there is a race condition when checking the state. For example, if only one token is in the storage buffer and two consumers find the buffer non-empty, then both will consume the same token and possibly increase the count of consumed tokens over produced counter.

- This example, as written, requires that UINT_MAX + 1 is evenly divisible by BUFFER_SIZE; if it is not evenly divisible, [Count % BUFFER_SIZE] produces the wrong buffer index after Count wraps past UINT_MAX back to zero. An alternate solution without this restriction would employ two additional Idx variables to track the current buffer index for the head (producer) and tail (consumer). These Idx variables would be used in place of [Count % BUFFER_SIZE], and each of them would have to be incremented at the same time as the respective Count variable is incremented, as follows: Idx = (Idx + 1) % BUFFER_SIZE.

```
volatile unsigned int produceCount = 0, consumeCount = 0;

TokenType buffer[BUFFER_SIZE];

void producer(void) {

    while (1) {

        while (produceCount - consumeCount == BUFFER_SIZE)

            sched_yield(); /* `buffer` is full */

        /* You must update the field in the buffer _before_ incrementing your

         * pointer.

         */

        buffer[produceCount % BUFFER_SIZE] = produceToken();

        ++produceCount;

    }

}

void consumer(void) {

    while (1) {

        while (produceCount - consumeCount == 0)

            sched_yield(); /* `buffer` is empty */

        consumeToken(&buffer[consumeCount % BUFFER_SIZE]);

        ++consumeCount;

    }

}
```

Hybrid Algorithm

A hybrid algorithm is an algorithm that combines two or more other algorithms that solve the same problem, either choosing one (depending on the data), or switching between them over the course of the algorithm. This is generally done to combine desired features of each, so that the overall algorithm is better than the individual components.

"Hybrid algorithm" does not refer to simply combining multiple algorithms to solve a different problem – many algorithms can be considered as combinations of simpler pieces – but only to combining algorithms that solve the same problem, but differ in other characteristics, notably performance.

Examples

In computer science, hybrid algorithms are very common in optimized real-world implementations of recursive algorithms, particularly implementations of divide and conquer or decrease and conquer algorithms, where the size of the data decreases as one moves deeper in the recursion. In this case, one algorithm is used for the overall approach (on large data), but deep in the recursion, it switches to a different algorithm, which is more efficient on small data. A common example is in sorting algorithms, where the insertion sort, which is inefficient on large data, but very efficient on small data (say, five to ten elements), is used as the final step, after primarily applying another algorithm, such as merge sort or quicksort. Merge sort and quicksort are asymptotically optimal on large data, but the overhead becomes significant if applying them to small data, hence the use of a different algorithm at the end of the recursion. A highly optimized hybrid sorting algorithm is Timsort, which combines merge sort, insertion sort, together with additional logic (including binary search) in the merging logic.

A general procedure for a simple hybrid recursive algorithm is *short-circuiting the base case,* also known as *arm's-length recursion.* In this case whether the next step will result in the base case is checked before the function call, avoiding an unnecessary function call. For example, in a tree, rather than recursing to a child node and then checking if it is null, checking null before recursing. This is useful for efficiency when the algorithm usually encounters the base case many times, as in many tree algorithms, but is otherwise considered poor style, particularly in academia, due to the added complexity.

Another example of hybrid algorithms for performance reasons are introsort and introselect, which combine one algorithm for fast average performance, falling back on another algorithm to ensure (asymptotically) optimal worst-case performance. Introsort begins with a quicksort, but switches to a heap sort if quicksort is not progressing well; analogously introselect begins with quickselect, but switches to median of medians if quickselect is not progressing well.

Centralized distributed algorithms can often be considered as hybrid algorithms, consisting of an individual algorithm (run on each distributed processor), and a combining algorithm (run on a centralized distributor) – these correspond respectively to running the entire algorithm on one processor, or running the entire computation on the distributor, combining trivial results (a one-element data set from each processor). A basic example of these algorithms are distribution sorts, particularly used for external sorting, which divide the data into separate subsets, sort the subsets, and then combine the subsets into totally sorted data; examples include bucket sort and flashsort.

However, in general distributed algorithms need not be hybrid algorithms, as individual algorithms or combining or communication algorithms may be solving different problems. For example, in models such as MapReduce, the Map and Reduce step solve different problems, and are combined to solve a different, third problem.

Recursion (Computer Science)

Tree created using the Logo programming language and relying heavily on recursion

Recursion in computer science is a method where the solution to a problem depends on solutions to smaller instances of the same problem (as opposed to iteration). The approach can be applied to many types of problems, and recursion is one of the central ideas of computer science.

"The power of recursion evidently lies in the possibility of defining an infinite set of objects by a finite statement. In the same manner, an infinite number of computations can be described by a finite recursive program, even if this program contains no explicit repetitions."

Most computer programming languages support recursion by allowing a function to call itself within the program text. Some functional programming languages do not define any looping constructs but rely solely on recursion to repeatedly call code. Computability theory proves that these recursive-only languages are Turing complete; they are as computationally powerful as Turing complete imperative languages, meaning they can solve the same kinds of problems as imperative languages even without iterative control structures such as "while" and "for".

Recursive Functions and Algorithms

A common computer programming tactic is to divide a problem into sub-problems of the same type as the original, solve those sub-problems, and combine the results. This is often referred to as the divide-and-conquer method; when combined with a lookup table that stores the results of solving sub-problems (to avoid solving them repeatedly and incurring extra computation time), it can be referred to as dynamic programming or memoization.

A recursive function definition has one or more *base cases*, meaning input(s) for which the function produces a result trivially (without recurring), and one or more *recursive cases*, meaning input(s) for which the program recurs (calls itself). For example, the factorial function can be defined recursively by the equations $0! = 1$ and, for all $n > 0$, $n! = n(n - 1)!$. Neither equation by itself constitutes a complete definition; the first is the base case, and the second is the recursive case. Because the base case breaks the chain of recursion, it is sometimes also called the "terminating case".

The job of the recursive cases can be seen as breaking down complex inputs into simpler ones. In a properly designed recursive function, with each recursive call, the input problem must be simplified in such a way that eventually the base case must be reached. (Functions that are not intended to terminate under normal circumstances—for example, some system and server processes—are an exception to this.) Neglecting to write a base case, or testing for it incorrectly, can cause an infinite loop.

For some functions (such as one that computes the series for $e = 1/0! + 1/1! + 1/2! + 1/3! + ...$) there is not an obvious base case implied by the input data; for these one may add a parameter (such as the number of terms to be added, in our series example) to provide a 'stopping criterion' that establishes the base case. Such an example is more naturally treated by co-recursion, where successive terms in the output are the partial sums; this can be converted to a recursion by using the indexing parameter to say "compute the nth term (nth partial sum)".

Recursive Data Types

Many computer programs must process or generate an arbitrarily large quantity of data. Recursion is one technique for representing data whose exact size the programmer does not know: the programmer can specify this data with a self-referential definition. There are two types of self-referential definitions: inductive and coinductive definitions.

Inductively Defined Data

An inductively defined recursive data definition is one that specifies how to construct instances of the data. For example, linked lists can be defined inductively (here, using Haskell syntax):

```
data ListOfStrings = EmptyList | Cons String ListOfStrings
```

The code above specifies a list of strings to be either empty, or a structure that contains a string and a list of strings. The self-reference in the definition permits the construction of lists of any (finite) number of strings.

Another example of inductive definition is the natural numbers (or positive integers):

```
A natural number is either 1 or n+1, where n is a natural number.
```

Similarly recursive definitions are often used to model the structure of expressions and statements in programming languages. Language designers often express grammars in a syntax such as Backus-Naur form; here is such a grammar, for a simple language of arithmetic expressions with multiplication and addition:

```
<expr> ::= <number>
```

```
    | (<expr> * <expr>)

    | (<expr> + <expr>)
```

This says that an expression is either a number, a product of two expressions, or a sum of two expressions. By recursively referring to expressions in the second and third lines, the grammar permits arbitrarily complex arithmetic expressions such as (5 * ((3 * 6) + 8)), with more than one product or sum operation in a single expression.

Coinductively Defined Data and Corecursion

A coinductive data definition is one that specifies the operations that may be performed on a piece of data; typically, self-referential coinductive definitions are used for data structures of infinite size.

A coinductive definition of infinite streams of strings, given informally, might look like this:

```
A stream of strings is an object s such that:

 head(s) is a string, and

 tail(s) is a stream of strings.
```

This is very similar to an inductive definition of lists of strings; the difference is that this definition specifies how to access the contents of the data structure—namely, via the accessor functions head and tail—and what those contents may be, whereas the inductive definition specifies how to create the structure and what it may be created from.

Corecursion is related to coinduction, and can be used to compute particular instances of (possibly) infinite objects. As a programming technique, it is used most often in the context of lazy programming languages, and can be preferable to recursion when the desired size or precision of a program's output is unknown. In such cases the program requires both a definition for an infinitely large (or infinitely precise) result, and a mechanism for taking a finite portion of that result. The problem of computing the first n prime numbers is one that can be solved with a corecursive program (e.g. here).

Types of Recursion

Single Recursion and Multiple Recursion

Recursion that only contains a single self-reference is known as single recursion, while recursion that contains multiple self-references is known as multiple recursion. Standard examples of single recursion include list traversal, such as in a linear search, or computing the factorial function, while standard examples of multiple recursion include tree traversal, such as in a depth-first search.

Single recursion is often much more efficient than multiple recursion, and can generally be replaced by an iterative computation, running in linear time and requiring constant space. Multiple recursion, by contrast, may require exponential time and space, and is more fundamentally recursive, not being able to be replaced by iteration without an explicit stack.

Multiple recursion can sometimes be converted to single recursion (and, if desired, thence to iteration). For example, while computing the Fibonacci sequence naively is multiple iteration, as each value requires two previous values, it can be computed by single recursion by passing two successive values as parameters. This is more naturally framed as corecursion, building up from the initial values, tracking at each step two successive values – see corecursion: examples. A more sophisticated example is using a threaded binary tree, which allows iterative tree traversal, rather than multiple recursion.

Indirect Recursion

Most basic examples of recursion, and most of the examples presented here, demonstrate *direct* recursion, in which a function calls itself. *Indirect* recursion occurs when a function is called not by itself but by another function that it called (either directly or indirectly). For example, if *f* calls *f*, that is direct recursion, but if *f* calls *g* which calls *f*, then that is indirect recursion of *f*. Chains of three or more functions are possible; for example, function 1 calls function 2, function 2 calls function 3, and function 3 calls function 1 again.

Indirect recursion is also called mutual recursion, which is a more symmetric term, though this is simply a difference of emphasis, not a different notion. That is, if *f* calls *g* and then *g* calls *f*, which in turn calls *g* again, from the point of view of *f* alone, *f* is indirectly recursing, while from the point of view of *g* alone, it is indirectly recursing, while from the point of view of both, *f* and *g* are mutually recursing on each other. Similarly a set of three or more functions that call each other can be called a set of mutually recursive functions.

Anonymous Recursion

Recursion is usually done by explicitly calling a function by name. However, recursion can also be done via implicitly calling a function based on the current context, which is particularly useful for anonymous functions, and is known as anonymous recursion.

Structural Versus Generative Recursion

Some authors classify recursion as either "structural" or "generative". The distinction is related to where a recursive procedure gets the data that it works on, and how it processes that data:

[Functions that consume structured data] typically decompose their arguments into their immediate structural components and then process those components. If one of the immediate components belongs to the same class of data as the input, the function is recursive. For that reason, we refer to these functions as (Structurally) Recursive Functions.

Thus, the defining characteristic of a structurally recursive function is that the argument to each recursive call is the content of a field of the original input. Structural recursion includes nearly all tree traversals, including XML processing, binary tree creation and search, etc. By considering the algebraic structure of the natural numbers (that is, a natural number is either zero or the successor of a natural number), functions such as factorial may also be regarded as structural recursion.

Generative recursion is the alternative:

Many well-known recursive algorithms generate an entirely new piece of data from the given data and recur on it. HtDP (How To Design Programs) refers to this kind as generative recursion. Examples of generative recursion include: gcd, quicksort, binary search, mergesort, Newton's method, fractals, and adaptive integration.

This distinction is important in proving termination of a function.

- All structurally recursive functions on finite (inductively defined) data structures can easily be shown to terminate, via structural induction: intuitively, each recursive call receives a smaller piece of input data, until a base case is reached.

- Generatively recursive functions, in contrast, do not necessarily feed smaller input to their recursive calls, so proof of their termination is not necessarily as simple, and avoiding infinite loops requires greater care. These generatively recursive functions can often be interpreted as corecursive functions – each step generates the new data, such as successive approximation in Newton's method – and terminating this corecursion requires that the data eventually satisfy some condition, which is not necessarily guaranteed.

- In terms of loop variants, structural recursion is when there is an obvious loop variant, namely size or complexity, which starts off finite and decreases at each recursive step.

- By contrast, generative recursion is when there is not such an obvious loop variant, and termination depends on a function, such as "error of approximation" that does not necessarily decrease to zero, and thus termination is not guaranteed without further analysis.

Recursive Programs

Factorial

A classic example of a recursive procedure is the function used to calculate the factorial of a natural number:

$$\text{fact}(n) = \begin{cases} 1 & \text{if } n = 0 \\ n \cdot \text{fact}(n-1) & \text{if } n > 0 \end{cases}$$

Pseudocode (recursive):

```
function factorial is:
input: integer n such that n >= 0

output: [n × (n-1) × (n-2) × … × 1]

    1. if n is 0, return 1

    2. otherwise, return [ n × factorial(n-1) ]

end factorial
```

The function can also be written as a recurrence relation:

$$b_n = nb_{n-1}$$

$$b_0 = 1$$

This evaluation of the recurrence relation demonstrates the computation that would be performed in evaluating the pseudocode above:

Computing the recurrence relation for n = 4:

```
b4          = 4 * b3

            = 4 * (3 * b2)

            = 4 * (3 * (2 * b1))

            = 4 * (3 * (2 * (1 * b0)))

            = 4 * (3 * (2 * (1 * 1)))

            = 4 * (3 * (2 * 1))

            = 4 * (3 * 2)

            = 4 * 6

            = 24
```

This factorial function can also be described without using recursion by making use of the typical looping constructs found in imperative programming languages:

Pseudocode (iterative):

```
function factorial is:
input: integer n such that n >= 0
output: [n × (n-1) × (n-2) × … × 1]

    1. create new variable called running_total with a value of 1

    2. begin loop

        1. if n is 0, exit loop

        2. set running_total to (running_total × n)

        3. decrement n

        4. repeat loop

    3. return running_total

end factorial
```

The imperative code above is equivalent to this mathematical definition using an accumulator variable *t:*

$$\mathrm{fact}(n) \quad = \quad \mathrm{fact}_{acc}(n, 1)$$

$$\mathrm{fact}_{acc}(n, t) \quad = \quad \begin{cases} t & \text{if } n = 0 \\ \mathrm{fact}_{acc}(n - 1, nt) & \text{if } n > 0 \end{cases}$$

The definition above translates straightforwardly to functional programming languages such as Scheme; this is an example of iteration implemented recursively.

Greatest Common Divisor

The Euclidean algorithm, which computes the greatest common divisor of two integers, can be written recursively.

Function definition:

$$\gcd(x, y) = \begin{cases} x & \text{if } y = 0 \\ \gcd(y, \text{remainder}(x, y)) & \text{if } y > 0 \end{cases}$$

Pseudocode (recursive):

```
function gcd is:

input: integer x, integer y such that x > 0 and y >= 0

    1. if y is 0, return x

    2. otherwise, return [ gcd( y, (remainder of x/y) ) ]

end gcd
```

Recurrence relation for greatest common divisor, where $x \% y$ expresses the remainder of x / y :

$$\gcd(x, y) = \gcd(y, x \% y) \text{ if } y \neq 0 \quad _{77}$$

$$\gcd(x, 0) = x$$

Computing the recurrence relation for x = 27 and y = 9:

```
gcd(27, 9)    = gcd(9, 27% 9)

              = gcd(9, 0)

              = 9
```

Computing the recurrence relation for x = 111 and y = 259:

```
gcd(111, 259)   = gcd(259, 111% 259)

                = gcd(259, 111)

                = gcd(111, 259% 111)

                = gcd(111, 37)

                = gcd(37, 111% 37)

                = gcd(37, 0)

                = 37
```

The recursive program above is tail-recursive; it is equivalent to an iterative algorithm, and the computation shown above shows the steps of evaluation that would be performed by a language that eliminates tail calls. Below is a version of the same algorithm using explicit iteration, suitable for a language that does not eliminate tail calls. By maintaining its state entirely in the variables x and y and using a looping construct, the program avoids making recursive calls and growing the call stack.

Pseudocode (iterative):

```
function gcd is:
input: integer x, integer y such that x >= y and y >= 0

    1. create new variable called remainder

    2. begin loop

            1. if y is zero, exit loop

            2. set remainder to the remainder of x/y

            3. set x to y

            4. set y to remainder

            5. repeat loop

    3. return x

end gcd
```

The iterative algorithm requires a temporary variable, and even given knowledge of the Euclidean algorithm it is more difficult to understand the process by simple inspection, although the two algorithms are very similar in their steps.

Towers of Hanoi

Towers of Hanoi

The Towers of Hanoi is a mathematical puzzle whose solution illustrates recursion. There are three pegs which can hold stacks of disks of different diameters. A larger disk may never be stacked on top of a smaller. Starting with n disks on one peg, they must be moved to another peg one at a time. What is the smallest number of steps to move the stack?

Function definition:

$$\text{hanoi}(n) = \begin{cases} 1 & \text{if } n = 1 \\ 2 \cdot \text{hanoi}(n-1) + 1 & \text{if } n > 1 \end{cases}$$

Recurrence relation for hanoi:

$$h_n = 2h_{n-1} + 1$$

$$h_1 = 1$$

Computing the recurrence relation for n = 4:

```
hanoi(4)      = 2*hanoi(3) + 1

              = 2*(2*hanoi(2) + 1) + 1

              = 2*(2*(2*hanoi(1) + 1) + 1) + 1

              = 2*(2*(2*1 + 1) + 1) + 1

              = 2*(2*(3) + 1) + 1

              = 2*(7) + 1

              = 15
```

Example implementations:

Pseudocode (recursive):

```
function hanoi is:

input: integer n, such that n >= 1

    1. if n is 1 then return 1

    2. return [2 * [call hanoi(n-1)] + 1]

end hanoi
```

Although not all recursive functions have an explicit solution, the Tower of Hanoi sequence can be reduced to an explicit formula.

An explicit formula for Towers of Hanoi:

```
h₁ = 1    = 2¹ - 1
```
$h_1 = 1 \quad = 2^1 - 1$

$h_2 = 3 \quad = 2^2 - 1$

$h_3 = 7 \quad = 2^3 - 1$

$h_4 = 15 \quad = 2^4 - 1$

$h_5 = 31 \quad = 2^5 - 1$

$h_6 = 63 \quad = 2^6 - 1$

$h_7 = 127 = 2^7 - 1$

In general:

$h_n = 2^n - 1$, for all n >= 1

Binary Search

The binary search algorithm is a method of searching a sorted array for a single element by cutting the array in half with each recursive pass. The trick is to pick a midpoint near the center of the array, compare the data at that point with the data being searched and then responding to one of three possible conditions: the data is found at the midpoint, the data at the midpoint is greater than the data being searched for, or the data at the midpoint is less than the data being searched for.

Recursion is used in this algorithm because with each pass a new array is created by cutting the old one in half. The binary search procedure is then called recursively, this time on the new (and smaller) array. Typically the array's size is adjusted by manipulating a beginning and ending index. The algorithm exhibits a logarithmic order of growth because it essentially divides the problem domain in half with each pass.

Example implementation of binary search in C:

```
/*
Call binary_search with proper initial conditions.
INPUT:
    data is an array of integers SORTED in ASCENDING order,
    toFind is the integer to search for,
    count is the total number of elements in the array
OUTPUT:
    result of binary_search
*/
int search(int *data, int toFind, int count)
{
    //  Start = 0 (beginning index)
    //  End = count - 1 (top index)
    return binary_search(data, toFind, 0, count-1);
}
/*
  Binary Search Algorithm.
  INPUT:
        data is a array of integers SORTED in ASCENDING order,
        toFind is the integer to search for,
        start is the minimum array index,
        end is the maximum array index
  OUTPUT:
        position of the integer toFind within array data,
        -1 if not found
*/
int binary_search(int *data, int toFind, int start, int end)
```

```
{
    //Get the midpoint.
    int mid = start + (end - start)/2;    //Integer division
    //Stop condition.
    if (start > end)
        return -1;
    else if (data[mid] == toFind)         //Found?
        return mid;
    else if (data[mid] > toFind)          //Data is greater than toFind, search lower half
        return binary_search(data, toFind, start, mid-1);
    else                                  //Data is less than toFind, search upper half
        return binary_search(data, toFind, mid+1, end);
}
```

Recursive Data Structures (Structural Recursion)

An important application of recursion in computer science is in defining dynamic data structures such as lists and trees. Recursive data structures can dynamically grow to a theoretically infinite size in response to runtime requirements; in contrast, the size of a static array must be set at compile time.

"Recursive algorithms are particularly appropriate when the underlying problem or the data to be treated are defined in recursive terms."

The examples in this section illustrate what is known as "structural recursion". This term refers to the fact that the recursive procedures are acting on data that is defined recursively.

As long as a programmer derives the template from a data definition, functions employ structural recursion. That is, the recursions in a function's body consume some immediate piece of a given compound value.

Linked Lists

Below is a C definition of a linked list node structure. Notice especially how the node is defined in terms of itself. The "next" element of *struct node* is a pointer to another *struct node*, effectively creating a list type.

```
struct node
{
    int data;          // some integer data
    struct node *next; // pointer to another struct node
};
```

Because the *struct node* data structure is defined recursively, procedures that operate on it can be implemented naturally as recursive procedures. The *list_print* procedure defined below walks down the list until the list is empty (i.e., the list pointer has a value of NULL). For each node it prints the data element (an integer). In the C implementation, the list remains unchanged by the *list_print* procedure.

```c
void list_print(struct node *list)
{
    if (list != NULL)              // base case
    {
        printf ("%d ", list->data);  // print integer data followed by a space
        list_print (list->next);     // recursive call on the next node
    }
}
```

Binary Trees

Below is a simple definition for a binary tree node. Like the node for linked lists, it is defined in terms of itself, recursively. There are two self-referential pointers: left (pointing to the left sub-tree) and right (pointing to the right sub-tree).

```c
struct node
{
    int data;             // some integer data
    struct node *left;    // pointer to the left subtree
    struct node *right;   // point to the right subtree
};
```

Operations on the tree can be implemented using recursion. Note that because there are two self-referencing pointers (left and right), tree operations may require two recursive calls:

```c
// Test if tree_node contains i; return 1 if so, 0 if not.
int tree_contains(struct node *tree_node, int i) {
    if (tree_node == NULL)
        return 0;  // base case
    else if (tree_node->data == i)
        return 1;
    else
        return tree_contains(tree_node->left, i) || tree_contains(tree_node->right, i);
}
```

At most two recursive calls will be made for any given call to *tree_contains* as defined above.

```c
// Inorder traversal:
void tree_print(struct node *tree_node) {
```

```
if (tree_node != NULL) {                    // base case
        tree_print(tree_node->left);        // go left
      printf("%d ", tree_node->data);       // print the integer followed by a space
        tree_print(tree_node->right);       // go right

    }

}
```

The above example illustrates an in-order traversal of the binary tree. A Binary search tree is a special case of the binary tree where the data elements of each node are in order.

Filesystem Traversal

Since the number of files in a filesystem may vary, recursion is the only practical way to traverse and thus enumerate its contents. Traversing a filesystem is very similar to that of tree traversal, therefore the concepts behind tree traversal are applicable to traversing a filesystem. More specifically, the code below would be an example of a preorder traversal of a filesystem.

```java
import java.io.*;

public class FileSystem {

        public static void main (String [] args) {

                traverse ();

        }

        /**

          * Obtains the filesystem roots

          * Proceeds with the recursive filesystem traversal

          */

        private static void traverse () {

                File [] fs = File.listRoots ();

                for (int i = 0; i < fs.length; i++) {

                        if (fs[i].isDirectory () && fs[i].canRead ()) {

                                rtraverse (fs[i]);

                        }

                }

        }

        /**

          * Recursively traverse a given directory

          *

          * @param fd indicates the starting point of traversal

          */
```

```
private static void rtraverse (File fd) {

        File [] fss = fd.listFiles ();

        for (int i = 0; i < fss.length; i++) {

                System.out.println (fss[i]);

                if (fss[i].isDirectory () && fss[i].canRead ()) {

                        rtraverse (fss[i]);

                }

        }

    }

}
```

This code blends the lines, at least somewhat, between recursion and iteration. It is, essentially, a recursive implementation, which is the best way to traverse a filesystem. It is also an example of direct and indirect recursion. The method "rtraverse" is purely a direct example; the method "traverse" is the indirect, which calls "rtraverse." This example needs no "base case" scenario due to the fact that there will always be some fixed number of files or directories in a given filesystem.

Implementation Issues

In actual implementation, rather than a pure recursive function (single check for base case, otherwise recursive step), a number of modifications may be made, for purposes of clarity or efficiency. These include:

- Wrapper function

- Short-circuiting the base case, aka "Arm's-length recursion"

- Hybrid algorithm – switching to a different algorithm once data is small enough

On the basis of elegance, wrapper functions are generally approved, while short-circuiting the base case is frowned upon, particularly in academia. Hybrid algorithms are often used for efficiency, to reduce the overhead of recursion in small cases, and arm's-length recursion is a special case of this.

Wrapper Function

A wrapper function is a function that is directly called but does not recurse itself, instead calling a separate auxiliary function which actually does the recursion.

Wrapper functions can be used to validate parameters (so the recursive function can skip these), perform initialization (allocate memory, initialize variables), particularly for auxiliary variables such as "level of recursion" or partial computations for memoization, and handle exceptions and errors. In languages that support nested functions, the auxiliary function can be nested inside the wrapper function and use a shared scope. In the absence of nested functions, auxiliary functions are instead a separate function, if possible private (as they are not called directly), and information is shared with the wrapper function by using pass-by-reference.

Short-circuiting the Base Case

Short-circuiting the base case, also known as arm's-length recursion, consists of checking the base case *before* making a recursive call – i.e., checking if the next call will be the base case, instead of calling and then checking for the base case. Short-circuiting is particularly done for efficiency reasons, to avoid the overhead of a function call that immediately returns. Note that since the base case has already been checked for (immediately before the recursive step), it does not need to be checked for separately, but one does need to use a wrapper function for the case when the overall recursion starts with the base case itself. For example, in the factorial function, properly the base case is 0! = 1, while immediately returning 1 for 1! is a short-circuit, and may miss 0; this can be mitigated by a wrapper function.

Short-circuiting is primarily a concern when many base cases are encountered, such as Null pointers in a tree, which can be linear in the number of function calls, hence significant savings for $O(n)$ algorithms; this is illustrated below for a depth-first search. Short-circuiting on a tree corresponds to considering a leaf (non-empty node with no children) as the base case, rather than considering an empty node as the base case. If there is only a single base case, such as in computing the factorial, short-circuiting provides only $O(1)$ savings.

Conceptually, short-circuiting can be considered to either have the same base case and recursive step, only checking the base case before the recursion, or it can be considered to have a different base case (one step removed from standard base case) and a more complex recursive step, namely "check valid then recurse", as in considering leaf nodes rather than Null nodes as base cases in a tree. Because short-circuiting has a more complicated flow, compared with the clear separation of base case and recursive step in standard recursion, it is often considered poor style, particularly in academia.

Depth-first Search

A basic example of short-circuiting is given in depth-first search (DFS) of a binary tree:

The standard recursive algorithm for a DFS is:

- base case: If current node is Null, return false
- recursive step: otherwise, check value of current node, return true if match, otherwise recurse on children

In short-circuiting, this is instead:

- check value of current node, return true if match,
- otherwise, on children, if not Null, then recurse.

In terms of the standard steps, this moves the base case check *before* the recursive step. Alternatively, these can be considered a different form of base case and recursive step, respectively. Note that this requires a wrapper function to handle the case when the tree itself is empty (root node is Null).

In the case of a perfect binary tree of height h, there are $2^{h+1}-1$ nodes and 2^{h+1} Null pointers as children (2 for each of the 2^h leaves), so short-circuiting cuts the number of function calls in half in the worst case.

In C, the standard recursive algorithm may be implemented as:

```
bool tree_contains(struct node *tree_node, int i) {

    if (tree_node == NULL)

        return false;  // base case

    else if (tree_node->data == i)

        return true;

    else

        return tree_contains(tree_node->left, i) ||

                tree_contains(tree_node->right, i);

}
```

The short-circuited algorithm may be implemented as:

```
// Wrapper function to handle empty tree

bool tree_contains(struct node *tree_node, int i) {

    if (tree_node == NULL)

        return false;  // empty tree

    else

        return tree_contains_do(tree_node, i);  // call auxiliary function

}

// Assumes tree_node != NULL

bool tree_contains_do(struct node *tree_node, int i) {

    if (tree_node->data == i)

        return true;  // found

    else  // recurse

        return (tree_node->left  && tree_contains_do(tree_node->left,  i)) ||

                (tree_node->right && tree_contains_do(tree_node->right, i));

}
```

Note the use of short-circuit evaluation of the Boolean && (AND) operators, so that the recursive call is only made if the node is valid (non-Null). Note that while the first term in the AND is a pointer to a node, the second term is a bool, so the overall expression evaluates to a bool. This is a common idiom in recursive short-circuiting. This is in addition to the short-circuit evaluation of the Boolean || (OR) operator, to only check the right child if the left child fails. In fact, the entire control flow of these functions can be replaced with a single Boolean expression in a return statement, but legibility suffers at no benefit to efficiency.

Hybrid Algorithm

Recursive algorithms are often inefficient for small data, due to the overhead of repeated function calls and returns. For this reason efficient implementations of recursive algorithms often start with the recursive algorithm, but then switch to a different algorithm when the input becomes small. An important example is merge sort, which is often implemented by switching to the non-recursive insertion sort when the data is sufficiently small, as in the tiled merge sort. Hybrid recursive algorithms can often be further refined, as in Timsort, derived from a hybrid merge sort/insertion sort.

Recursion Versus Iteration

Recursion and iteration are equally expressive: recursion can be replaced by iteration with an explicit stack, while iteration can be replaced with tail recursion. Which approach is preferable depends on the problem under consideration and the language used. In imperative programming, iteration is preferred, particularly for simple recursion, as it avoids the overhead of function calls and call stack management, but recursion is generally used for multiple recursion. By contrast, in functional languages recursion is preferred, with tail recursion optimization leading to little overhead, and sometimes explicit iteration is not available.

Compare the templates to compute x_n defined by $x_n = f(n, x_{n-1})$ from x_{base}:

function recursive(n)	function iterative(n)
if n==base	x = xbase
return xbase	for i = n downto base
else	x = f(i, x)
return f(n, recursive(n-1))	return x

For imperative language the overhead is to define the function, for functional language the overhead is to define the accumulator variable x.

For example, the factorial function may be implemented iteratively in C by assigning to an loop index variable and accumulator variable, rather than passing arguments and returning values by recursion:

```
unsigned int factorial(unsigned int n) {

  unsigned int product = 1; // empty product is 1

  while (n) {

    product *= n;

    --n;

  }

  return product;

}
```

Expressive Power

Most programming languages in use today allow the direct specification of recursive functions and procedures. When such a function is called, the program's runtime environment keeps track of the various instances of the function (often using a call stack, although other methods may be used). Every recursive function can be transformed into an iterative function by replacing recursive calls with iterative control constructs and simulating the call stack with a stack explicitly managed by the program.

Conversely, all iterative functions and procedures that can be evaluated by a computer can be expressed in terms of recursive functions; iterative control constructs such as while loops and do loops are routinely rewritten in recursive form in functional languages. However, in practice this rewriting depends on tail call elimination, which is not a feature of all languages. C, Java, and Python are notable mainstream languages in which all function calls, including tail calls, may cause stack allocation that would not occur with the use of looping constructs; in these languages, a working iterative program rewritten in recursive form may overflow the call stack, although tail call elimination may be a feature that is not covered by a language's specification, and different implementations of the same language may differ in tail call elimination capabilities.

Performance Issues

In languages (such as C and Java) that favor iterative looping constructs, there is usually significant time and space cost associated with recursive programs, due to the overhead required to manage the stack and the relative slowness of function calls; in functional languages, a function call (particularly a tail call) is typically a very fast operation, and the difference is usually less noticeable.

As a concrete example, the difference in performance between recursive and iterative implementations of the "factorial" example above depends highly on the compiler used. In languages where looping constructs are preferred, the iterative version may be as much as several orders of magnitude faster than the recursive one. In functional languages, the overall time difference of the two implementations may be negligible; in fact, the cost of multiplying the larger numbers first rather than the smaller numbers (which the iterative version given here happens to do) may overwhelm any time saved by choosing iteration.

Stack Space

In some programming languages, the stack space available to a thread is much less than the space available in the heap, and recursive algorithms tend to require more stack space than iterative algorithms. Consequently, these languages sometimes place a limit on the depth of recursion to avoid stack overflows; Python is one such language. Note the caveat below regarding the special case of tail recursion.

Multiply Recursive Problems

Multiply recursive problems are inherently recursive, because of prior state they need to track. One example is tree traversal as in depth-first search; contrast with list traversal and linear search in a list, which is singly recursive and thus naturally iterative. Other examples include divide-and-conquer algorithms such as Quicksort, and functions such as the Ackermann function. All of these algorithms can be implemented iteratively with the help of an explicit stack, but the programmer effort involved in managing the stack, and the complexity of the resulting program, arguably outweigh any advantages of the iterative solution.

Tail-recursive Functions

Tail-recursive functions are functions in which all recursive calls are tail calls and hence do not build up any deferred operations. For example, the gcd function (shown again below) is tail-recursive. In contrast, the factorial function (also below) is not tail-recursive; because its recursive call is not in tail position, it builds up deferred multiplication operations that must be performed after the final recursive call completes. With a compiler or interpreter that treats tail-recursive calls as jumps rather than function calls, a tail-recursive function such as gcd will execute using constant space. Thus the program is essentially iterative, equivalent to using imperative language control structures like the "for" and "while" loops.

Tail recursion:	Augmenting recursion:
``//INPUT: Integers x, y such that x >= y and y > 0

int gcd(int x, int y)

{

  if (y == 0)

    return x;

  else

    return gcd(y, x % y);

}``` | ```//INPUT: n is an Integer such that n >= 0

int fact(int n)

{

  if (n == 0)

    return 1;

  else

    return n * fact(n - 1);

}``` |

The significance of tail recursion is that when making a tail-recursive call (or any tail call), the caller's return position need not be saved on the call stack; when the recursive call returns, it will branch directly on the previously saved return position. Therefore, in languages that recognize this property of tail calls, tail recursion saves both space and time.

Order of Execution

In the simple case of a function calling itself only once, instructions placed before the recursive call are executed once per recursion before any of the instructions placed after the recursive call. The latter are executed repeatedly after the maximum recursion has been reached. Consider this example:

Function 1

```
void recursiveFunction(int num) {

    printf("%d\n", num);
```

```
   if (num < 4)

       recursiveFunction(num + 1);

}
```

1	recursiveFunction(0)
2	printf(0)
3	recursiveFunction(0+1)
4	printf(1)
5	recursiveFunction(1+1)
6	printf(2)
7	recursiveFunction(2+1)
8	printf(3)
9	recursiveFunction(3+1)
10	printf(4)

Function 2 with Swapped Lines

```
void recursiveFunction(int num) {

   if (num < 4)

       recursiveFunction(num + 1);

   printf("%d\n", num);

}
```

1	recursiveFunction(0)
2	recursiveFunction(0+1)
3	recursiveFunction(1+1)
4	recursiveFunction(2+1)
5	recursiveFunction(3+1)
6	printf(4)
7	printf(3)
8	printf(2)
9	printf(1)
10	printf(0)

Time-efficiency of Recursive Algorithms

The time efficiency of recursive algorithms can be expressed in a recurrence relation of Big O notation. They can (usually) then be simplified into a single Big-Oh term.

Shortcut Rule (Master Theorem)

If the time-complexity of the function is in the form

$$T(n) = a \cdot T(n/b) + f(n)$$

Then the Big-Oh of the time-complexity is thus:

- If $f(n) = O(n^{\log_b a - \epsilon})$ for some constant $\epsilon > 0$, then $T(n) = \Theta(n^{\log_b a})$

- If $f(n) = \Theta(n^{\log_b a})$, then $T(n) = \Theta(n^{\log_b a} \log n)$

- If $f(n) = \Omega(n^{\log_b a + \epsilon})$ for some constant $\epsilon > 0$, and if $a \cdot f(n/b) \leq c \cdot f(n)$ for some constant $c < 1$ and all sufficiently large n, then $T(n) = \Theta(f(n))$

where a represents the number of recursive calls at each level of recursion, b represents by what factor smaller the input is for the next level of recursion (i.e. the number of pieces you divide the problem into), and $f(n)$ represents the work the function does independent of any recursion (e.g. partitioning, recombining) at each level of recursion.

Characteristics of Algorithm

An algorithm model is the representation of a parallel algorithm by selecting a strategy for dividing the data and processing technique and applying the appropriate method to reduce interactions. The various models available are:

1) The data parallel model

2) The task graph model

3) The work pool model

4) The master slave model

5) The pipeline or producer consumer model

6) Hybrid models

Asymptotic Analysis

In mathematical analysis, asymptotic analysis is a method of describing limiting behavior. The method has applications across science. Examples are:

- In applied mathematics, asymptotic analysis is used to build numerical methods to approximate equation solutions.

- In mathematical statistics and probability theory, asymptotics are used in analysis of long-run or large-sample behaviour of random variables and estimators.

- In computer science in the analysis of algorithms, considering the performance of algorithms when applied to very very big input datasets.

- The behavior of physical systems when they are very large, an example being statistical mechanics.

- In accident analysis when identifying the causation of crash through count modeling with large number of crash counts in a given time and space.

A simple illustration, when considering a function $f(n)$, is when there is a need to describe its properties as n becomes very large. Thus, if $f(n) = n^2 + 3n$, the term $3n$ becomes insignificant compared to n^2, when n is very large. The function $f(n)$ is said to be "asymptotically equivalent to n^2 as $n \to \infty$", and this is written symbolically as $f(n) \sim n^2$.

Definition

Formally, given functions f and g of a natural number variable n, one defines a binary relation

$$f \sim g \quad (\text{as } n \to \infty)$$

if and only if (according to Erdelyi, 1956)

$$\lim_{n \to \infty} \frac{f(n)}{g(n)} = 1 \ .$$

This relation is an equivalence relation on the set of functions of n. The equivalence class of f informally consists of all functions g which are approximately equal to f in a relative sense, in the limit.

Properties

If $f \sim g$, then

$f^r \sim g^r$ for any real r, and

$\log(f) \sim \log(g)$.

If $f \sim g$ and $a \sim b$, then

$f \times a \sim g \times b$, and

$f / a \sim g / b$.

This allows asymptotically equivalent functions to be freely exchanged in many algebraic expressions.

Asymptotic Expansion

An asymptotic expansion of a function $f(x)$ is in practice an expression of that function in terms of a series, the partial sums of which do not necessarily converge, but such that taking any initial partial sum provides an asymptotic formula for f. The idea is that successive terms provide an increasingly accurate description of the order of growth of f. An example is Stirling's approximation.

In symbols, it means we have

$$f \sim g_1$$

but also

$$f - g_1 \sim g_2$$

and

$$f - g_1 - \cdots - g_{k-1} \sim g_k$$

for each *fixed k*.

In view of the definition of the $\sim$ symbol, the last equation means

$$f - (g_1 + \cdots + g_k) = o(g_k)$$

in the little o notation, i.e.,

$f - (g_1 + \cdots + g_k)$ is much smaller than g_k.

The relation

$f - g_1 - \cdots - g_{k-1} \sim g_k$ takes its full meaning if $\forall k, g_{k+1} = o(g_k)$,

which means the g_k form an asymptotic scale.

In that case, some authors may abusively write

$$f \sim g_1 + \cdots + g_k$$

to denote the statement

$$f - (g_1 + \cdots + g_k) = o(g_k).$$

One should however be careful that this is not a standard use of the $\sim$ symbol, and that it does not correspond to the definition given in § Definition.

In the present situation, this relation $g_k = o(g_{k-1})$ actually follows from combining steps k and $(k-1)$, by subtracting $f - g_1 - \cdots - g_{k-2} = g_{k-1} + o(g_{k-1})$ from $f - g_1 - \cdots - g_{k-2} - g_{k-1} = g_k + o(g_k)$ one gets

$$g_k + o(g_k) = o(g_{k-1}),$$

i.e., $g_k = o(g_{k-1})$.

In case the asymptotic expansion does not converge, for any particular value of the argument there will be a particular partial sum which provides the best approximation and adding additional terms will decrease the accuracy. However, this optimal partial sum will usually have more terms as the argument approaches the limit value.

Asymptotic expansions typically arise in the approximation of certain integrals (Laplace's method, saddle-point method, method of steepest descent) or in the approximation of probability distributions (Edgeworth series). The famous Feynman graphs in quantum field theory are another example of asymptotic expansions which often do not converge.

Use in Applied Mathematics

Asymptotic analysis is a key tool for exploring the ordinary and partial differential equations which arise in the mathematical modelling of real-world phenomena. An illustrative example is the derivation of the boundary layer equations from the full Navier-Stokes equations governing fluid flow. In many cases, the asymptotic expansion is in power of a small parameter, ε: in the boundary layer case, this is the nondimensional ratio of the boundary layer thickness to a typical lengthscale of the problem. Indeed, applications of asymptotic analysis in mathematical modelling often centre around a nondimensional parameter which has been shown, or assumed, to be small through a consideration of the scales of the problem at hand.

Method of Dominant Balance

The method of dominant balance is used to determine the asymptotic behavior of solutions to an ODE without fully solving it. The process is iterative, in that the result obtained by performing the method once can be used as input when the method is repeated, to obtain as many terms in the asymptotic expansion as desired.

The process goes as follows:

1. Assume that the asymptotic behavior has the form

    $$y(x) \sim e^{S(x)} .$$

2. Make an informed guess as to which terms in the ODE might be negligible in the limit of interest.

3. Drop these terms and solve the resulting simpler ODE.

4. Check that the solution is consistent with step 2. If this is the case, then one has the controlling factor of the asymptotic behavior; otherwise, one needs try dropping different terms in step 2, instead.

5. Repeat the process to higher orders, relying on the above result as the leading term in the solution.

Example. For arbitrary constants c and a, consider

$$xy'' + (c - x)y' - ay = 0 .$$

This differential equation cannot be solved exactly. However, it is useful to consider how the solutions behave for large x: it turns out that y behaves like e^x as $x \to \infty$.

More rigorously, we will have $\log(y) \sim x$, not $y \sim e^x$. Since we are interested in the behavior of y in the large x limit, we change variables to $y = \exp(S(x))$, and re-express the ODE in terms of $S(x)$,

$$xS'' + xS'^2 + (c - x)S' - a = 0 ,$$

or

$$S'' + S'^2 + \left(\frac{c}{x} - 1\right)S' - \frac{a}{x} = 0$$

where we have used the product rule and chain rule to evaluate the derivatives of y.

Now *suppose* first that a solution to this ODE satisfies

$$S'^2 \sim S' ,$$

as $x \to \infty$, so that

$$S'', \frac{c}{x}S', \frac{a}{x} = o(S'^2), o(S')$$

as $x \to \infty$. Obtain then the dominant asymptotic behaviour by setting

$$S_0'^2 = S_0' .$$

If S_0 satisfies the above asymptotic conditions, then the above assumption is consistent. The terms we dropped will have been negligible with respect to the ones we kept.

S_0 is not a solution to the ODE for S, but it represents *the dominant asymptotic behavior*, which is what we are interested in. Check that this choice for S_0 is consistent,

$$S'_0 = 1$$
$$S'^2_0 = 1$$
$$S''_0 = 0 = o(S'_0)$$
$$\frac{c}{x}S'_0 = \frac{c}{x} = o(S'_0)$$
$$\frac{a}{x} = o(S'_0)$$

Everything is indeed consistent.

Thus the dominant asymptotic behaviour of a solution to our ODE has been found,

$$S_0 \sim x$$
$$\log(y) \sim x .$$

By convention, the full asymptotic series is written as

$$y \sim Ax^p e^{\lambda x^r}\left(1 + \frac{u_1}{x} + \frac{u_2}{x^2} \cdots + \frac{u_k}{x^k} + o\left(\frac{1}{x^k}\right)\right),$$

so to get at least the first term of this series we have to take a further step to see if there is a power of x out the front.

Proceed by introducing a new subleading dependent variable,

$$S(x) \equiv S_0(x) + C(x)$$

and then seek asymptotic solutions for $C(x)$. Substituting into the above ODE for $S(x)$ we find

$$C'' + C'^2 + C' + \frac{c}{x}C' + \frac{c-a}{x} = 0 \ .$$

Repeating the same process as before, we keep C' and $(c-a)/x$ to find that

$$C_0 = \log x^{a-c} \ .$$

The leading asymptotic behaviour is then

$$y \sim x^{a-c}e^x \ .$$

Big O Notation

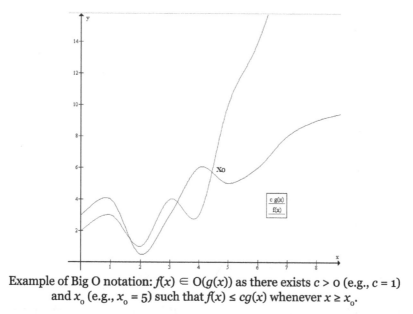

Example of Big O notation: $f(x) \in O(g(x))$ as there exists $c > 0$ (e.g., $c = 1$)
and x_0 (e.g., $x_0 = 5$) such that $f(x) \le cg(x)$ whenever $x \ge x_0$.

Big O notation is a mathematical notation that describes the limiting behavior of a function when the argument tends towards a particular value or infinity. It is a member of a family of notations invented by Paul Bachmann, Edmund Landau, and others, collectively called Bachmann–Landau notation or asymptotic notation.

In computer science, big O notation is used to classify algorithms according to how their running time or space requirements grow as the input size grows. In analytic number theory, big O notation is often used to express a bound on the difference between an arithmetical function and a better understood approximation; a famous example of such a difference is the remainder term in the prime number theorem.

Big O notation characterizes functions according to their growth rates: different functions with the same growth rate may be represented using the same O notation.

The letter O is used because the growth rate of a function is also referred to as order of the function. A description of a function in terms of big O notation usually only provides an upper bound on the growth rate of the function. Associated with big O notation are several related notations, using the symbols o, Ω, ω, and Θ, to describe other kinds of bounds on asymptotic growth rates.

Big O notation is also used in many other fields to provide similar estimates.

Formal Definition

Let f and g be two functions defined on some subset of the real numbers. One writes

$$f(x) = O(g(x)) \text{ as } x \to \infty$$

if and only if there is a positive constant M such that for all sufficiently large values of x, the absolute value of $f(x)$ is at most M multiplied by the absolute value of $g(x)$. That is, $f(x) = O(g(x))$ if and only if there exists a positive real number M and a real number x_0 such that

$$|f(x)| \leq M|g(x)| \text{ for all } x \geq x_0.$$

In many contexts, the assumption that we are interested in the growth rate as the variable x goes to infinity is left unstated, and one writes more simply that

$$f(x) = O(g(x)).$$

The notation can also be used to describe the behavior of f near some real number a (often, $a = 0$): we say

$$f(x) = O(g(x)) \text{ as } x \to a$$

if and only if there exist positive numbers δ and M such that

$$|f(x)| \leq M|g(x)| \text{ when } 0 < |x - a| < \delta.$$

If $g(x)$ is non-zero for values of x sufficiently close to a, both of these definitions can be unified using the limit superior:

$$f(x) = O(g(x)) \text{ as } x \to a$$

if and only if

$$\limsup_{x \to a} \left| \frac{f(x)}{g(x)} \right| < \infty.$$

Example

In typical usage, the formal definition of O notation is not used directly; rather, the O notation for a function f is derived by the following simplification rules:

- If $f(x)$ is a sum of several terms, if there is one with largest growth rate, it can be kept, and all others omitted.

- If $f(x)$ is a product of several factors, any constants (terms in the product that do not depend on x) can be omitted.

For example, let $f(x) = 6x^4 - 2x^3 + 5$, and suppose we wish to simplify this function, using O notation, to describe its growth rate as x approaches infinity. This function is the sum of three terms: $6x^4$, $-2x^3$, and 5. Of these three terms, the one with the highest growth rate is the one with the largest exponent as a function of x, namely $6x^4$. Now one may apply the second rule: $6x^4$ is a product of 6 and x^4 in which the first factor does not depend on x. Omitting this factor results in the simplified form x^4. Thus, we say that $f(x)$ is a "big-oh" of (x^4). Mathematically, we can write $f(x) = O(x^4)$. One may confirm this calculation using the formal definition: let $f(x) = 6x^4 - 2x^3 + 5$ and $g(x) = x^4$. Applying the formal definition from above, the statement that $f(x) = O(x^4)$ is equivalent to its expansion,

$$|f(x)| \le M|x^4|$$

for some suitable choice of x_0 and M and for all $x > x_0$. To prove this, let $x_0 = 1$ and $M = 13$. Then, for all $x > x_0$:

$$|6x^4 - 2x^3 + 5| \le 6x^4 + |2x^3| + 5$$
$$\le 6x^4 + 2x^4 + 5x^4$$
$$= 13x^4$$

so

$$|6x^4 - 2x^3 + 5| \le 13x^4.$$

Usage

Big O notation has two main areas of application. In mathematics, it is commonly used to describe how closely a finite series approximates a given function, especially in the case of a truncated Taylor series or asymptotic expansion. In computer science, it is useful in the analysis of algorithms. In both applications, the function $g(x)$ appearing within the $O(...)$ is typically chosen to be as simple as possible, omitting constant factors and lower order terms. There are two formally close, but noticeably different, usages of this notation: infinite asymptotics and infinitesimal asymptotics. This distinction is only in application and not in principle, however—the formal definition for the "big O" is the same for both cases, only with different limits for the function argument.

Infinite Asymptotics

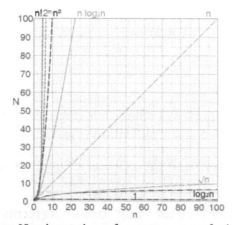

Graphs of number of operations, N vs input size, n for common complexities, assuming a coefficient of 1

Big O notation is useful when analyzing algorithms for efficiency. For example, the time (or the number of steps) it takes to complete a problem of size n might be found to be $T(n) = 4n^2 - 2n + 2$. As n grows large, the n^2 term will come to dominate, so that all other terms can be neglected—for instance when $n = 500$, the term $4n^2$ is 1000 times as large as the $2n$ term. Ignoring the latter would have negligible effect on the expression's value for most purposes. Further, the coefficients become irrelevant if we compare to any other order of expression, such as an expression containing a term n^3 or n^4. Even if $T(n) = 1,000,000n^2$, if $U(n) = n^3$, the latter will always exceed the former once n grows larger than 1,000,000 ($T(1,000,000) = 1,000,000^3 = U(1,000,000)$). Additionally, the number of steps depends on the details of the machine model on which the algorithm runs, but different types of machines typically vary by only a constant factor in the number of steps needed to execute an algorithm. So the big O notation captures what remains: we write either

$$T(n) = O(n^2)$$

or

$$T(n) \in O(n^2)$$

and say that the algorithm has *order of n^2* time complexity. Note that "=" is not meant to express "is equal to" in its normal mathematical sense, but rather a more colloquial "is", so the second expression is sometimes considered more accurate while the first is considered by some as an Abuse of notation.

Infinitesimal Asymptotics

Big O can also be used to describe the error term in an approximation to a mathematical function. The most significant terms are written explicitly, and then the least-significant terms are summarized in a single big O term. Consider, for example, the exponential series and two expressions of it that are valid when x is small:

$$e^x = 1 + x + \frac{x^2}{2!} + \frac{x^3}{3!} + \frac{x^4}{4!} + \cdots \qquad \text{for all } x$$

$$= 1 + x + \frac{x^2}{2} + O(x^3) \qquad \text{as } x \to 0$$

$$= 1 + x + O(x^2) \qquad \text{as } x \to 0$$

The second expression (the one with $O(x^3)$) means the absolute-value of the error $e^x - (1 + x + x^2/2)$ is at most some constant times $|x^3|$ when x is close enough to 0.

Properties

If the function f can be written as a finite sum of other functions, then the fastest growing one determines the order of $f(n)$. For example,

$$f(n) = 9 \log n + 5(\log n)^3 + 3n^2 + 2n^3 = O(n^3), \qquad \text{as } n \to \infty.$$

In particular, if a function may be bounded by a polynomial in n, then as n tends to *infinity*, one may disregard *lower-order* terms of the polynomial. Another thing to notice is the sets $O(n^c)$ and $O(c^n)$ are very different. If c is greater than one, then the latter grows much faster. A function that grows faster than n^c for any c is called *superpolynomial*. One that grows more slowly than any exponential function of the form c^n is called *subexponential*. An algorithm can require time that is both superpolynomial and subexponential; examples of this include the fastest known algorithms for integer factorization and the function $n^{\log n}$.

We may ignore any powers of n inside of the logarithms. The set $O(\log n)$ is exactly the same as $O(\log(n^c))$. The logarithms differ only by a constant factor (since $\log(n^c) = c \log n$) and thus the big O notation ignores that. Similarly, logs with different constant bases are equivalent. On the other hand, exponentials with different bases are not of the same order. For example, 2^n and 3^n are not of the same order.

Changing units may or may not affect the order of the resulting algorithm. Changing units is equivalent to multiplying the appropriate variable by a constant wherever it appears. For example, if an algorithm runs in the order of n^2, replacing n by cn means the algorithm runs in the order of c^2n^2, and the big O notation ignores the constant c^2. This can be written as $c^2n^2 = O(n^2)$. If, however, an algorithm runs in the order of 2^n, replacing n with cn gives $2^{cn} = (2^c)^n$. This is not equivalent to 2^n in general. Changing variables may also affect the order of the resulting algorithm. For example, if an algorithm's run time is $O(n)$ when measured in terms of the number n of *digits* of an input number x, then its run time is $O(\log x)$ when measured as a function of the input number x itself, because $n = O(\log x)$.

Product

$$f_1 = O(g_1) \text{ and } f_2 = O(g_2) \Rightarrow f_1 f_2 = O(g_1 g_2)$$

$$f \cdot O(g) = O(fg)$$

Sum

$$f_1 = O(g_1) \text{ and } f_2 = O(g_2) \Rightarrow f_1 + f_2 = O(|g_1| + |g_2|)$$

This implies $f_1 = O(g)$ and $f_2 = O(g) \Rightarrow f_1 + f_2 \in O(g)$, which means that $O(g)$ is a convex cone.

If f and g are positive functions, $f + O(g) = O(f + g)$

Multiplication by a Constant

Let k be a constant. Then:

$$O(kg) = O(g) \text{ if } k \text{ is nonzero.}$$

$$f = O(g) \Rightarrow kf = O(g).$$

Multiple Variables

Big O (and little o, and Ω...) can also be used with multiple variables. To define Big O formally for multiple variables, suppose f and g are two functions defined on some subset of $\mathbb{R}^n$. We say

$$f(\vec{x}) \text{ is } O(g(\vec{x})) \text{ as } \vec{x} \to \infty$$

if and only if

$$\exists M \exists C > 0 \text{ such that for all } \vec{x} \text{ with } x_i \geq M \text{ for some } i, |f(\vec{x})| \leq C |g(\vec{x})|.$$

Equivalently, the condition that $x_i \geq M$ for some i can be replaced with the condition that $\|\vec{x}\|_\infty \geq M$, where $\|\vec{x}\|_\infty$ denotes the Chebyshev norm. For example, the statement

$$f(n,m) = n^2 + m^3 + O(n+m) \text{ as } n,m \to \infty$$

asserts that there exist constants C and M such that

$$\forall \|(n,m)\|_\infty \geq M : |g(n,m)| \leq C |n+m|,$$

where $g(n,m)$ is defined by

$$f(n,m) = n^2 + m^3 + g(n,m).$$

Note that this definition allows all of the coordinates of $\vec{x}$ to increase to infinity. In particular, the statement

$$f(n,m) = O(n^m) \text{ as } n,m \to \infty$$

(i.e., $\exists C \exists M \forall n \forall m \ldots$) is quite different from

$$\forall m : f(n,m) = O(n^m) \text{ as } n \to \infty$$

$$\text{(i.e., } \forall m \exists C \exists M \forall n \ldots).$$

This is not the only generalization of big O to multivariate functions, and in practice, there is some inconsistency in the choice of definition.

Matters of Notation

Equals Sign

The statement "$f(x)$ is $O(g(x))$" as defined above is usually written as $f(x) = O(g(x))$. Some consider this to be an abuse of notation, since the use of the equals sign could be misleading as it suggests a symmetry that this statement does not have. As de Bruijn says, $O(x) = O(x^2)$ is true but $O(x^2) = O(x)$ is not. Knuth describes such statements as "one-way equalities", since if the sides could be reversed, "we could deduce ridiculous things like $n = n^2$ from the identities $n = O(n^2)$ and $n^2 = O(n^2)$."

For these reasons, it would be more precise to use set notation and write $f(x) \in O(g(x))$, thinking of $O(g(x))$ as the class of all functions $h(x)$ such that $|h(x)| \leq C|g(x)|$ for some constant C. However, the use of the equals sign is customary. Knuth pointed out that "mathematicians customarily use the = sign as they use the word 'is' in English: Aristotle is a man, but a man isn't necessarily Aristotle."

Other Arithmetic Operators

Big O notation can also be used in conjunction with other arithmetic operators in more complicated equations. For example, $h(x) + O(f(x))$ denotes the collection of functions having the growth of $h(x)$ plus a part whose growth is limited to that of $f(x)$. Thus,

$$g(x) = h(x) + O(f(x))$$

expresses the same as

$$g(x) - h(x) = O(f(x)).$$

Example

Suppose an algorithm is being developed to operate on a set of n elements. Its developers are interested in finding a function $T(n)$ that will express how long the algorithm will take to run (in some arbitrary measurement of time) in terms of the number of elements in the input set. The algorithm works by first calling a subroutine to sort the elements in the set and then perform its own operations. The sort has a known time complexity of $O(n^2)$, and after the subroutine runs the algorithm must take an additional $55n^3 + 2n + 10$ steps before it terminates. Thus the overall time complexity of the algorithm can be expressed as $T(n) = 55n^3 + O(n^2)$. Here the terms $2n+10$ are subsumed within the faster-growing $O(n^2)$. Again, this usage disregards some of the formal meaning of the "=" symbol, but it does allow one to use the big O notation as a kind of convenient placeholder.

Declaration of Variables

Another feature of the notation, although less exceptional, is that function arguments may need to be inferred from the context when several variables are involved. The following two right-hand side big O notations have dramatically different meanings:

$$f(m) = O(m^n),$$

$$g(n) = O(m^n).$$

The first case states that $f(m)$ exhibits polynomial growth, while the second, assuming $m > 1$, states that $g(n)$ exhibits exponential growth. To avoid confusion, some authors use the notation

$$g(x) = O(f(x)).$$

rather than the less explicit

$$g = O(f),$$

Multiple usages

In more complicated usage, O can appear in different places in an equation, even several times on each side. For example, the following are true for $n \to \infty$

$$(n+1)^2 = n^2 + O(n)$$

$$(n+O(n^{1/2}))(n+O(\log n))^2 = n^3 + O(n^{5/2})$$

$$n^{O(1)} = O(e^n).$$

The meaning of such statements is as follows: for *any* functions which satisfy each $O(...)$ on the left side, there are *some* functions satisfying each $O(...)$ on the right side, such that substituting all these functions into the equation makes the two sides equal. For example, the third equation above means: "For any function $f(n) = O(1)$, there is some function $g(n) = O(e^n)$ such that $n^{f(n)} = g(n)$." In terms of the "set notation" above, the meaning is that the class of functions represented by the left side is a subset of the class of functions represented by the right side. In this use the "=" is a formal symbol that unlike the usual use of "=" is not a symmetric relation. Thus for example $n^{O(1)} = O(e^n)$ does not imply the false statement $O(e^n) = n^{O(1)}$

Orders of Common Functions

Here is a list of classes of functions that are commonly encountered when analyzing the running time of an algorithm. In each case, c is a positive constant and n increases without bound. The slower-growing functions are generally listed first.

Notation	Name	Example
$O(1)$	constant	Determining if a binary number is even or odd; Calculating $(-1)^n$; Using a constant-size lookup table
$O(\log \log n)$	double logarithmic	Number of comparisons spent finding an item using interpolation search in a sorted array of uniformly distributed values
$O(\log n)$	logarithmic	Finding an item in a sorted array with a binary search or a balanced search tree as well as all operations in a Binomial heap
$O((\log n)^c)$	polylogarithmic	Matrix chain ordering can be solved in polylogarithmic time on a Parallel Random Access Machine.
$O(n^c)$	fractional power	Searching in a kd-tree
$O(n)$	linear	Finding an item in an unsorted list or in an unsorted array; adding two n-bit integers by ripple carry
$O(n \log^* n)$	n log-star n	Performing triangulation of a simple polygon using Seidel's algorithm, or the union–find algorithm. Note that $\log^*(n) = \begin{cases} 0, & \text{if } n \leq 1 \\ 1 + \log^*(\log n), & \text{if } n > 1 \end{cases}$

$O(n \log n) = O(\log n!)$	linearithmic, loglinear, or quasilinear	Performing a fast Fourier transform; Fastest possible comparison sort; heapsort and merge sort
$O(n^2)$	quadratic	Multiplying two n-digit numbers by a simple algorithm; simple sorting algorithms, such as bubble sort, selection sort and insertion sort; bound on some usually faster sorting algorithms such as quicksort, Shellsort, and tree sort
$O(n^c)$	polynomial or algebraic	Tree-adjoining grammar parsing; maximum matching for bipartite graphs; finding the determinant with LU decomposition
$L_n[\alpha,c] = e^{(c+o(1))(\ln n)^\alpha (\ln \ln n)^{1-\alpha}}$ $0<\alpha<1$	L-notation or sub-exponential	Factoring a number using the quadratic sieve or number field sieve
$O(c^n)$ $c>1$	exponential	Finding the (exact) solution to the travelling salesman problem using dynamic programming; determining if two logical statements are equivalent using brute-force search
$O(n!)$	factorial	Solving the travelling salesman problem via brute-force search; generating all unrestricted permutations of a poset; finding the determinant with Laplace expansion; enumerating all partitions of a set

The statement $f(n) = O(n!)$ is sometimes weakened to $f(n) = O\left(n^n\right)$ to derive simpler formulas for asymptotic complexity. For any $k > 0$ and $c > 0$, $O(n^c (\log n)^k)$ is a subset of $O(n^{c+\varepsilon})$ for any $\varepsilon > 0$, so may be considered as a polynomial with some bigger order.

Related Asymptotic Notations

Big O is the most commonly used asymptotic notation for comparing functions, although in many cases Big O may be replaced with Big Theta Θ for asymptotically tighter bounds. Here, we define some related notations in terms of Big O, progressing up to the family of Bachmann–Landau notations to which Big O notation belongs.

Little-o Notation

The informal assertion "$f(x)$ is little-o of $g(x)$" is formally written

$$f(x) = o(g(x)),$$

or in set notation $f(x) \in o(g(x))$. Intuitively, it means that $g(x)$ *grows much faster than* $f(x)$, or similarly, that the growth of $f(x)$ is nothing compared to that of $g(x)$.

It assumes that f and g are both functions of one variable. Formally, $f(n) = o(g(n))$ (or $f(n) \in o(g(n))$) as $n \to \infty$ means that for every positive constant ε there exists a constant N such that

$$|f(n)| \le \varepsilon |g(n)| \qquad \text{for all } n \ge N.$$

Note the difference between the earlier formal definition for the big-O notation, and the present definition of little-o: while the former has to be true for *at least one* constant M the latter must hold for *every* positive constant ε, however small. In this way, little-o notation makes a *stronger statement* than the corresponding big-O notation: every function that is little-o of g is also big-O of g, but not every function that is big-O of g is also little-o of g (for instance g itself is not, unless it is identically zero near ∞).

If $g(x)$ is nonzero, or at least becomes nonzero beyond a certain point, the relation $f(x) = o(g(x))$ is equivalent to

$$\lim_{x \to \infty} \frac{f(x)}{g(x)} = 0.$$

For example,

- $2x = o(x^2)$

- $2x^2 \neq o(x^2)$

- $1/x = o(1)$

Little-o notation is common in mathematics but rarer in computer science. In computer science, the variable (and function value) is most often a natural number. In mathematics, the variable and function values are often real numbers. The following properties (expressed in the more recent, set-theoretical notation) can be useful:

- $c \cdot o(f) = o(f)$ for $c \neq 0$

- $o(f)o(g) \subseteq o(fg)$

- $o(o(f)) \subseteq o(f)$

- $o(f) \subset O(f)$ (and thus the above properties apply with most combinations of o and O).

As with big O notation, the statement "$f(x)$ is $o(g(x))$ " is usually written as $f(x) = o(g(x))$, which some consider an abuse of notation.

Big Omega Notation

There are two very widespread and incompatible definitions of the statement

$$f(x) = \Omega(g(x)) \, (x \to a),$$

where a is some real number, ∞, or $-\infty$, where f and g are real functions defined in a neighbourhood of a, and where g is positive in this neighbourhood.

The first one (chronologically) is used in analytic number theory, and the other one in computational complexity theory. When the two subjects meet, this situation is bound to generate confusion.

The Hardy–Littlewood Definition

In 1914 G.H. Hardy and J.E. Littlewood introduced the new symbol Ω, which is defined as follows:

$$f(x) = \Omega(g(x)) \, (x \to \infty) \Leftrightarrow \limsup_{x \to \infty} \left| \frac{f(x)}{g(x)} \right| > 0.$$

Thus $f(x) = \Omega(g(x))$ is the negation of $f(x) = o(g(x))$.

In 1916 the same authors introduced the two new symbols Ω_R and Ω_L, thus defined:

$$f(x) = \Omega_R(g(x)) \; (x \to \infty) \Leftrightarrow \limsup_{x \to \infty} \frac{f(x)}{g(x)} > 0 \; ;$$

$$f(x) = \Omega_L(g(x)) \; (x \to \infty) \Leftrightarrow \liminf_{x \to \infty} \frac{f(x)}{g(x)} < 0 \, .$$

Hence $f(x) = \Omega_R(g(x))$ is the negation of $f(x) < o(g(x))$, and $f(x) = \Omega_L(g(x))$ is the negation of $f(x) > o(g(x))$.

Contrary to a later assertion of D.E. Knuth, Edmund Landau did use these three symbols, with the same meanings, in 1924.

These Hardy-Littlewood symbols are prototypes, which after Landau were never used again exactly thus.

$$\Omega_R \text{ became } \Omega_+ \text{, and } \Omega_L \text{ became } \Omega_- .$$

These three symbols $\Omega, \Omega_+, \Omega_-$, as well as $f(x) = \Omega_\pm(g(x))$ (meaning that $f(x) = \Omega_+(g(x))$ and $f(x) = \Omega_-(g(x))$ are both satisfied), are now currently used in analytic number theory.

Simple examples

We have

$$\sin x = \Omega(1) \; (x \to \infty),$$

and more precisely

$$\sin x = \Omega_\pm(1) \; (x \to \infty).$$

We have

$$\sin x + 1 = \Omega(1) \; (x \to \infty),$$

and more precisely

$$\sin x + 1 = \Omega_+(1) \; (x \to \infty);$$

however

$$\sin x + 1 \neq \Omega_-(1) \; (x \to \infty).$$

The Knuth Definition

In 1976 Donald Knuth published a paper to justify his use of the Ω-symbol to describe a stronger property. Knuth wrote: "For all the applications I have seen so far in computer science, a stronger requirement [...] is much more appropriate". He defined

$$f(x) = \Omega(g(x)) \Leftrightarrow g(x) = O(f(x))$$

with the comment: "Although I have changed Hardy and Littlewood's definition of Ω, I feel justified in doing so because their definition is by no means in wide use, and because there are other ways to say what they want to say in the comparatively rare cases when their definition applies".

Use in Computer Science

Informally, especially in computer science, the Big O notation often is permitted to be somewhat abused to describe an asymptotic tight bound where using Big Theta Θ notation might be more factually appropriate in a given context. For example, when considering a function $T(n) = 73n^3 + 22n^2 + 58$, all of the following are generally acceptable, but tighter bounds (i.e., numbers 2 and 3 below) are usually strongly preferred over looser bounds (i.e., number 1 below).

1. $T(n) = O(n^{100})$

2. $T(n) = O(n^3)$

3. $T(n) = \Theta(n^3)$

The equivalent English statements are respectively:

1. $T(n)$ grows asymptotically no faster than n^{100}

2. $T(n)$ grows asymptotically no faster than n^3

3. $T(n)$ grows asymptotically as fast as n^3.

So while all three statements are true, progressively more information is contained in each. In some fields, however, the big O notation (number 2 in the lists above) would be used more commonly than the Big Theta notation (bullets number 3 in the lists above). For example, if $T(n)$ represents the running time of a newly developed algorithm for input size n, the inventors and users of the algorithm might be more inclined to put an upper asymptotic bound on how long it will take to run without making an explicit statement about the lower asymptotic bound.

Other Notation

In their book *Introduction to Algorithms*, Cormen, Leiserson, Rivest and Stein consider the set of functions g to which some function f belongs when it satisfies

$$f(n) = O(g(n)) \, (n \to \infty).$$

In a correct notation this set can for instance be called $O(g)$, where

$$O(g) = \{f : \text{there exist positive constants } c \text{ and } n_0 \text{ such that } 0 \le f(n) \le cg(n) \text{ for all } n \ge n_0\}.$$

The authors state that the use of equality operator (=) to denote set membership rather than the set membership operator ($\in$) is an abuse of notation, but that doing so has advantages. Inside an equation or inequality, the use of asymptotic notation stands for an anonymous function in the set $O(g)$, which eliminates lower-order terms, and helps to reduce inessential clutter in equations, for example:

$$2n^2 + 3n + 1 = 2n^2 + O(n).$$

Extensions to the Bachmann–Landau Notations

Another notation sometimes used in computer science is $\tilde{O}$ (read *soft-O*): $f(n) = \tilde{O}(g(n))$ is shorthand for $f(n) = O(g(n) \log^k g(n))$ for some k. Essentially, it is big O notation, ignoring logarithmic factors because the growth-rate effects of some other super-logarithmic function indicate a growth-rate explosion for large-sized input parameters that is more important to predicting bad run-time performance than the finer-point effects contributed by the logarithmic-growth factor(s). This notation is often used to obviate the "nitpicking" within growth-rates that are stated as too tightly bounded for the matters at hand (since $\log^k n$ is always $o(n^\varepsilon)$ for any constant k and any $\varepsilon > 0$).

Also the L notation, defined as

$$L_n[\alpha, c] = e^{(c + o(1))(\ln n)^\alpha (\ln \ln n)^{1-\alpha}}$$

is convenient for functions that are between polynomial and exponential in terms of $\ln n$.

Generalizations and Related Usages

The generalization to functions taking values in any normed vector space is straightforward (replacing absolute values by norms), where f and g need not take their values in the same space. A generalization to functions g taking values in any topological group is also possible. The "limiting process" $x \to x_0$ can also be generalized by introducing an arbitrary filter base, i.e. to directed nets f and g. The o notation can be used to define derivatives and differentiability in quite general spaces, and also (asymptotical) equivalence of functions,

$$f \sim g \Leftrightarrow (f - g) \in o(g)$$

which is an equivalence relation and a more restrictive notion than the relationship "f is $\Theta(g)$" from above. (It reduces to $\lim f / g = 1$ if f and g are positive real valued functions.) For example, $2x$ is $\Theta(x)$, but $2x - x$ is not $o(x)$.

History (Bachmann–Landau, Hardy, and Vinogradov Notations)

The symbol O was first introduced by number theorist Paul Bachmann in 1894, in the second volume of his book *Analytische Zahlentheorie* ("analytic number theory"), the first volume of which (not yet containing big O notation) was published in 1892. The number theorist Edmund Landau adopted it, and was thus inspired to introduce in 1909 the notation o; hence both are now called Landau symbols. These notations were used in applied mathematics during the 1950s for asymptotic analysis. The symbol Ω (in the sense "is not an o of") was introduced in 1914 by Hardy and Littlewood. Hardy and Littlewood also introduced in 1918 the symbols Ω_R ("right") and Ω_L ("left"), precursors of the modern symbols Ω_+ ("is not smaller than a small o of") and Ω_- ("is not larger than a small o of"). Thus the Omega symbols (with their original meanings) are sometimes also referred to as "Landau symbols". This notation Ω became commonly used in number theory at least since the 1950s. In the 1970s the big O was popularized in computer science by Donald Knuth, who introduced the related Theta notation, and proposed a different definition for the Omega notation.

Landau never used the Big Theta and small omega symbols.

Hardy's symbols were (in terms of the modern O notation)

$$f \preceq g \Leftrightarrow f \in O(g) \text{ and } f \prec g \Leftrightarrow f \in o(g);$$

(Hardy however never defined or used the notation $\prec\prec$, nor $\ll$, as it has been sometimes reported). It should also be noted that Hardy introduces the symbols $\preceq$ and $\prec$ (as well as some other symbols) in his 1910 tract "Orders of Infinity", and makes use of it only in three papers (1910–1913). In his nearly 400 remaining papers and books he consistently uses the Landau symbols O and o.

Hardy's notation is not used anymore. On the other hand, in the 1930s, the Russian number theorist Ivan Matveyevich Vinogradov introduced his notation $\ll$, which has been increasingly used in number theory instead of the O notation. We have

$$f \ll g \Leftrightarrow f \in O(g),$$

and frequently both notations are used in the same paper.

The big-O originally stands for "order of" ("Ordnung", Bachmann 1894), and is thus a Latin letter. Neither Bachmann nor Landau ever call it "Omicron". The symbol was much later on (1976) viewed by Knuth as a capital omicron, probably in reference to his definition of the symbol Omega. The digit zero should not be used.

Omega Network

An Omega network is a network configuration often used in parallel computing architectures. It is an indirect topology that relies on the perfect shuffle interconnection algorithm.

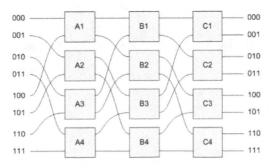

Omega network with 8 processing elements

Connection Architecture

An 8x8 Omega network is a multistage interconnection network, meaning that processing elements (PEs) are connected using multiple stages of switches. Inputs and outputs are given addresses as shown in the figure. The outputs from each stage are connected to the inputs of the next stage using a perfect shuffle connection system. This means that the connections at each stage represent the movement of a deck of cards divided into 2 equal decks and then shuffled together, with each card from one deck alternating with the corresponding card from the other deck. In terms of binary representation of the PEs, each stage of the perfect shuffle can be thought of as a cyclic logical left shift; each bit in the address is shifted once to the left, with the most significant bit moving to the least significant bit.

At each stage, adjacent pairs of inputs are connected to a simple exchange element, which can be set either straight (pass inputs directly through to outputs) or crossed (send top input to bottom output, and vice versa). For N processing element, an Omega network contains N/2 switches at each stage, and $\log_2 N$ stages. The manner in which these switches are set determines the connection paths available in the network at any given time. Two such methods are destination-tag routing and XOR-tag routing, discussed in detail below.

The Omega Network is highly blocking, though one path can always be made from any input to any output in a free network.

Destination-tag Routing

In destination-tag routing, switch settings are determined solely by the message destination. The most significant bit of the destination address is used to select the output of the switch in the first stage; if the most significant bit is 0, the upper output is selected, and if it is 1, the lower output is selected. The next-most significant bit of the destination address is used to select the output of the switch in the next stage, and so on until the final output has been selected.

For example, if a message's destination is PE 001, the switch settings are: upper, upper, lower. If a message's destination is PE 101, the switch settings are: lower, upper, lower. These switch settings hold regardless of the PE sending the message.

XOR-tag Routing

In XOR-tag routing, switch settings are based on (source PE) XOR (destination PE). This XOR-tag contains 1s in the bit positions that must be swapped and 0s in the bit positions that both source and destination have in common. The most significant bit of the XOR-tag is used to select the setting of the switch in the first stage; if the most significant bit is 0, the switch is set to pass-through, and if it is 1, the switch is crossed. The next-most significant bit of the tag is used to set the switch in the next stage, and so on until the final output has been selected.

For example, if PE 001 wishes to send a message to PE 010, the XOR-tag will be 011 and the appropriate switch settings are: A2 straight, B3 crossed, C2 crossed.

Applications

In multiprocessing, omega networks may be used as connectors between the central processing units (CPUs) and their shared memory, in order to decrease the probability that the *CPU-to-memory* connection becomes a bottleneck.

This class of networks has been built into the Illinois Cedar Multiprocessor, into the IBM RP3, and into the NYU Ultracomputer.

Performance Metrics for Parallel Systems

In Parallel computing paradigm number of metrics is important to evaluate the performance of parallel systems. The parallel runtime is the time that elapses from the moment a parallel computation starts to the moment the last processing element finishes execution. The parallel time is represented by T_p. We define overhead function or *total overhead* of a parallel system as the total time collectively spent by all the processing elements over and above that required by the fastest known sequential algorithm for solving the same problem on a single processing element. We denote the overhead function of a parallel system by the symbol *To*. The total time spent in solving a problem summed over all processing elements is *pTP*. *TS* units of this time are spent performing useful work, and the remainder is overhead. We formally define the *speedup S* as the ratio of the serial runtime of the best sequential algorithm for solving a problem to the time taken by the parallel algorithm to solve the same problem on *p* processing elements

Consider the example of parallelizing bubble sort. Assume that a serial version of bubble sort of 105 records takes 150 seconds and a serial quicksort can sort the same list in 30 seconds. If a parallel version of bubble sort, also called odd-even sort, takes 40 seconds on four processing elements, it would appear that the parallel odd-even sort algorithm results in a speedup of 150/40 or 3.75. However, this conclusion is misleading, as in reality the parallel algorithm results in a speedup of 30/40 or 0.75 with respect to the best serial algorithm.

Theoretically, speedup can never exceed the number of processing elements, *p*. If the best sequential algorithm takes *TS* units of time to solve a given problem on a single processing element, then a speedup of *p* can be obtained on *p* processing elements if none of the processing elements spends more than time *TS* /*p*. A speed up greater than *p* is possible only if each processing element spends less than time *TS* /*p* solving the problem. In this case, a single processing element could emulate the *p* processing elements and solve the problem in fewer than *TS* units of time. This is a contradiction because speedup, by definition, is computed with respect to the best sequential algorithm. If *TS* is the serial runtime of the algorithm, then the problem cannot be solved in less than time *TS* on a single processing element.

We define the *cost* of solving a problem on a parallel system as the product of parallel runtime and the number of processing elements used. Cost reflects the sum of the time that each processing element spends solving the problem. Efficiency can also be expressed as the ratio of the execution time of the fastest known sequential algorithm for solving a problem to the cost of solving the same problem on *p* processing elements. The cost of solving a problem on a single processing element is the execution time of the fastest known sequential algorithm. A parallel system is said to be *cost-optimal* if the cost of solving a problem on a parallel computer has the same asymptotic growth (in Q terms) as a function of the input size as the fastest-known sequential algorithm on a single processing element. Since efficiency is the ratio of sequential cost to parallel cost, a cost- optimal parallel system has an efficiency of Q (1). Cost is sometimes referred to as *work* or *processor-time product*, and a cost-optimal system is also known as a *pTP* -optimal system.

Consider a method for adding n numbers using p processing elements for $n = 16$ and $p = 4$. In the first step of this algorithm, each processing element locally adds its n/p numbers in time $Q(n/p)$. Now the problem is reduced to adding the p partial sums on p processing elements, which can be done in time $Q(\log p)$. The parallel runtime of this algorithm is

$$T_p=\theta(n/p+\log p)$$

and its cost is $Q(n + p \log p)$. As long as $n = \Omega(p \log p)$, the cost is $Q(n)$, which is the same as the serial runtime. Hence, this parallel system is cost-optimal. Thus the parallel analysis is performed.

References

- Kowalski, Robert (1979). "Algorithm=Logic+Control". Communications of the ACM. 22 (7): 424–436. doi:10.1145/359131.359136

- Bell, C. Gordon and Newell, Allen (1971), Computer Structures: Readings and Examples, McGraw–Hill Book Company, New York. ISBN 0-07-004357-4

- Tausworthe, Robert C (1977). Standardized Development of Computer Software Part 1 Methods. Englewood Cliffs NJ: Prentice–Hall, Inc. ISBN 0-13-842195-1

- Blelloch, Guy E.; Maggs, Bruce M. "Parallel Algorithms" (PDF). USA: School of Computer Science, Carnegie Mellon University. Retrieved 2015-07-27

- Duncan H. Lawrie (1975): "Access and Alignment of Data in an Array Processor", IEEE Transactions on Computers, Volume C-24, Number 12, pp. 1145– 1155, December 1975 doi:10.1109/T-C.1975.224157

- Quinn, Michael J. (2007). Parallel programming in C with MPI and openMP (Tata McGraw-Hill ed. ed.). New Delhi: Tata McGraw-Hill Pub. ISBN 0070582017

- Bender, C.M.; Orszag, S.A. (1999). Advanced mathematical methods for scientists and engineers. Springer. pp. 549–568. ISBN 0-387-98931-5

- Shuang Yu (8 May 2012). "IEEE APPROVES NEW IEEE 802.1aq™ SHORTEST PATH BRIDGING STANDARD". IEEE. Retrieved 2 June 2012

- Hardy, G. H.; Littlewood, J. E. (1914). "Some problems of diophantine approximation: Part II. The trigonometrical series associated with the elliptic -functions". Acta Mathematica. 37: 225. doi:10.1007/BF02401834

- Boyer, L. L; Pawley, G. S (1988-10-01). "Molecular dynamics of clusters of particles interacting with pairwise forces using a massively parallel computer". Journal of Computational Physics. 78 (2): 405–423. doi:10.1016/0021-9991(88)90057-5

- Scott, Michael L. (2009). Programming Language Pragmatics (3rd ed.). Morgan Kaufmann Publishers/Elsevier. ISBN 978-0-12-374514-9

- Peter Ashwood-Smith (24 Feb 2011). "Shortest Path Bridging IEEE 802.1aq Overview" (PDF). Huawei. Retrieved 11 May 2012

- Vitányi, Paul; Meertens, Lambert (April 1985). "Big Omega versus the wild functions" (PDF). ACM SIGACT News. 16 (4): 56–59. doi:10.1145/382242.382835

- Kleene, Stephen C. (1991) [1952]. Introduction to Metamathematics (Tenth ed.). North-Holland Publishing Company. ISBN 0-7204-2103-9. Excellent—accessible, readable—reference source for mathematical "foundations"

- Jim Duffy (11 May 2012). "Largest Illinois healthcare system uproots Cisco to build $40M private cloud". PC Advisor. Retrieved 11 May 2012

- Blelloch, Guy (1996). "Programming Parallel Algorithms" (PDF). Communications of the ACM. 39 (3): 85–97. doi:10.1145/227234.227246

- Cormen, Thomas H.; Leiserson, Charles E.; Rivest, Ronald L.; Stein, Clifford (2009) [1990]. Introduction to Algorithms (3rd ed.). MIT Press and McGraw-Hill. pp. 779–784. ISBN 0-262-03384-4

- "IEEE Approves New IEEE 802.1aq Shortest Path Bridging Standard". Tech Power Up. 7 May 2012. Retrieved 11 May 2012

Dense and Space Matrix Algorithms

Data decomposition is important in parallel computing algorithms. Matrices and vectors are used to divide tasks. Processor arrays are storage spaces that contain elements required for data processing. The chapter strategically encompasses and incorporates the major components and key concepts of dense and space matrix algorithms, providing a complete understanding.

Introduction to Processor Arrays

- At the end of this section, the learner would be able to:

  - Define a Vector Computer

  - Understand the methods for implementing a vector computer

  - Determine the performance of a Processor Array.

Vector Computer

> A computer that is capable of carrying out operations on vectors and scalars.

Two Important Ways of Implementing a Vector Computer

1. Pipelined Vector Processor: A processor that manipulates vectors using pipelined units is called a vector processor. Example: CRAY-1, Cyber-205

2. Processor Array: It is a vector computer where a set of identical synchronized processing elements concurrently do the same operation on different data.

Types of Processor Arrays

> Processor arrays can be organized as follows:

1. hypercubes

2. shuffle exchange network

3. cube connected cycles and

4. 2D mesh.

Vector Processor

In computing, a vector processor or array processor is a central processing unit (CPU) that implements an instruction set containing instructions that operate on one-dimensional arrays of data called *vectors*, compared to scalar processors, whose instructions operate on single data items. Vector processors can greatly improve performance on certain workloads, notably numerical simulation and similar tasks. Vector machines appeared in the early 1970s and dominated supercomputer design through the 1970s into the 1990s, notably the various Cray platforms. The rapid fall in the price-to-performance ratio of conventional microprocessor designs led to the vector supercomputer's demise in the later 1990s.

As of 2015 most commodity CPUs implement architectures that feature instructions for a form of vector processing on multiple (vectorized) data sets, typically known as SIMD (Single Instruction, Multiple Data). Common examples include Intel x86's MMX, SSE and AVX instructions, Sparc's VIS extension, PowerPC's AltiVec and MIPS' MSA. Vector processing techniques also operate in video-game console hardware and in graphics accelerators. In 2000, IBM, Toshiba and Sony collaborated to create the Cell processor, consisting of one scalar processor and eight SIMD processors, which found use in the Sony PlayStation 3 among other applications.

Other CPU designs may include some multiple instructions for vector processing on multiple (vectorised) data sets, typically known as MIMD (Multiple Instruction, Multiple Data) and realized with VLIW (Very Long Instruction Word). Such designs are usually dedicated to a particular application and not commonly marketed for general-purpose computing. The Fujitsu FR-V VLIW/ *vector processor* combines both technologies.

History

Early Work

Vector processing development began in the early 1960s at Westinghouse in their "Solomon" project. Solomon's goal was to dramatically increase math performance by using a large number of simple math co-processors under the control of a single master CPU. The CPU fed a single common instruction to all of the arithmetic logic units (ALUs), one per cycle, but with a different data point for each one to work on. This allowed the Solomon machine to apply a single algorithm to a large data set, fed in the form of an array.

In 1962, Westinghouse cancelled the project, but the effort was restarted at the University of Illinois as the ILLIAC IV. Their version of the design originally called for a 1 GFLOPS machine with 256 ALUs, but, when it was finally delivered in 1972, it had only 64 ALUs and could reach only 100 to 150 MFLOPS. Nevertheless, it showed that the basic concept was sound, and, when used on data-intensive applications, such as computational fluid dynamics, the ILLIAC was the fastest machine in the world. The ILLIAC approach of using separate ALUs for each data element is not common to later designs, and is often referred to under a separate category, massively parallel computing.

A computer for operations with functions was presented and developed by Kartsev in 1967.

Supercomputers

The first *successful* implementation of vector processing appears to be the Control Data Corporation STAR-100 and the Texas Instruments Advanced Scientific Computer (ASC). The basic ASC (i.e., "one pipe") ALU used a pipeline architecture that supported both scalar and vector computations, with peak performance reaching approximately 20 MFLOPS, readily achieved when processing long vectors. Expanded ALU configurations supported "two pipes" or "four pipes" with a corresponding 2X or 4X performance gain. Memory bandwidth was sufficient to support these expanded modes. The STAR was otherwise slower than CDC's own supercomputers like the CDC 7600, but at data related tasks they could keep up while being much smaller and less expensive. However the machine also took considerable time decoding the vector instructions and getting ready to run the process, so it required very specific data sets to work on before it actually sped anything up.

The vector technique was first fully exploited in 1976 by the famous Cray-1. Instead of leaving the data in memory like the STAR and ASC, the Cray design had eight vector registers, which held sixty-four 64-bit words each. The vector instructions were applied between registers, which is much faster than talking to main memory. The Cray design used pipeline parallelism to implement vector instructions rather than multiple ALUs. In addition the design had completely separate pipelines for different instructions, for example, addition/subtraction was implemented in different hardware than multiplication. This allowed a batch of vector instructions themselves to be pipelined, a technique they called *vector chaining*. The Cray-1 normally had a performance of about 80 MFLOPS, but with up to three chains running it could peak at 240 MFLOPS – far faster than any machine of the era.

Cray J90 processor module with four scalar/vector processors

Other examples followed. Control Data Corporation tried to re-enter the high-end market again with its ETA-10 machine, but it sold poorly and they took that as an opportunity to leave the supercomputing field entirely. In the early and mid-1980s Japanese companies (Fujitsu, Hitachi and Nippon Electric Corporation (NEC) introduced register-based vector machines similar to the Cray-1, typically being slightly faster and much smaller. Oregon-based Floating Point Systems (FPS) built add-on array processors for minicomputers, later building their own minisupercomputers.

Throughout, Cray continued to be the performance leader, continually beating the competition with a series of machines that led to the Cray-2, Cray X-MP and Cray Y-MP. Since then, the supercomputer market has focused much more on massively parallel processing rather than better implementations of vector processors. However, recognising the benefits of vector processing IBM developed Virtual Vector Architecture for use in supercomputers coupling several scalar processors to act as a vector processor.

SIMD

Vector processing techniques have since been added to almost all modern CPU designs, although they are typically referred to as SIMD(differing in that a single instruction always drives a single operation across a vector register, as opposed to the more flexible latency hiding approach in true vector processors). In these implementations, the vector unit runs beside the main scalar CPU, providing a separate set of vector registers, and is fed data from vector instruction aware programs.

GPGPU

Modern GPUs include an array of shader pipelines which may be driven by compute kernels, which can be considered vector processors (using a similar strategy for hiding memory latencies).

Description

In general terms, CPUs are able to manipulate one or two pieces of data at a time. For instance, most CPUs have an instruction that essentially says "add A to B and put the result in C". The data for A, B and C could be—in theory at least—encoded directly into the instruction. However, in efficient implementation things are rarely that simple. The data is rarely sent in raw form, and is instead "pointed to" by passing in an address to a memory location that holds the data. Decoding this address and getting the data out of the memory takes some time, during which the CPU traditionally would sit idle waiting for the requested data to show up. As CPU speeds have increased, this *memory latency* has historically become a large impediment to performance.

In order to reduce the amount of time consumed by these steps, most modern CPUs use a technique known as instruction pipelining in which the instructions pass through several sub-units in turn. The first sub-unit reads the address and decodes it, the next "fetches" the values at those addresses, and the next does the math itself. With pipelining the "trick" is to start decoding the next instruction even before the first has left the CPU, in the fashion of an assembly line, so the address decoder is constantly in use. Any particular instruction takes the same amount of time to complete, a time known as the *latency*, but the CPU can process an entire batch of operations much faster and more efficiently than if it did so one at a time.

Vector processors take this concept one step further. Instead of pipelining just the instructions, they also pipeline the data itself. The processor is fed instructions that say not just to add A to B, but to add all of the numbers "from here to here" to all of the numbers "from there to there". Instead of constantly having to decode instructions and then fetch the data needed to complete them, the processor reads a single instruction from memory, and it is simply implied in the definition of the instruction *itself* that the instruction will operate again on another item of data, at an address one increment larger than the last. This allows for significant savings in decoding time.

To illustrate what a difference this can make, consider the simple task of adding two groups of 10 numbers together. In a normal programming language one would write a "loop" that picked up each of the pairs of numbers in turn, and then added them. To the CPU, this would look something like this:

```
execute this loop 10 times

   read the next instruction and decode it

   fetch this number

   fetch that number

   add them

   put the result here

end loop
```

But to a vector processor, this task looks considerably different:

```
read instruction and decode it

fetch these 10 numbers

fetch those 10 numbers

add them

put the results here
```

There are several savings inherent in this approach. For one, only two address translations are needed. Depending on the architecture, this can represent a significant savings by itself. Another saving is fetching and decoding the instruction itself, which has to be done only one time instead of ten. The code itself is also smaller, which can lead to more efficient memory use.

But more than that, a vector processor may have multiple functional units adding those numbers in parallel. The checking of dependencies between those numbers is not required as a vector instruction specifies multiple independent operations. This simplifies the control logic required, and can improve performance by avoiding stalls.

As mentioned earlier, the Cray implementations took this a step further, allowing several different types of operations to be carried out at the same time. Consider code that adds two numbers and then multiplies by a third; in the Cray, these would all be fetched at once, and both added and multiplied in a single operation. Using the pseudocode above, the Cray did:

```
read instruction and decode it

fetch these 10 numbers

fetch those 10 numbers

fetch another 10 numbers

add and multiply them

put the results here
```

The math operations thus completed far faster overall, the limiting factor being the time required to fetch the data from memory.

Not all problems can be attacked with this sort of solution. Including these types of instructions necessarily adds complexity to the core CPU. That complexity typically makes *other* instructions run slower—i.e., whenever it is not adding up many numbers in a row. The more complex instructions also add to the complexity of the decoders, which might slow down the decoding of the more common instructions such as normal adding.

In fact, vector processors work best only when there are large amounts of data to be worked on. For this reason, these sorts of CPUs were found primarily in supercomputers, as the supercomputers themselves were, in general, found in places such as weather prediction centres and physics labs, where huge amounts of data are "crunched".

Performance and Speed Up

Let r be the vector speed ratio and f be the vectorization ratio. If the time taken for the vector unit to add an array of 64 numbers is 10 times faster than its equivalent scalar counterpart, r = 10. Also, if the total number of operations in a program is 100, out of which only 10 are scalar (after vectorization), then f = 90, i.e., 90% of the work is done by the vector unit. It follows the achievable speed up of:

$$r / [(1 - f) * r + f]$$

So, even if the performance of the vector unit is very high ($r = \infty$) we get a speedup less than $1 / (1 - f)$, which suggests that the ratio f is crucial to the performance. This ratio depends on the efficiency of the compilation like adjacency of the elements in memory.

Real-world Example: Vector Instructions Usage with the x86 Architecture

Shown below is an actual x86 architecture example for vector instruction usage with the SSE instruction set. The example multiplies two arrays of single precision floating point numbers. It's written in the C language with inline assembly code parts for compilation with GCC (32bit).

```
//SSE simd function for vectorized multiplication of 2 arrays with single-precision
floating point numbers

//1st param pointer on source/destination array, 2nd param 2. source array, 3rd param
number of floats per array
 void mul_asm(float* out, float* in, unsigned int leng)
 {    unsigned int count, rest;

      //compute if array is big enough for vector operation
      rest  = (leng*4)%16;

      count = (leng*4)-rest;

     // vectorized part; 4 floats per loop iteration
      if (count>0){
      __asm __volatile__   (".intel_syntax noprefix\n\t"
      "loop:                  \n\t"
      "movups xmm0,[ebx+ecx] ;loads 4 floats in first register (xmm0)\n\t"
```

```
"movups xmm1,[eax+ecx] ;loads 4 floats in second register (xmm1)\n\t"

"mulps xmm0,xmm1        ;multiplies both vector registers\n\t"

"movups [eax+ecx],xmm0 ;write back the result to memory\n\t"

"sub ecx,16             ;increase address pointer by 4 floats\n\t"

"jnz loop              \n\t"

".att_syntax prefix     \n\t"

  : : "a" (out), "b" (in), "c"(count), "d"(rest): "xmm0","xmm1");

}

// scalar part; 1 float per loop iteration

if (rest!=0)

{

  __asm __volatile__  (".intel_syntax noprefix\n\t"

"add eax,ecx           \n\t"

"add ebx,ecx           \n\t"

"rest:                 \n\t"

"movss xmm0,[ebx+edx]  ;load 1 float in first register (xmm0)\n\t"

"movss xmm1,[eax+edx]  ;load 1 float in second register (xmm1)\n\t"

"mulss xmm0,xmm1       ;multiplies both scalar parts of registers\n\t"

"movss [eax+edx],xmm0  ;write back the result\n\t"

"sub edx,4             \n\t"

"jnz rest              \n\t"

".att_syntax prefix     \n\t"

  : : "a" (out), "b" (in), "c"(count), "d"(rest): "xmm0","xmm1");

}

return;

}
```

Programming Heterogeneous Computing Architectures

Various machines were designed to include both traditional processors and vector processors, such as the Fujitsu AP1000 and AP3000. Programming such heterogeneous machines can be difficult since developing programs that make best use of characteristics of different processors increases the programmer's burden. It increases code complexity and decreases portability of the code by requiring hardware specific code to be interleaved throughout application code. Balancing the application workload across processors can be problematic, especially given that they typically have different performance characteristics. There are different conceptual models to deal with the problem, for example using a coordination language and program building blocks (programming libraries or higher order functions). Each block can have a different native implementation for each processor type. Users simply program using these abstractions and an intelligent compiler chooses the best implementation based on the context.

Instruction Pipelining

Instr. No.	Pipeline Stage						
1	IF	ID	EX	MEM	WB		
2		IF	ID	EX	MEM	WB	
3			IF	ID	EX	MEM	WB
4				IF	ID	EX	MEM
5					IF	ID	EX
Clock Cycle	1	2	3	4	5	6	7

Basic five-stage pipeline (IF = Instruction Fetch, ID = Instruction Decode, EX = Execute, MEM = Memory access, WB = Register write back). In the fourth clock cycle (the green column), the earliest instruction is in MEM stage, and the latest instruction has not yet entered the pipeline.

Instruction pipelining is a technique that implements a form of parallelism called instruction-level parallelism within a single processor. It therefore allows faster CPU throughput (the number of instructions that can be executed in a unit of time) than would otherwise be possible at a given clock rate. The basic instruction cycle is broken up into a series called a pipeline. Rather than processing each instruction sequentially (finishing one instruction before starting the next), each instruction is split up into a sequence of dependent steps so different steps can be executed in parallel and instructions can be processed concurrently (starting one instruction before finishing the previous one).

The first step is always to fetch the instruction from memory; the final step is usually writing the results of the instruction to processor registers or to memory. Pipelining seeks to let the processor work on as many instructions as there are dependent steps, just as an assembly line builds many vehicles at once, rather than waiting until one vehicle has passed through the line before admitting the next one. Just as the goal of the assembly line is to keep each assembler productive at all times, pipelining seeks to keep every portion of the processor busy with some instruction. Pipelining lets the computer's cycle time be the time of the slowest step, and ideally lets one instruction complete in every cycle.

Pipelining increases instruction throughput by performing multiple operations at the same time, but does not reduce latency, the time needed to complete a single instruction. Indeed, pipelining may increase latency due to additional overhead from breaking the computation into separate steps, and depending on how often the pipeline stalls or needs to be flushed.

The term pipeline is an analogy to the fact that there is fluid in each link of a pipeline, as each part of the processor is occupied with work.

Introduction

Central processing units (CPUs) are driven by a clock. Each clock pulse need not do the same thing; rather, logic in the CPU directs successive pulses to different places to perform a useful sequence. There are many reasons that the entire execution of a machine instruction cannot happen at once; in pipelining, effects that cannot happen at the same time are made into dependent steps of the instruction.

For example, if one clock pulse latches a value into a register or begins a calculation, it will take some time for the value to be stable at the outputs of the register or for the calculation to complete. As another example, reading an instruction out of a memory unit cannot be done at the same time that an instruction writes a result to the same memory unit.

Number of Steps

The number of dependent steps varies with the machine architecture. For example:

- The 1956-1961 IBM Stretch project proposed the terms Fetch, Decode, and Execute that have become common.

- The classic RISC pipeline comprises:

  1. Instruction fetch

  2. Instruction decode and register fetch

  3. Execute

  4. Memory access

  5. Register write back

- The Atmel AVR and the PIC microcontroller each have a two-stage pipeline.

- Many designs include pipelines as long as 7, 10 and even 20 stages (as in the Intel Pentium 4).

- The later "Prescott" and "Cedar Mill" Netburst cores from Intel, used in the latest Pentium 4 models and their Pentium D and Xeon derivatives, have a long 31-stage pipeline.

- The Xelerated X10q Network Processor has a pipeline more than a thousand stages long, although in this case 200 of these stages represent independent CPUs with individually programmed instructions. The remaining stages are used to coordinate accesses to memory and on-chip function units.

As the pipeline is made "deeper" (with a greater number of dependent steps), a given step can be implemented with simpler circuitry, which may let the processor clock run faster. Such pipelines may be called *superpipelines*.

A processor is said to be *fully pipelined* if it can fetch an instruction on every cycle. Thus, if some instructions or conditions require delays that inhibit fetching new instructions, the processor is not fully pipelined.

Hazards

The model of sequential execution assumes that each instruction completes before the next one begins; this assumption is not true on a pipelined processor. A situation where the expected result is problematic is known as a hazard. Imagine the following two register instructions to a hypothetical processor:

```
1: add 1 to R5
```

```
2: copy R5 to R6
```

If the processor has the 5 steps listed in the initial illustration, instruction 1 would be fetched at time t_1 and its execution would be complete at t_5. Instruction 2 would be fetched at t_2 and would be complete at t_6. The first instruction might deposit the incremented number into R5 as its fifth step (register write back) at t_5. But the second instruction might get the number from R5 (to copy to R6) in its second step (instruction decode and register fetch) at time t_3. It seems that the first instruction would not have incremented the value by then. The above code invokes a hazard.

Writing computer programs in a compiled language might not raise these concerns, as the compiler could be designed to generate machine code that avoids hazards.

Workarounds

In some early DSP and RISC processors, the documentation advises programmers to avoid such dependencies in adjacent and nearly adjacent instructions (called delay slots), or declares that the second instruction uses an old value rather than the desired value (in the example above, the processor might counter-intuitively copy the unincremented value), or declares that the value it uses is undefined. The programmer may have unrelated work that the processor can do in the meantime; or, to ensure correct results, the programmer may insert NOPs into the code, partly negating the advantages of pipelining.

Solutions

Pipelined processors commonly use three techniques to work as expected when the programmer assumes that each instruction completes before the next one begins:

- Processors that can compute the presence of a hazard may *stall*, delaying processing of the second instruction (and subsequent instructions) until the values it requires as input are ready. This creates a *bubble* in the pipeline, also partly negating the advantages of pipelining.

- Some processors can not only compute the presence of a hazard but can compensate by having additional data paths that provide needed inputs to a computation step before a subsequent instruction would otherwise compute them, an attribute called operand forwarding.

- Some processors can determine that instructions other than the next sequential one are not dependent on the current ones and can be executed without hazards. Such processors may perform out-of-order execution.

Branches

A branch out of the normal instruction sequence often involves a hazard. Unless the processor can give effect to the branch in a single time cycle, the pipeline will continue fetching instructions sequentially. Such instructions cannot be allowed to take effect because the programmer has diverted control to another part of the program.

A conditional branch is even more problematic. The processor may or may not branch, depending on a calculation that has not yet occurred. Various processors may stall, may attempt branch prediction, and may be able to begin to execute two different program sequences (eager execution), both assuming the branch is and is not taken, discarding all work that pertains to the incorrect guess.

A processor with an implementation of branch prediction that usually makes correct predictions can minimize the performance penalty from branching. However, if branches are predicted poorly, it may create more work for the processor, such as flushing from the pipeline the incorrect code path that has begun execution before resuming execution at the correct location.

Programs written for a pipelined processor deliberately avoid branching to minimize possible loss of speed. For example, the programmer can handle the usual case with sequential execution and branch only on detecting unusual cases. Using programs such as gcov to analyze code coverage lets the programmer measure how often particular branches are actually executed and gain insight with which to optimize the code.

Special Situations

Self-modifying programs

The technique of self-modifying code can be problematic on a pipelined processor. In this technique, one of the effects of a program is to modify its own upcoming instructions. If the processor has an instruction cache, the original instruction may already have been copied into a prefetch input queue and the modification will not take effect.

Uninterruptible instructions

An instruction may be uninterruptible to ensure its atomicity, such as when it swaps two items. A sequential processor permits interrupts between instructions, but a pipelining processor overlaps instructions, so executing an uninterruptible instruction renders portions of ordinary instructions uninterruptible too. The Cyrix coma bug would hang a single-core system using an infinite loop in which an uninterruptible instruction was always in the pipeline.

Design Considerations

Speed

Pipelining keeps all portions of the processor occupied and increases the amount of useful work the processor can do in a given time. Pipelining typically reduces the processor's cycle time and increases the throughput of instructions. The speed advantage is diminished to the extent that execution encounters hazards that require execution to slow below its ideal rate. A non-pipelined processor executes only a single instruction at a time. The start of the next instruction is delayed not based on hazards but unconditionally.

A pipelined processor's need to organize all its work into modular steps may require the duplication of registers that increases the latency of some instructions.

Economy

By making each dependent step simpler, pipelining can enable complex operations more economically than adding complex circuitry, such as for numerical calculations. However, a processor that declines to pursue increased speed with pipelining may be simpler and cheaper to manufacture.

Predictability

Compared to environments where the programmer needs to avoid or work around hazards, use of a non-pipelined processor may make it easier to program and to train programmers. The non-pipelined processor also makes it easier to predict the exact timing of a given sequence of instructions.

Example

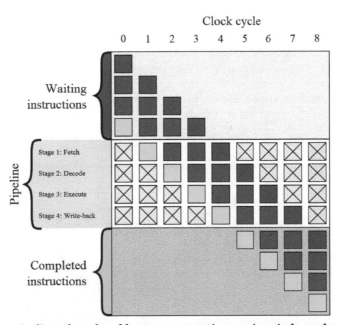

Generic 4-stage pipeline; the colored boxes represent instructions independent of each other

To the right is a generic pipeline with four stages: fetch, decode, execute and write-back. The top gray box is the list of instructions waiting to be executed, the bottom gray box is the list of instructions that have had their execution completed, and the middle white box is the pipeline.

The execution is as follows:

Time	Execution
0	Four instructions are waiting to be executed
1	• The green instruction is fetched from memory
2	• The green instruction is decoded • The purple instruction is fetched from memory
3	• The green instruction is executed (actual operation is performed) • The purple instruction is decoded • The blue instruction is fetched
4	• The green instruction's results are written back to the register file or memory • The purple instruction is executed • The blue instruction is decoded • The red instruction is fetched
5	• The execution of green instruction is completed • The purple instruction is written back • The blue instruction is executed • The red instruction is decoded
6	• The execution of purple instruction is completed • The blue instruction is written back • The red instruction is executed
7	• The execution of blue instruction is completed • The red instruction is written back
8	• The execution of red instruction is completed
9	The execution of all four instructions is completed

Pipeline Bubble

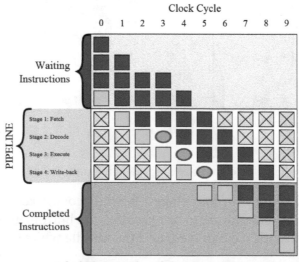

A bubble in cycle 3 delays execution.

A pipelined processor may deal with hazards by stalling and creating a bubble in the pipeline, resulting in one or more cycles in which nothing useful happens.

In the illustration at right, in cycle 3, the processor cannot decode the purple instruction, perhaps because the processor determines that decoding depends on results produced by the execution of the green instruction. The green instruction can proceed to the Execute stage and then to the Write-back stage as scheduled, but the purple instruction is stalled for one cycle at the Fetch stage. The blue instruction, which was due to be fetched during cycle 3, is stalled for one cycle, as is the red instruction after it.

Because of the bubble (the blue ovals in the illustration), the processor's Decode circuitry is idle during cycle 3. Its Execute circuitry is idle during cycle 4 and its Write-back circuitry is idle during cycle 5.

When the bubble moves out of the pipeline (at cycle 6), normal execution resumes. But everything now is one cycle late. It will take 8 cycles (cycle 1 through 8) rather than 7 to completely execute the four instructions shown in colors.

History

Seminal uses of pipelining were in the ILLIAC II project and the IBM Stretch project, though a simple version was used earlier in the Z1 in 1939 and the Z3 in 1941.

Pipelining began in earnest in the late 1970s in supercomputers such as vector processors and array processors. One of the early supercomputers was the Cyber series built by Control Data Corporation. Its main architect, Seymour Cray, later headed Cray Research. Cray developed the XMP line of supercomputers, using pipelining for both multiply and add/subtract functions. Later, Star Technologies added parallelism (several pipelined functions working in parallel), developed by Roger Chen. In 1984, Star Technologies added the pipelined divide circuit developed by James Bradley. By the mid 1980s, supercomputing was used by many different companies around the world.

Today, pipelining and most of the above innovations are implemented by the instruction unit of most microprocessors.

Types of Processor Arrays

Processor arrays can be organized as follows:

1. hypercubes

2. shuffle exchange network

3. cube connected cycles and

4. 2D mesh.

Performance of a Processor Array

Now we will identify a method to determine the performance of a processor array.

- It is measured as the number of operations per second.

- It is based on the processor utilization.

- The size of the data structure that is currently manipulated is directly proportional to the performance.

Mesh Network

Mesh Network: A set of nodes arranged in the form of a p dimensional lattice is called a mesh network. In a mesh network only neighbouring nodes can communicate with each other. Therefore interior nodes can communicate with 2p other nodes.

Evaluation of a Mesh Network

Let us assume that the mesh has no wraparound connection. A mesh network can be evaluated using two factors (i) Diameter and (ii)Bisection width.

(i) Diameter:A diameter of a mesh network is the longest distance between two nodes. The diameter of a p dimensional mesh with k^p nodes is p(k-1).

(ii) Bisection width:It is defined as the minimum number of edges to be removed to divide the network into two halves. The bisection width of a p dimensional mesh with k^p nodes is k^{p-1}.

Matrix Multiplication using 2D Mesh

Given a 2D mesh SIMD model with wraparound connections it is easy to devise an algorithm that uses n^2 processors to multiply two nxn arrays in theta(n) time.

Initial Location of Matrix Elements to Processing Elements

Let each Processing Element $PE_{i,j}$ represents two elements $a_{i,j}$, $b_{i,j}$

In the original state there are only n processing elements containing a pair of scalars suitable for multiplica- tion.

Stagger matrices A and B so that every processor has a pair of scalars that need to be multiplied.

The elements of A will move in leftward rotation and the elements of B move in upward rotation. These movements present each PE with a new pair of values to be multiplied.

Now let us look at the actions of a single processing element. After matrices A and B have been staggered, the PE P(1,2) performs the multiplications and additions form the dot product $C_{1,2}$.

The pseudo code for the matrix multiplication is given below. The first phase of the parallel algorithm staggers two matrices. The second phase computes all products a_{ik} X b_{kj} and accumulate sums when the phase II is complete.

Algorithm

Procedure MATRIXMULT

Begin

for k = 1 to n-1 step 1 do

begin

for all Pi,j where i and j ranges from 1 to n do

if i is greater than k then

rotate a in the east direction

end if

if j is greater than k then

rotate b in the south direction

end if

end

for all Pi,j where i and j lies between 1 and n do

compute the product of a and b and store it in c

for k= 1 to n-1 step 1 do for all Pi,j where i and j ranges from 1 to n do

rotate a in the east

rotate b in the south

c=c+aXb

end

Explanation with an example

Let us consider the following two matrices.

$$A = \begin{pmatrix} 1 & 2 \\ 3 & 4 \end{pmatrix}$$

$$B = \begin{pmatrix} 5 & 6 \\ 7 & 8 \end{pmatrix}$$

The matrix elements are stored in a two dimensional mesh as follows. The elements of the matrix A are in red and the elements of the matrix B are in green.

$$Mesh = \begin{pmatrix} a11|b11 & a12|b12 \\ a21|b21 & a22|b22 \end{pmatrix}$$

That is,

$$Mesh = \begin{pmatrix} 1|5 & 2|6 \\ 3|7 & 4|8 \end{pmatrix}$$

Let the number of processors be $n^2=4$. Let the processors be P(1,1), P(1,2), P(2,1) and P(2,2). Let k ranges from 1 to 2-1=1.

According to the algorithm, P(1,2), P(2,1) and P(2,2) will carry out the movements. That is there is no change in a11 and b11. b12 and b22 are moved up while a21 and a22 are moved left. Now the resultant Mesh after column movement is given below.

$$Mesh = \begin{pmatrix} & 6 & \\ 1|5 & 2|8 \\ 3|7 & 4 \end{pmatrix}$$

Now the element 6 wraparound to the bottom.

$$Mesh = \begin{pmatrix} 1|5 & 2|8 \\ 3|7 & 4|6 \end{pmatrix}$$

Now P(2,1) and P(2,2) will move $a_{2,1}$ and $a_{2,2}$ towards its left respectively. Therefore the resultant Mesh will be

$$Mesh = \begin{pmatrix} 1|5 & 2|8 \\ 4|7 & 3|6 \end{pmatrix}$$

The processors P_{ij} i,j ranges from 1 to 2 will compute the product of a_{ij} and b_{ij} respectively The resultant matrix after computing the product will be

$$C = \begin{pmatrix} 5 & 16 \\ 28 & 18 \end{pmatrix}$$

Next all P_{ij} will move its a_{ij} and b_{ij} left and up respectively. The resultant Mesh will be

$$Mesh = \begin{pmatrix} 2|7 & 1|6 \\ 3|5 & 4|8 \end{pmatrix}$$

Now all the processors P_{ij} compute the product of a_{ij} and b_{ij} respectively and add with the old value of C_{ij}.

Hence the resultant product matrix will be

$$C = \begin{pmatrix} 19 & 22 \\ 43 & 50 \end{pmatrix}$$

Analysis

Communication

Let us assume that the given matrices A and B are divided into sub matrices each of order m x m, where m is the number of processes or processors. Each process will have q x q sub matrices where q=n/m. The initial alignment requires a maximum of q-1 shift operations for both A and B.

Next there will be q-1 shift operations for A and B each. Each shift operation involves m^2 elements. $T_{Communication} = 4(q\text{-}1)(\text{startuptime} + m^2\text{datatime})=O(qm^2)=O(mn)$ since q=n/m

Computation

Each sub matrix multiplication requires m^3 multiplication and m^3 addition. Therefore with q-1 shifts, $T_{Computation} = 2qm^3=2m^2n$. Hence $T_{Computation}=O(m^2n)$.

Network Topology

Network topology is the arrangement of the various elements (links, nodes, etc.) of a computer network. Essentially, it is the topological structure of a network and may be depicted physically or logically. *Physical topology* is the placement of the various components of a network, including device location and cable installation, while *logical topology* illustrates how data flows within a network, regardless of its physical design. Distances between nodes, physical interconnections, transmission rates, or signal types may differ between two networks, yet their topologies may be identical.

An example is a local area network (LAN). Any given node in the LAN has one or more physical links to other devices in the network; graphically mapping these links results in a geometric shape that can be used to describe the physical topology of the network. Conversely, mapping the data flow between the components determines the logical topology of the network.

Topology

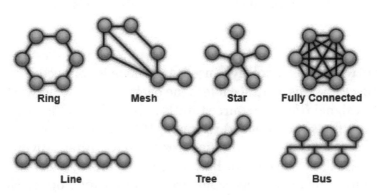

Diagram of different network topologies.

Two basic categories of network topologies exist, physical topologies and logical topologies.

The cabling layout used to link devices is the physical topology of the network. This refers to the layout of cabling, the locations of nodes, and the interconnections between the nodes and the cabling. The physical topology of a network is determined by the capabilities of the network access devices and media, the level of control or fault tolerance desired, and the cost associated with cabling or telecommunications circuits.

In contrast, logical topology is the way that the signals act on the network media, or the way that the data passes through the network from one device to the next without regard to the physical interconnection of the devices. A network's logical topology is not necessarily the same as its physical topology. For example, the original twisted pair Ethernet using repeater hubs was a logical bus topology carried on a physical star topology. Token ring is a logical ring topology, but is wired as a physical star from the media access unit. Logical topologies are often closely associated with media access control methods and protocols. Some networks are able to dynamically change their logical topology through configuration changes to their routers and switches.

Classification

The study of network topology recognizes eight basic topologies: point-to-point, bus, star, ring or circular, mesh, tree, hybrid, or daisy chain.

Point-to-point

The simplest topology with a dedicated link between two endpoints. Easiest to understand, of the variations of point-to-point topology, is a point-to-point communications channel that appears, to the user, to be permanently associated with the two endpoints. A child's tin can telephone is one example of a *physical dedicated* channel.

Using circuit-switching or packet-switching technologies, a point-to-point circuit can be set up dynamically and dropped when no longer needed. Switched point-to-point topologies are the basic model of conventional telephony.

The value of a permanent point-to-point network is unimpeded communications between the two endpoints. The value of an on-demand point-to-point connection is proportional to the number of potential pairs of subscribers and has been expressed as Metcalfe's Law.

Bus

In local area networks where bus topology is used, each node is connected to a single cable, by the help of interface connectors. This central cable is the backbone of the network and is known as the bus (thus the name). A signal from the source travels in both directions to all machines connected on the bus cable until it finds the intended recipient. If the machine address does not match the intended address for the data, the machine ignores the data. Alternatively, if the data matches the machine address, the data is accepted. Because the bus topology consists of only one wire, it is rather inexpensive to implement when compared to other topologies. However, the low cost of implementing the technology is offset by the high cost of managing the network. Additionally, because only one cable is utilized, it can be the single point of failure. In this topology data being transferred may be accessed by any workstation.

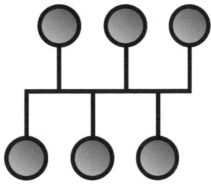

Bus network topology

Linear Bus

The type of network topology in which all of the nodes of the network are connected to a common transmission medium which has exactly two endpoints (this is the 'bus', which is also commonly referred to as the backbone, or trunk) – all data that is transmitted between nodes in the network is transmitted over this common transmission medium and is able to be received by all nodes in the network simultaneously.

Note: When the electrical signal reaches the end of the bus, the signal is reflected back down the line, causing unwanted interference. As a solution, the two endpoints of the bus are normally terminated with a device called a terminator that prevents this reflection.

Distributed Bus

The type of network topology in which all of the nodes of the network are connected to a common transmission medium which has more than two endpoints that are created by adding branches to the main section of the transmission medium – the physical distributed bus topology functions in exactly the same fashion as the physical linear bus topology (i.e., all nodes share a common transmission medium).

Star

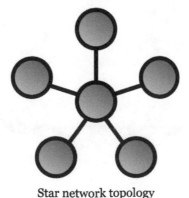

Star network topology

In local area networks with a star topology, each network host is connected to a central hub with a point-to-point connection. So it can be said that every computer is indirectly connected to every other node with the help of the hub. In Star topology, every node (computer workstation or any other peripheral) is connected to a central node called hub, router or switch. The switch is the server and the peripherals are the clients. The network does not necessarily have to resemble a star to be classified as a star network, but all of the nodes on the network must be connected to one central device. All traffic that traverses the network passes through the central hub. The hub acts as a signal repeater. The star topology is considered the easiest topology to design and implement. An advantage of the star topology is the simplicity of adding additional nodes. The primary disadvantage of the star topology is that the hub represents a single point of failure.

Extended Star

A type of network topology in which a network that is based upon the physical star topology has one or more repeaters between the central node and the peripheral or 'spoke' nodes, the repeaters being used to extend the maximum transmission distance of the point-to-point links between the central node and the peripheral nodes beyond that which is supported by the transmitter power of the central node or beyond that which is supported by the standard upon which the physical layer of the physical star network is based.

If the repeaters in a network that is based upon the physical extended star topology are replaced with hubs or switches, then a hybrid network topology is created that is referred to as a physical hierarchical star topology, although some texts make no distinction between the two topologies.

Distributed Star

A type of network topology that is composed of individual networks that are based upon the physical star topology connected in a linear fashion – i.e., 'daisy-chained' – with no central or top level connection point (e.g., two or more 'stacked' hubs, along with their associated star connected nodes or 'spokes').

Ring

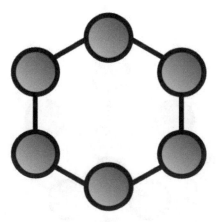

Ring network topology

A ring topology is a bus topology in a closed loop. Data travels around the ring in one direction. When one node sends data to another, the data passes through each intermediate node on the ring until it reaches its destination. The intermediate nodes repeat (re transmit) the data to keep the signal strong. Every node is a peer; there is no hierarchical relationship of clients and servers. If one node is unable to re transmit data, it severs communication between the nodes before and after it in the bus.

Advantages:

- When the load on the network increases, its performance is better than bus topology.

- There is no need of network server to control the connectivity between workstations.

Mesh

The value of fully meshed networks is proportional to the exponent of the number of subscribers, assuming that communicating groups of any two endpoints, up to and including all the endpoints, is approximated by Reed's Law.

Fully Connected Network

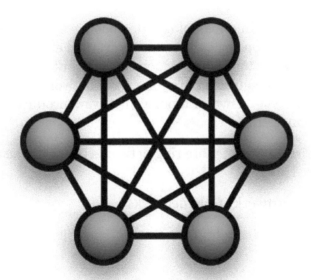

Fully connected mesh topology

In a *fully connected network*, all nodes are interconnected. (In graph theory this is called a complete graph.) The simplest fully connected network is a two-node network. A fully connected network doesn't need to use packet switching or broadcasting. However, since the number of connections grows quadratically with the number of nodes:

$$c = \frac{n(n-1)}{2}.$$

This makes it impractical for large networks.

Partially Connected Network

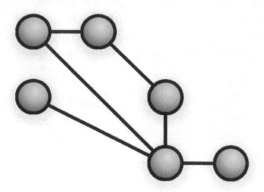

Partially connected mesh topology

In a partially connected network, certain nodes are connected to exactly one other node; but some nodes are connected to two or more other nodes with a point-to-point link. This makes it possible to make use of some of the redundancy of mesh topology that is physically fully connected, without the expense and complexity required for a connection between every node in the network.

Hybrid

Hybrid networks combine two or more topologies in such a way that the resulting network does not exhibit one of the standard topologies (e.g., bus, star, ring, etc.). For example, a tree network (or *star-bus network*) is a hybrid topology in which star networks are interconnected via bus networks. However, a tree network connected to another tree network is still topologically a tree network, not a distinct network type. A hybrid topology is always produced when two different basic network topologies are connected.

A *star-ring* network consists of two or more ring networks connected using a multistation access unit (MAU) as a centralized hub.

Snowflake topology is a star network of star networks.

Two other hybrid network types are *hybrid mesh* and *hierarchical star*.

Daisy Chain

Except for star-based networks, the easiest way to add more computers into a network is by daisy-chaining, or connecting each computer in series to the next. If a message is intended for a computer partway down the line, each system bounces it along in sequence until it reaches the destination. A daisy-chained network can take two basic forms: linear and ring.

- A linear topology puts a two-way link between one computer and the next. However, this was expensive in the early days of computing, since each computer (except for the ones at each end) required two receivers and two transmitters.

- By connecting the computers at each end, a ring topology can be formed. An advantage of the ring is that the number of transmitters and receivers can be cut in half, since a message will eventually loop all of the way around. When a node sends a message, the message is processed by each computer in the ring. If the ring breaks at a particular link then the transmission can be sent via the reverse path thereby ensuring that all nodes are always connected in the case of a single failure.

Centralization

The star topology reduces the probability of a network failure by connecting all of the peripheral nodes (computers, etc.) to a central node. When the physical star topology is applied to a logical bus network such as Ethernet, this central node (traditionally a hub) rebroadcasts all transmissions received from any peripheral node to all peripheral nodes on the network, sometimes including the originating node. All peripheral nodes may thus communicate with all others by transmitting to, and receiving from, the central node only. The failure of a transmission line linking any peripheral node to the central node will result in the isolation of that peripheral node from all others, but the remaining peripheral nodes will be unaffected. However, the disadvantage is that the failure of the central node will cause the failure of all of the peripheral nodes.

If the central node is *passive*, the originating node must be able to tolerate the reception of an echo of its own transmission, delayed by the two-way round trip transmission time (i.e. to and from the central node) plus any delay generated in the central node. An *active* star network has an active central node that usually has the means to prevent echo-related problems.

A tree topology (a.k.a. hierarchical topology) can be viewed as a collection of star networks arranged in a hierarchy. This tree has individual peripheral nodes (e.g. leaves) which are required to transmit to and receive from one other node only and are not required to act as repeaters or regenerators. Unlike the star network, the functionality of the central node may be distributed.

As in the conventional star network, individual nodes may thus still be isolated from the network by a single-point failure of a transmission path to the node. If a link connecting a leaf fails, that leaf is isolated; if a connection to a non-leaf node fails, an entire section of the network becomes isolated from the rest.

To alleviate the amount of network traffic that comes from broadcasting all signals to all nodes, more advanced central nodes were developed that are able to keep track of the identities of the nodes that are connected to the network. These network switches will "learn" the layout of the network by "listening" on each port during normal data transmission, examining the data packets and recording the address/identifier of each connected node and which port it is connected to in a lookup table held in memory. This lookup table then allows future transmissions to be forwarded to the intended destination only.

Decentralization

In a partially connected mesh topology, there are at least two nodes with two or more paths between them to provide redundant paths in case the link providing one of the paths fails. Decentralization is often used to compensate for the single-point-failure disadvantage that is present when using a single device as a central node (e.g., in star and tree networks). A special kind of mesh, limiting the number of hops between two nodes, is a hypercube. The number of arbitrary forks in mesh networks makes them more difficult to design and implement, but their decentralized nature makes them very useful. In 2012 the Institute of Electrical and Electronics Engineers (IEEE) published the Shortest Path Bridging protocol to ease configuration tasks and allows all paths to be active which increases bandwidth and redundancy between all devices.

This is similar in some ways to a grid network, where a linear or ring topology is used to connect systems in multiple directions. A multidimensional ring has a toroidal topology, for instance.

A *fully connected network, complete topology*, or *full mesh topology* is a network topology in which there is a direct link between all pairs of nodes. In a fully connected network with n nodes, there are n(n-1)/2 direct links. Networks designed with this topology are usually very expensive to set up, but provide a high degree of reliability due to the multiple paths for data that are provided by the large number of redundant links between nodes. This topology is mostly seen in military applications.

Hypercube Network

Now let us start with the definition of a cube connected network.

Definition 1. *Cube Connected Network: It is also called as a binary n-cube network consists of 2^k nodes that forms a k-dimensional hypercube. The nodes are named from 0 to 2^k-1. Two nodes n_1 and n_2 are said to be adjacent iff their labels differ in exactly one bit position.*

Some Important Features of Hypercubes

1. The diameter of a hypercube with 2^k nodes = k

2. The bisection width of a hypercube with 2^k nodes = 2^{k-1}

3. Number of edges=k

4. BitComplement(n,k): It is used to complement the kth bit position of an integer n. Example:BitComplement(4,1)=BitCom

5. nCUBE is building systems based on hypercube topology.

6. Connection Machine-200(CM-200) are connected in a hypercube.

Now let us analyze how to route messages in a hypercube.

Two nodes whose name differ in exactly one bit position are always linked by edges.

For example 0101 will be connected with 0001,1101,0111 and 0100. Using this one can identify the shortest path between source and destination. The shortest path to reach 0011 from 0101 is via 0001.

Matrix Multiplication on the Hypercube

- Let us consider the following specification for a hypercube interconnection network

  - Let N= 2^k be the total number of processors. Let it be P_0, P_1, etc upto P_{N-1}.

  - Let j and j^b be two integers ranging from 0 to N-2 whose binary representation differ only in position b, where b ranges from 0 to k-1.

  - Let us compute the product of the following two matrices.

$$A = \begin{pmatrix} 1 & 2 \\ 3 & 4 \end{pmatrix}$$

$$B = \begin{pmatrix} 5 & 6 \\ 7 & 8 \end{pmatrix}$$

Initial Step 1: Let the elements of A and B are arranged in a hypercube as shown in Figure.

- Step 2: The nodes labelled 000,001,010 and 011 will send their data to its neighbours labelled 100,101,110 and 111 respectively. That is A(0,j,k) and B(0,j,k) will send the data to the Processing Element(i,j,k). This is shown in Figur.

- Step 3: The processing elements with identical first and third bits will send the elements of A to their neighbours. That is 101 will send to 100, 000 will send to 001, 010 will send to 011 and 111 will send to 110 respectively. This is shown in Figure.

- Step 4: The Processing elements with identical first and second bits will send the elements of B to their neighbours. That is 110 will send to 100, 111 will send to 101, 000 will send to 010 and 001 will send to 011 respectively. This is shown in Figure.

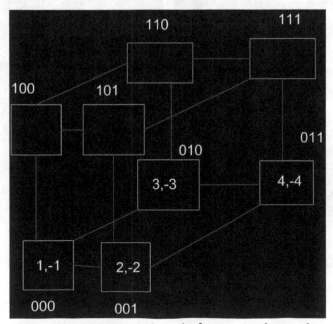

Step 1: An arrangement of matrix elements in a hypercube

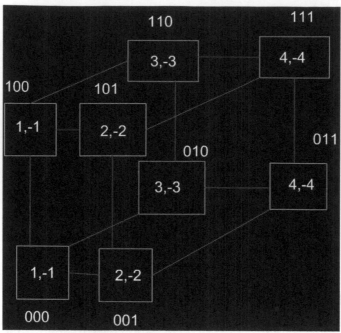

Step 2: A data routing in a hypercube

- Step 5:Each Processing Element $P_{i,j,k}$ will compute the product of its elements. This is shown in Figure.

- Step 6: The Processing Elements $P_{i,j,k}$ that differ in the Most significant bit will sum up their elements and the result will be stored in the Processing Element $P_{o,j,k}$. This is shown in Figure

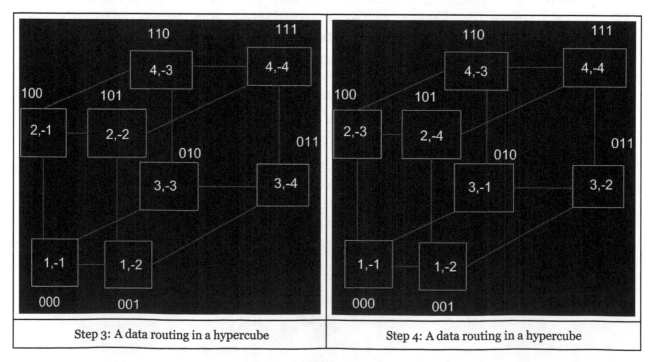

| Step 3: A data routing in a hypercube | Step 4: A data routing in a hypercube |

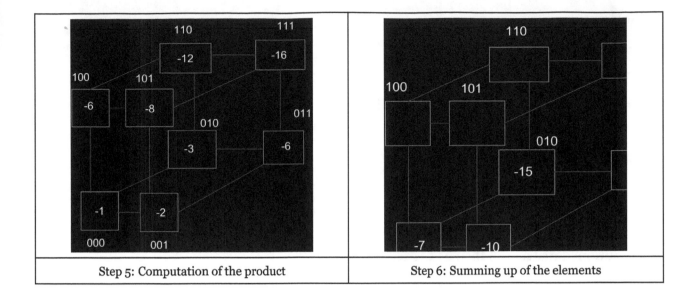

| Step 5: Computation of the product | Step 6: Summing up of the elements |

Block Matrix

In mathematics, a block matrix or a partitioned matrix is a matrix that is *interpreted* as having been broken into sections called blocks or submatrices. Intuitively, a matrix interpreted as a block matrix can be visualized as the original matrix with a collection of horizontal and vertical lines, which break it up, or partition it, into a collection of smaller matrices. Any matrix may be interpreted as a block matrix in one or more ways, with each interpretation defined by how its rows and columns are partitioned.

This notion can be made more precise for an n by m matrix M by partitioning   into a collection *colgroups* , and then partitioning m into a collection *colgroups* . The original matrix is then considered as the "total" of these groups, in the sense that the (i, j) entry of the original matrix corresponds in a 1-to-1 way with some (s, t) offset entry of some (x, y), where $x \in rowgroups$ and $y \in colgroups$.

Block matrix algebra arises in general from biproducts in categories of matrices.

Example

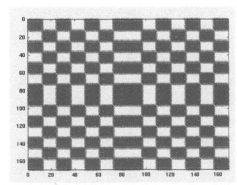

A 168×168 element block matrix with 12×12, 12×24, 24x12, and 24×24 sub-Matrices.
Non-zero elements are in blue, zero elements are grayed.

The matrix

$$\mathbf{P} = \begin{bmatrix} 1 & 1 & 2 & 2 \\ 1 & 1 & 2 & 2 \\ 3 & 3 & 4 & 4 \\ 3 & 3 & 4 & 4 \end{bmatrix}$$

can be partitioned into 4 2×2 blocks

$$\mathbf{P}_{11} = \begin{bmatrix} 1 & 1 \\ 1 & 1 \end{bmatrix}, \mathbf{P}_{12} = \begin{bmatrix} 2 & 2 \\ 2 & 2 \end{bmatrix}, \mathbf{P}_{21} = \begin{bmatrix} 3 & 3 \\ 3 & 3 \end{bmatrix}, \mathbf{P}_{22} = \begin{bmatrix} 4 & 4 \\ 4 & 4 \end{bmatrix}.$$

The partitioned matrix can then be written as

$$\mathbf{P} = \begin{bmatrix} \mathbf{P}_{11} & \mathbf{P}_{12} \\ \mathbf{P}_{21} & \mathbf{P}_{22} \end{bmatrix}.$$

Block Matrix Multiplication

It is possible to use a block partitioned matrix product that involves only algebra on submatrices of the factors. The partitioning of the factors is not arbitrary, however, and requires "conformable partitions" between two matrices A and B such that all submatrix products that will be used are defined. Given an $(m \times p)$ matrix $\mathbf{A}$ with q row partitions and s column partitions

$$\mathbf{A} = \begin{bmatrix} \mathbf{A}_{11} & \mathbf{A}_{12} & \cdots & \mathbf{A}_{1s} \\ \mathbf{A}_{21} & \mathbf{A}_{22} & \cdots & \mathbf{A}_{2s} \\ \vdots & \vdots & \ddots & \vdots \\ \mathbf{A}_{q1} & \mathbf{A}_{q2} & \cdots & \mathbf{A}_{qs} \end{bmatrix}$$

and a $(p \times n)$ matrix $\mathbf{B}$ with s row partitions and r column partitions

$$\mathbf{B} = \begin{bmatrix} \mathbf{B}_{11} & \mathbf{B}_{12} & \cdots & \mathbf{B}_{1r} \\ \mathbf{B}_{21} & \mathbf{B}_{22} & \cdots & \mathbf{B}_{2r} \\ \vdots & \vdots & \ddots & \vdots \\ \mathbf{B}_{s1} & \mathbf{B}_{s2} & \cdots & \mathbf{B}_{sr} \end{bmatrix},$$

that are compatible with the partitions of A, the matrix product

$$\mathbf{C} = \mathbf{AB}$$

can be formed blockwise, yielding $\mathbf{C}$ as an $(m \times n)$ matrix with q row partitions and r column partitions. The matrices in the resulting matrix $\mathbf{C}$ are calculated by multiplying:

$$C_{\alpha\beta} = \sum_{\gamma=1}^{s} A_{\alpha\gamma} B_{\gamma\beta}.$$

Or, using the Einstein notation that implicitly sums over repeated indices:

$$C_{\alpha\beta} = A_{\alpha\gamma} B_{\gamma\beta}.$$

Block Matrix Inversion

If a matrix is partitioned into four blocks, it can be inverted blockwise as follows:

$$\begin{bmatrix} \mathbf{A} & \mathbf{B} \\ \mathbf{C} & \mathbf{D} \end{bmatrix}^{-1} = \begin{bmatrix} \mathbf{A}^{-1} + \mathbf{A}^{-1}\mathbf{B}(\mathbf{D}-\mathbf{C}\mathbf{A}^{-1}\mathbf{B})^{-1}\mathbf{C}\mathbf{A}^{-1} & -\mathbf{A}^{-1}\mathbf{B}(\mathbf{D}-\mathbf{C}\mathbf{A}^{-1}\mathbf{B})^{-1} \\ -(\mathbf{D}-\mathbf{C}\mathbf{A}^{-1}\mathbf{B})^{-1}\mathbf{C}\mathbf{A}^{-1} & (\mathbf{D}-\mathbf{C}\mathbf{A}^{-1}\mathbf{B})^{-1} \end{bmatrix},$$

where A, B, C and D have arbitrary size. (A and D must be square, so that they can be inverted. Furthermore, A and D−CA⁻¹B must be nonsingular.)

Equivalently,

$$\begin{bmatrix} \mathbf{A} & \mathbf{B} \\ \mathbf{C} & \mathbf{D} \end{bmatrix}^{-1} = \begin{bmatrix} (\mathbf{A}-\mathbf{B}\mathbf{D}^{-1}\mathbf{C})^{-1} & -(\mathbf{A}-\mathbf{B}\mathbf{D}^{-1}\mathbf{C})^{-1}\mathbf{B}\mathbf{D}^{-1} \\ -\mathbf{D}^{-1}\mathbf{C}(\mathbf{A}-\mathbf{B}\mathbf{D}^{-1}\mathbf{C})^{-1} & \mathbf{D}^{-1}+\mathbf{D}^{-1}\mathbf{C}(\mathbf{A}-\mathbf{B}\mathbf{D}^{-1}\mathbf{C})^{-1}\mathbf{B}\mathbf{D}^{-1} \end{bmatrix}.$$

Block Diagonal Matrices

A block diagonal matrix is a block matrix that is a square matrix, and having main diagonal blocks square matrices, such that the off-diagonal blocks are zero matrices. A block diagonal matrix A has the form

$$\mathbf{A} = \begin{bmatrix} \mathbf{A}_1 & 0 & \cdots & 0 \\ 0 & \mathbf{A}_2 & \cdots & 0 \\ \vdots & \vdots & \ddots & \vdots \\ 0 & 0 & \cdots & \mathbf{A}_n \end{bmatrix}$$

where A_k is a square matrix; in other words, it is the direct sum of A_1, ..., A_n. It can also be indicated as $A_1 \oplus A_2 \oplus \ldots \oplus A_n$ or $\mathrm{diag}(A_1, A_2, \ldots, A_n)$ (the latter being the same formalism used for a diagonal matrix). Any square matrix can trivially be considered a block diagonal matrix with only one block.

For the determinant and trace, the following properties hold

$$\det \mathbf{A} = \det \mathbf{A}_1 \times \ldots \times \det \mathbf{A}_n,$$

$$\mathrm{tr}\, \mathbf{A} = \mathrm{tr}\, \mathbf{A}_1 + \cdots + \mathrm{tr}\, \mathbf{A}_n.$$

The inverse of a block diagonal matrix is another block diagonal matrix, composed of the inverse of each block, as follows:

$$
\begin{pmatrix}
\mathbf{A}_1 & 0 & \cdots & 0 \\
0 & \mathbf{A}_2 & \cdots & 0 \\
\vdots & \vdots & \ddots & \vdots \\
0 & 0 & \cdots & \mathbf{A}_n
\end{pmatrix}^{-1}
=
\begin{pmatrix}
\mathbf{A}_1^{-1} & 0 & \cdots & 0 \\
0 & \mathbf{A}_2^{-1} & \cdots & 0 \\
\vdots & \vdots & \ddots & \vdots \\
0 & 0 & \cdots & \mathbf{A}_n^{-1}
\end{pmatrix}.
$$

The eigenvalues and eigenvectors of A are simply those of A_1 and A_2 and ... and A_n (combined).

Block Tridiagonal Matrices

A block tridiagonal matrix is another special block matrix, which is just like the block diagonal matrix a square matrix, having square matrices (blocks) in the lower diagonal, main diagonal and upper diagonal, with all other blocks being zero matrices. It is essentially a tridiagonal matrix but has submatrices in places of scalars. A block tridiagonal matrix A has the form

$$
\mathbf{A} =
\begin{bmatrix}
\mathbf{B}_1 & \mathbf{C}_1 & & & \cdots & & 0 \\
\mathbf{A}_2 & \mathbf{B}_2 & \mathbf{C}_2 & & & & \\
& \ddots & \ddots & \ddots & & & \vdots \\
& & \mathbf{A}_k & \mathbf{B}_k & \mathbf{C}_k & & \\
\vdots & & & \ddots & \ddots & \ddots & \\
& & & & \mathbf{A}_{n-1} & \mathbf{B}_{n-1} & \mathbf{C}_{n-1} \\
0 & & \cdots & & & \mathbf{A}_n & \mathbf{B}_n
\end{bmatrix}
$$

where A_k, B_k and C_k are square sub-matrices of the lower, main and upper diagonal respectively.

Block tridiagonal matrices are often encountered in numerical solutions of engineering problems (e.g., computational fluid dynamics). Optimized numerical methods for LU factorization are available and hence efficient solution algorithms for equation systems with a block tridiagonal matrix as coefficient matrix. The Thomas algorithm, used for efficient solution of equation systems involving a tridiagonal matrix can also be applied using matrix operations to block tridiagonal matrices.

Block Toeplitz Matrices

A block Toeplitz matrix is another special block matrix, which contains blocks that are repeated down the diagonals of the matrix, as a Toeplitz matrix has elements repeated down the diagonal. The individual block matrix elements, A_{ij}, must also be a Toeplitz matrix.

A Block Toeplitz Matrix A has the Form

$$
\mathbf{A} =
\begin{bmatrix}
\mathbf{A}_{(1,1)} & \mathbf{A}_{(1,2)} & & & \cdots & \mathbf{A}_{(1,n-1)} & \mathbf{A}_{(1,n)} \\
\mathbf{A}_{(2,1)} & \mathbf{A}_{(1,1)} & \mathbf{A}_{(1,2)} & & & & \mathbf{A}_{(1,n-1)} \\
& \ddots & \ddots & \ddots & & & \vdots \\
& & \mathbf{A}_{(2,1)} & \mathbf{A}_{(1,1)} & \mathbf{A}_{(1,2)} & & \\
\vdots & & & \ddots & \ddots & \ddots & \\
\mathbf{A}_{(n-1,1)} & & & & \mathbf{A}_{(2,1)} & \mathbf{A}_{(1,1)} & \mathbf{A}_{(1,2)} \\
\mathbf{A}_{(n,1)} & \mathbf{A}_{(n-1,1)} & \cdots & & & \mathbf{A}_{(2,1)} & \mathbf{A}_{(1,1)}
\end{bmatrix}.
$$

Direct Sum

For any arbitrary matrices A (of size $m \times n$) and B (of size $p \times q$), we have the direct sum of A and B, denoted by A $\oplus$ B and defined as

$$\mathbf{A} \oplus \mathbf{B} = \begin{bmatrix} a_{11} & \cdots & a_{1n} & 0 & \cdots & 0 \\ \vdots & \cdots & \vdots & \vdots & \cdots & \vdots \\ a_{m1} & \cdots & a_{mn} & 0 & \cdots & 0 \\ 0 & \cdots & 0 & b_{11} & \cdots & b_{1q} \\ \vdots & \cdots & \vdots & \vdots & \cdots & \vdots \\ 0 & \cdots & 0 & b_{p1} & \cdots & b_{pq} \end{bmatrix}.$$

For instance,

$$\begin{bmatrix} 1 & 3 & 2 \\ 2 & 3 & 1 \end{bmatrix} \oplus \begin{bmatrix} 1 & 6 \\ 0 & 1 \end{bmatrix} = \begin{bmatrix} 1 & 3 & 2 & 0 & 0 \\ 2 & 3 & 1 & 0 & 0 \\ 0 & 0 & 0 & 1 & 6 \\ 0 & 0 & 0 & 0 & 1 \end{bmatrix}.$$

This operation generalizes naturally to arbitrary dimensioned arrays (provided that A and B have the same number of dimensions).

Note that any element in the direct sum of two vector spaces of matrices could be represented as a direct sum of two matrices.

Direct Product

Application

In linear algebra terms, the use of a block matrix corresponds to having a linear mapping thought of in terms of corresponding 'bunches' of basis vectors. That again matches the idea of having distinguished direct sum decompositions of the domain and range. It is always particularly significant if a block is the zero matrix; that carries the information that a summand maps into a sub-sum.

Given the interpretation *via* linear mappings and direct sums, there is a special type of block matrix that occurs for square matrices (the case $m = n$). For those we can assume an interpretation as an endomorphism of an n-dimensional space V; the block structure in which the bunching of rows and columns is the same is of importance because it corresponds to having a single direct sum decomposition on V (rather than two). In that case, for example, the diagonal blocks in the obvious sense are all square. This type of structure is required to describe the Jordan normal form.

This technique is used to cut down calculations of matrices, column-row expansions, and many computer science applications, including VLSI chip design. An example is the Strassen algorithm for fast matrix multiplication, as well as the Hamming(7,4) encoding for error detection and recovery in data transmissions.

References

- Sosinsky, Barrie A. (2009). "Network Basics". Networking Bible. Indianapolis: Wiley Publishing. p. 16. ISBN 978-0-470-43131-3. OCLC 359673774. Retrieved 2016-03-26

- John Darlinton; Moustafa Ghanem; Yike Guo; Hing Wing To (1996), "Guided Resource Organisation in Heterogeneous Parallel Computing", Journal of High Performance Computing, 4 (1): 13–23

- Glaskowsky, Peter (Aug 18, 2003). "Xelerated's Xtraordinary NPU — World's First 40Gb/s Packet Processor Has 200 CPUs". Microprocessor Report. 18 (8): 12–14. Retrieved 20 March 2017

- Bicsi, B. (2002). Network Design Basics for Cabling Professionals. McGraw-Hill Professional. ISBN 9780071782968

- ATIS committee PRQC. "mesh topology". ATIS Telecom Glossary 2007. Alliance for Telecommunications Industry Solutions. Retrieved 2008-10-10

- Kunzman, D. M.; Kale, L. V. (2011). "Programming Heterogeneous Systems". 2011 IEEE International Symposium on Parallel and Distributed Processing Workshops and Phd Forum. p. 2061. doi:10.1109/IPDPS.2011.377. ISBN 978-1-61284-425-1

- Bradley, Ray. Understanding Computer Science (for Advanced Level): The Study Guide. Cheltenham: Nelson Thornes. p. 244. ISBN 978-0-7487-6147-0. OCLC 47869750. Retrieved 2016-03-26

- Peter Ashwood-Smith (24 February 2011). "Shortest Path Bridging IEEE 802.1aq Overview" (PDF). Huawei. Retrieved 11 May 2012

- D. Fedyk, Ed.,; P. Ashwood-Smith, Ed.,; D. Allan, A. Bragg,; P. Unbehagen (April 2012). "IS-IS Extensions Supporting IEEE 802.1aq". IETF. Retrieved 12 May 2012

Processing Techniques of Parallel Algorithms

A significant amount of time is consumed in a single processing system if a query, which is decomposed into segments, is processed. Therefore, it is easier and time-saving to process a query in a parallel processing system. The section explores the 15 puzzle problem, discrete event simulation and dither as well. Parallel computing is best understood in confluence with the major topics listed in the following chapter.

Parallel Query

Query is processed using single processor or multiple processors. When executing a composite query it is decomposed into segments. These segments if it is executed in single processor it takes time. Further when the query involves I/O, it is going to be the bottleneck. Hence, composite query can be executed using parallel processors.

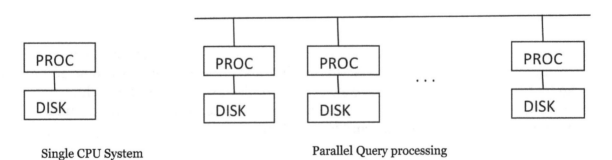

Single CPU System   Parallel Query processing

When multiple CPUs are available, SQL Server provides parallel queries to optimize query execution and index operations for these computers. Because SQL Server can perform a query or index operation in parallel by using several operating system threads, the operation can be completed quickly and efficiently.

SQL Server looks for queries or index operations that might benefit from parallel execution, during query execution. For such queries, SQL Server inserts exchange operators into the query execution plan to prepare the query for parallel execution. An exchange operator is an operator in a query execution plan that provides process management, data redistribution, and flow control. The exchange operator includes the Distribute Streams, Repartition Streams, and Gather Streamslogical operators as subtypes, one or more of which can appear in the Showplan output of a query plan for a parallel query.

Once the exchange operators are inserted, the result obtained is a parallel-query execution plan. A parallel-query execution plan can use more than one thread. A serial execution plan, used by a non-parallel query, uses only one thread for its execution. The actual number of threads used by a parallel query is determined at query plan execution initialization and is determined by the complexity of the plan and the degree of parallelism. Degree of parallelism determines the maximum number of CPUs that are being used.It does not mean the number of threads that are being used. The degree of parallelism value is set at the server level and can be modified by using the sp_configure system stored procedure.

The SQL Server query optimizer does not use a parallel execution plan for a query if any one of the following conditions is true:

- The serial execution cost of the query is not high

- A serial execution plan is considered faster than any possible parallel execution plan

- The query contains scalar or relational operators that cannot be run in parallel.

There are several multiprocessor architectures possible for parallel query processing. They are:

- Shared Memory Architectures

- Shared Disk Architectures

- Shared Nothing Architectures

- Hybrid Architectures

Shared Memory Architectures

In this architecture there are multiple processors are available. There is only one memory module. Any processor can access the memory module or disk unit. Thus the queries can be decomposed into fragments and these fragments are executed in parallel. Figure shows the architecture of this model. The advantages of this model are simplicity and load balancing. The disadvantages of this model are high cost, little extensibility and low availability.

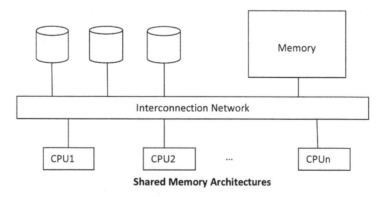

Shared Memory Architectures

Shared Disk Architecture

In contrast to the shared memory architecture the shared disk architecture consists of multiple memory modules. Each CPU has its own memory module. Using the interconnection network the multiple CPUs are able to access the disk modules. Figure shows the shared disk architecture. The advantages of this model are low cost, extensibility, load balancing, availability and easy migration. But this model has potential performance problem. This model has higher complexity.

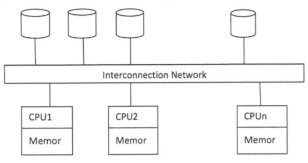

Shared Disk Architectures

Shared Nothing Architectures

In this architecture each CPU will have its own Memory and disk. The interconnection network is still used to establish communication between various CPUS. The architecture is shown in the diagram below.

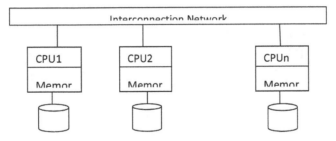

Shared Nothing Architecture

The advantages of this model are low cost, extensibility and availability. The disadvantages are higher complexity and load balancing.

Hybrid Architectures

The hybrid architectures combine the advantages of different architectures. It uses different processing elements in the system. The system is nothing but shared nothing architecture where each node is a multicomputer system of any architecture.

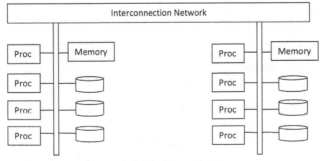

Hybrid Architectures

Parallel Relational Operators

There are three parallel relational operators. They are data partitioning, parallelization of relational operators and Join.

Data Partitioning

The data partitioning is nothing but the distribution of tuples of a relation over several disks. The goal of the data partitioning is allowing parallel databases to exploit the I/O bandwidth of multiple disks by reading them and writing them in parallel. Relations are horizontally partitioned using three functions namely:

- Round-robin
- Range index
- Hash function.

Round Robin Partitioning.

It maps the ith tuple to the disk I mod n. It sequentially scans all the tuples in each query.

Range Index Partitioning

It clusters all the tuples with same attributes in the same partition. There is a sequential scan of all tuples in each query. It also performs associative search for data and clustering of data.

Hash Partitioning

This method uses a hash function to group the tuples. Hash randomizes the data rather than cluster it. It searches the data associatively.

Parallel Relational Operators

Relational algebra allows parallel processing due to its properties. It is a set oriented processing. The relational operators perform simple operations. These operations are limited in nature. The basic idea is that it uses the parallel data streams and uses the sequential relational operators in parallel. Each relational operator has a set of input ports on which the input tuples arrive and an output port to which the operator's output stream is sent. The parallel dataflow works by partitioning and merging data streams into these sequential ports.

15 Puzzle Problem

During the last several years, there has been increasing interest in studying how humans solve combinatorial problems, such as the traveling salesman problem (TSP) and 15 puzzle problems and so on. In this section we will concentrate on 15 puzzle problem. The 15-puzzle has different-sized variants. The smallest size involves a board 2 X 3 and is called the 5-puzzle. The 8-puzzle involves a board 3X 3. The 35-puzzle involves aboard 6 X 6 (boards of other shapes—e.g., 4X 9—could also be used). The family of these puzzles will be called the *n-puzzle*, where *n* stands for the number of tiles. In all of the *n*-puzzles we used, the tiles in the goal state were ordered from left to right and from top to bottom, with an empty space located in the bottom right corner (previous studies of the 8-puzzle have usually used a goal state in which the empty space was in the center and the eight tiles were ordered around the boundary of the 3X 3 board). Previous research on the n-puzzle has concentrated on the 8-puzzle . It is known that the family of n puzzles belongs to the class of NP complete problems, which means that the number of paths grows exponentially with the number of tiles and that finding the shortest path from the start to the goal may require performing an exhaustive search.

Let us consider an example of 15 puzzle. We are defined with the start state and goal state as shown in the figure below.

1	2	3	4
5	6		8
9	10	7	11
13	14	15	12

Start State

1	2	3	4
5	6	7	8
7	10	11	12
13	14	15	

Goal State

Solution

1	2	3	4
5	6	↑	8
9	10	7	11
13	14	15	12

Step1

1	2	3	4
5	6	7	8
9	10	←	11
13	14	15	12

Step2

1	2	3	4
5	6	7	8
9	10	11	
13	14	15	12

step3

1	2	3	4
5	6	7	8
9	10	11	12
13	14	15	

Target

The 15 puzzle can have any start state. First the start state is evaluated to check if it can lead to a goal state. Once this thing is verified, next we explore the state space to find the solution. There may be more than one solution to a given initial state. Among this we have to find the minimum distance as the heuristic. The iterative deepening A* algorithm is used to find the solution in the state space.

Depth First Iterative Deepening A*

Of the brute-force searches, depth-first iterative-deepening A*(DFIDA*) is the most practical, because it combines breadth-first optimality with the low space complexity of depth-first search. Its basic idea is as simple as conducting a series of independent depth- first (backtracking) searches, each with the look-ahead horizon extended by an additional tree level. With the iterative approach, DFIDA* is guaranteed to find the shortest solution path, just as a breadth-first search would.

But in contrast to the latter, DFIDA* needs negligible memory space. Its space complexity grows only linearly with the search depth.

```
algorithm Iterative Deepening; begin

bound := h(root);    //f initial bound is heuristic estimate g repeat

DFS g

bound := DepthFirstSearch (root; bound); //f perform iterative-deepening

end.

until solved;

function DepthFirstSearch (n, bound): integer; //f returns next cost bound g begin

if h(n) = 0 then begin
```

```
end;

solved := true; return (0);          //f found a solution: return cost g

new bound := 1;

for each successor ni of n do begin

if c(n; ni) + h(ni) _ bound then

b := c(n; ni) + DepthFirstSearch (ni; bound ⊂ (n;    ni));//f search deeper g

else

b := c(n; ni) + h(ni); f cuto_ g if solved then return (b);

new bound := min (new bound; b);

//f compute next iteration's bound g

end;

end;

return (new bound); //f return next iteration's bound g
```

Iterative-Deepening A*, IDA* for short, performs a series of cost-bounded depth-first searches with successively increased cost-thresholds. The total cost f(n) of a node n is made up of g(n), the cost already spent in reaching that node, plus h(n), the estimated cost of the path to the nearest goal. At each iteration, IDA* does the search, cutting off all nodes that exceed a fixed cost bound. At the beginning, the cost bound is set to the heuristic estimate of the initial state,h(root). Then, for each iteration, the bound is increased to the minimum path value that exceeds the previous bound.

The algorithm consists of a main Iterative Deepening routine that sets up the cost bounds for the single iterations, and a Depth First Search function, that actually does the search. The maximum search depth is controlled by the parameter bound. When the estimated solution costc(n; ni) + h(ni) of a path going from node n via successor ni to a (yet unknown) goal node does not exceed the current bound, the search is deepened by recursively calling Depth First Search. Otherwise, subtree ni is cut off and the node expansion continues with the next successor ni+1. Of all path values that exceed the current bound, the smallest is used as a cost bound for the next iteration. It is computed by recursively backing up the cost values of all subtrees originating in the current node and storing the minimum value in the variable new bound. Note, that these backed-up values are revised cost bounds, which are usually higher and thus more valuable than a direct heuristic estimate. In the simple IDA* algorithm shown in above the revised cost bounds are only used to determine the cost threshold for the next iteration.

In conjunction with a transposition table they can also serve to increase the cut offs. With an admissible heuristic estimate function (i.e. one that never overestimates), IDA* is guaranteed to find the shortest solution path. Moreover, it has been proved that IDA* obeys the same asymptotic branching factor asA*, if the number of nodes grows exponentially with the solution depth.

This growth rate is called the heuristic branching factor bh. On the average IDA* requires bh=(bh1) times as many operations as A*. While the search overhead diminishes with increasing bh (e.g., 11% overhead at bh = 10,1% at bh = 100), IDA* benefits from the elimination of unnecessary node re examinations in the shallow tree parts (all iterations before the last).

Discrete Event Simulation

Parallel discrete event simulation is nothing but the discrete event simulation on parallel computers. Parallel discrete event simulation has dominated the serial execution in reducing the time and memory. It is used to solve large-scale composite models. Simulation systems are nothing but models of mathematical and logical relationships. In simulation, computers are used to evaluate the models numerically, where data is gathered and used to estimate the behavior of target systems. A simulation model depicts the state evolution over time. The target system can be viewed as a continuous system, discrete system or as a hybrid system.

In continuous systems, state changes continuously with respect to time. In discrete system the state changes only at specific period of time. The hybrid system is a combination of both continuous system and discrete system. There are two simulation methods available. They are time driven simulation and event driven simulation. In a time driven (or time-stepping) simulation, time is measured at small intervals giving the impression that the system evolves continuously over time. As such, it is naturally more suitable for simulating continuous systems. In an event-driven (or discrete-event) simulation, time leaps through distinct points in time, which we call events. Consequently, event-driven simulation is more appropriate for simulating discrete systems. Note that one can combine both types of simulations, for example, in a computer network simulation, using discrete events to represent detail network transactions, such as sending and receiving packets, and using continuous simulation to capture the fluid dynamics of overall network traffic.

A discrete-event simulation maintains a data structure called the event-list, which is basically a priority queue that sorts events according to the time at which they are scheduled to happen in the simulated future. A clock variable T is used to denote the current time in simulation. At the heart of the program is a loop; the simulator repeatedly removes an event with the smallest timestamp from the event list, sets the clock variable T to the timestamp of this event, and processes the event. Processing an event typically changes the state of the model and may generate more future events to be inserted into the event-list. The loop continues until the simulation termination condition is met, for example, when the event- list becomes empty or when the simulation clock has reached a designated simulation completion time.

Parallel Discrete Event Simulation

Parallel Discrete Event Simulation (PDES) is a research area is parallel simulation and high performance computing. PDES is nothing but execution single event simulation on parallel systems like clusters, shared memory multiprocessors or a combination of both. As such, PDES can bring substantial benefit to time-critical simulations, and simulations of large-scale systems that demand an immense amount of computing resources. The simplest form of parallel simulation is called replicated trials, which executes multiple instances of a sequential simulation program concurrently on parallel computers. This approach has the obvious advantage of simplicity and it can expedite the exploration of a large parameter space. The disadvantage is that each replicated trial does not provide any speed up and cannot overcome the memory limit due to sequential execution. To address the latter problem, Hybinette and Fujimoto introduced a cloning method as an efficient parallel computation technique to allow simultaneous exploration of different simulation branches resulted from alternative decisions made in simulation. Another form of parallel simulation is to assign different functions of a simulation program, such as random number generation and event handling, to separate processors. This method is called functional decomposition. The main problem is the lack of ample parallelism. Also, the tight coupling of the simulation functions creates an excessive demand for communication and synchronization among the parallel components, which can easily defeat the parallelization effort.

More generally, one can view simulation as a set of state variables that evolve over time. Chandy and Sherman presented a space-time view of simulation, where each event can be characterized by a temporal coordinate, indicated by the the timestamp of the event, and a spatial coordinate, indicated by the location of the state variables affected by the event. Accordingly, the state space of a discrete-event simulation can be perceived as consisting of a continuous time axis and a discrete space axis; the objective of the simulation is therefore to compute the value at each point in the space-time continuum. This space-time view provides a high-level unifying concept for parallel simulation, where one can divide the space-time graph into regions of arbitrary shape and assign them to separate processors for parallel processing. For example, Bagrodia, Chandy, and Liao presented a distributed algorithm using fixed-point computations.

A special case of the space-time view is the time-parallel approach, which is based on temporal decomposition of the time-space continuum. Time- parallel simulation divides the space-time graph along the time axis into non-overlapping time intervals, and assigns them to different processors for parallel processing. Due to the obvious dependency issue, that is, the initial state of a time interval must match the final state of the preceding time interval, the efficiency of this approach relies heavily on the model's ability of either rapidly computing the initial state or achieving fast convergence under relaxation. For this reason, only a limited number of cases using time-parallel simulation exist in the literature. Successful examples include trace- driven cache simulations, queuing network and Petri net simulations, and road traffic simulations.

Orthogonal to the time-parallel approach, space-parallel simulation is based on data decomposition, where the target system is divided into a collection of subsystems, each simulated by a logical process (LP). Each LP maintains its own simulation clock and event-list, and is only capable of processing events pertaining to the subsystem to which it is assigned. These LPs can be assigned to different processors and executed concurrently. Communications between the LPs take place exclusively by exchanging time stamped events. Space-parallel simulation is in general more robust than the other parallelization approaches, mainly because data decomposition is naturally applicable to most models.

In discrete event simulation the events must be processed in the non decreasing time stamp order. If the events with small timestamp affects the events with a larger time stamp it is referred to as the causality constraint. In the case of parallel simulation, there are a lot of event lists. Each logical process has its own event list and the simulation clock to handle the simulation. Each Logical Process has to maintain its own event list and timestamp ordering. Here the fundamental challenge is therefore associated with the difficulty of preserving the local causality constraint at each LP without the use of a global simulation clock.

Conservative Synchronization

The first parallel simulation synchronization protocol is the CMB algorithm proposed independently by Chandy and Misra, and Bryant. In CMB,LPs are connected via directional links, through which events are transferred from one LP to another in chronological order (with non decreasing time stamps). Events are enqueued at the receiving LPs—there is one input queue for each incoming link at an LP. Also, each input queue is associated with a clock variable, set to be either the timestamp of the first event in the queue, or, if the queue is empty, the timestamp of the last processed event (or zero initially). Each LP maintains a loop: at each iteration, the LP selects an input queue with smallest clock value and processes the event at the beginning of the input queue; if the input queue is empty, the LP blocks until an event arrives at the queue and then continues at the next iteration. Since LPs block on empty input queues (with the smallest clock value),deadlock may happens once a waiting cycle is formed, in which case no progress will be made even if there are events in other input queues. The CMB algorithm uses null messages to avoid this pathological situation. A null message does not represent any real activities in the model; it carries only a timestamp and is regarded as a guarantee from the sending LP that it won't send events in the future with timestamps smaller than the time stamp of the null message. Upon receiving a null message, an LP can advance the clock associated with the input queue. The LP can further propagate the time advancement to its successor LPs, possibly by sending out more null messages. Consequently, no waiting cycle is formed and deadlock is avoided. It is important to note that the use of null messages is not the only way to prevent deadlocks. Alternatively, one can allow deadlock to happen, and subsequently detect and recover from deadlock situations. Deadlock recovery is based on the observation that events with the smallest time stamp in the system can always be processed safely. In cases where deadlock shappen more frequently, however, this may result in a significant amount of sequential execution that can adversely affect the overall performance.

Optimistic Synchronization

Optimistic synchronization enforces the local causality constraint differently from its conservative counterpart: an LP is allowed to process events that arrive in the simulated past, as long as the simulation is able to detect such causality errors, rewind the simulation clock, and roll back the erroneous computations.

Time Warp Algorithm

In Time Warp, each LP saves the events received from other LPs in the input queue, and those sent to other LPs in the output queue. Also, the state variables are saved in the state queue each time before an event is processed. When an event arrives with a timestamp smaller than the current simulation clock (called the straggler event), the LP must be rolled back to the saved state immediately before the timestamp of the straggler event. All actions that the LP might have affected on other LPs later than the timestamp of the straggler event must also be canceled. This can be achieved by sending anti-messages corresponding to the original messages that are stored at the output queue. Upon receiving an anti-message, the LP will annihilate the corresponding message in the input queue. If the anti-message carries a timestamp smaller than the LP's current simulation clock (and thus become a straggler event), the LP will also be rolled back accordingly. PDES has been applied in many areas, such as military applications (including war games and training exercises), on-line gaming, business operations, manufacturing, logistics and distribution, transportation, computer systems and computer networks. Thus PDES plays an important part in computing.

Dither

A grayscale image represented in 1 bit black-and-white space with dithering

Dither is an intentionally applied form of noise used to randomize quantization error, preventing large-scale patterns such as color banding in images. Dither is routinely used in processing of both digital audio and video data, and is often one of the last stages of mastering audio to a CD.

A typical use of dither is converting a greyscale image to black and white, such that the density of black dots in the new image approximates the average grey level in the original.

Etymology

...[O]ne of the earliest [applications] of dither came in World War II. Airplane bombers used mechanical computers to perform navigation and bomb trajectory calculations. Curiously, these computers (boxes filled with hundreds of gears and cogs) performed more accurately when flying on board the aircraft, and less well on ground. Engineers realized that the vibration from the aircraft reduced the error from sticky moving parts. Instead of moving in short jerks, they moved more continuously. Small vibrating motors were built into the computers, and their vibration was called dither from the Middle English verb "didderen," meaning "to tremble." Today, when you tap a mechanical meter to increase its accuracy, you are applying dither, and modern dictionaries define dither as a highly nervous, confused, or agitated state. In minute quantities, dither successfully makes a digitization system a little more analog in the good sense of the word.

— *Ken Pohlmann, Principles of Digital Audio*

The term "dither" was published in books on analog computation and hydraulically controlled guns shortly after the Second World War. The concept of dithering to reduce quantization patterns was first applied by Lawrence G. Roberts in his 1961 MIT master's thesis and 1962 article though he did not use the term *dither*. By 1964 dither was being used in the modern sense described in this article.

In Digital Processing and Waveform Analysis

Dither is often used in digital audio and video processing. It is utilized in many different fields where digital processing and analysis are used. These uses include systems using digital signal processing, such as digital audio, digital video, digital photography, seismology, radar, weather forecasting systems and many more.

The premise is that quantization yields error. If that error is repeating and *correlated* to the signal, the error that results is repeating, cyclical, and mathematically determinable. In some fields, especially where the receptor is sensitive to such artifacts, cyclical errors yield undesirable artifacts. In these fields introducing dither results in less determinable artifacts. The field of audio is a primary example of this. The human ear functions much like a Fourier transform, wherein it hears individual frequencies. The ear is therefore very sensitive to *distortion,* or additional frequency content that "colors" the sound differently, but far less sensitive to random noise at all frequencies such as found in a dithered signal.

Digital Audio

In audio, dither can be useful to break up periodic limit cycles, which are a common problem in digital filters. Random noise is typically less objectionable than the harmonic tones produced by limit cycles.

In a seminal paper published in the AES Journal, Lipshitz and Vanderkooy pointed out that different noise types, with different probability density functions (PDFs) behave differently when used as dither signals, and suggested optimal levels of dither signal for audio. Gaussian noise requires a higher level of added noise for full elimination of distortion than do rectangular PDF or triangular PDF noise. Triangular PDF noise also minimizes "noise modulation" - audible changes in the volume level of residual noise behind quiet music that draw attention to the noise.

In an analog system, the signal is *continuous,* but in a PCM digital system, the amplitude of the signal out of the digital system is limited to one of a set of fixed values or numbers. This process is called quantization. Each coded value is a discrete step... if a signal is quantized without using dither, there will be quantization distortion related to the original input signal... In order to prevent this, the signal is "dithered", a process that mathematically removes the harmonics or other highly undesirable distortions entirely, and that replaces it with a constant, fixed noise level.

The final version of audio that goes onto a compact disc contains only 16 bits per sample, but throughout the production process a greater number of bits are typically used to represent the sample. In the end, the digital data must be reduced to 16 bits for pressing onto a CD and distributing.

There are multiple ways to do this. One can, for example, simply discard the excess bits – called *truncation.* One can also *round* the excess bits to the nearest value. Each of these methods, however, results in predictable and determinable errors in the result. Take, for example, a waveform that consists of the following values:

1 2 3 4 5 6 7 8

If the waveform is reduced by, say, 20% then the following are the new values:

0.8 1.6 2.4 3.2 4.0 4.8 5.6 6.4

If these values are truncated it results in the following data:

0 1 2 3 4 4 5 6

If these values are rounded instead it results in the following data:

1 2 2 3 4 5 6 6

For any original waveform, the process of reducing the waveform amplitude by 20% results in regular errors. Take for example a sine wave that, for some portion, matches the values above. Every time the sine wave's value hit 3.2, the truncated result would be off by 0.2, as in the sample data above. Every time the sine wave's value hit 4.0, there would be no error since the truncated result would be off by 0.0, also shown above. The magnitude of this error changes regularly and repeatedly throughout the sine wave's cycle. It is precisely this error which manifests itself as distortion. What the ear hears as distortion is the additional content at discrete frequencies created by the regular and repeated quantization error.

A plausible solution would be to take the 2 digit number (say, 4.8) and round it one direction or the other. For example, it could be rounded to 5 one time and then 4 the next time. This would make the long-term average 4.5 instead of 4, so that over the long-term the value is closer to its actual value. This, on the other hand, still results in determinable (though more complicated) error. Every other time the value 4.8 comes up the result is an error of 0.2, and the other times it is −0.8. This still results in a repeating, quantifiable error.

Another plausible solution would be to take 4.8 and round it so that the first four times out of five it is rounded up to 5, and the fifth time it is rounded to 4. This would average out to exactly 4.8 over the long term. Unfortunately, however, it still results in repeatable and determinable errors, and those errors still manifest themselves as distortion to the ear (though oversampling can reduce this).

This leads to the *dither* solution. Rather than predictably rounding up or down in a repeating pattern, it is possible to round up or down in a random pattern. Dithering is a way to randomly toggle the results between 4 and 5 so that 80% of the time it ended up on 5 then it would average 4.8 over the long run but would have random, non-repeating error in the result.

If a series of random numbers between 0.0 and 0.9 (ex: 0.6, 0.1, 0.3, 0.6, 0.9, etc.) are calculated and added to the results of the equation, two times out of ten the result will truncate back to 4 (if 0.0 or 0.1 are added to 4.8) and the rest of the times it will truncate to 5, but each given situation has a random 20% chance of rounding to 4 or 80% chance of rounding to 5. Over the long haul this will result in results that average to 4.8 and a quantization error that is random — or noise. This "noise" result is less offensive to the ear than the determinable distortion that would result otherwise.

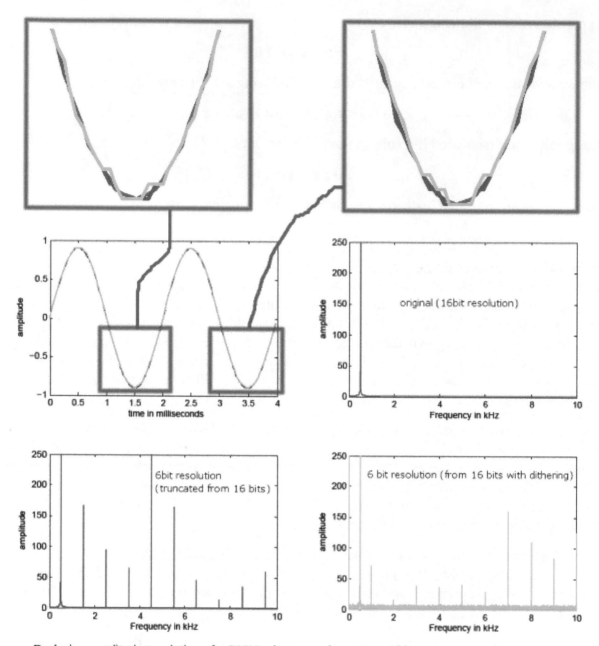

Reducing amplitude resolution of a 500Hz sine wave from 16 to 6 bits:

The Blue spectrum shows the original sine at 500Hz.
Truncating to 6 bits introduces harmonics/distortion (multiples of 500Hz) - red spectrum
Dithering reduces the amplitude of these distortions, but introduces background noise - green spectrum
(please note that the spectral plots above have been clipped at 250. The amplitude at 500Hz has thus
been clipped and is actually much larger than can be seen here)

The sine wave at the top shows that truncation (red) always rounds values the same way
while dithering randomizes the choice of rounding up or down (green)

Usage

Dither should be added to any low-amplitude or highly periodic signal before any quantization or
re-quantization process, in order to de-correlate the quantization noise from the input signal and

to prevent non-linear behavior (distortion); the lesser the bit depth, the greater the dither must be. The result of the process still yields distortion, but the distortion is of a random nature so the resulting noise is, effectively, de-correlated from the intended signal. Any bit-reduction process should add dither to the waveform before the reduction is performed.

Different Types

RPDF stands for "Rectangular Probability Density Function," equivalent to a roll of a die. Any number has the same random probability of surfacing.

TPDF stands for "Triangular Probability Density Function," equivalent to a roll of two dice (the sum of two independent samples of RPDF).

Gaussian PDF is equivalent to a roll of a large number of dice. The relationship of probabilities of results follows a bell-shaped, or Gaussian curve, typical of dither generated by analog sources such as microphone preamplifiers. If the bit depth of a recording is sufficiently great, that preamplifier noise will be sufficient to dither the recording.

Colored dither is sometimes mentioned as dither that has been filtered to be different from white noise. Some dither algorithms use noise that has more energy in the higher frequencies so as to lower the energy in the critical audio band.

Noise shaping is a filtering process that shapes the spectral energy of quantisation error, typically to either de-emphasise frequencies to which the ear is most sensitive or separate the signal and noise bands completely. If dither is used, its final spectrum depends on whether it is added inside or outside the feedback loop of the noise shaper: if inside, the dither is treated as part of the error signal and shaped along with actual quantisation error; if outside, the dither is treated as part of the original signal and linearises quantisation without being shaped itself. In this case, the final noise floor is the sum of the flat dither spectrum and the shaped quantisation noise. While real-world noise shaping usually includes in-loop dithering, it is also possible to use it without adding dither at all, in which case the usual harmonic-distortion effects still appear at low signal levels.

Which Types to Use

If the signal being dithered is to undergo further processing, then it should be processed with a triangular-type dither that has an amplitude of two quantisation steps; for example, so that the dither values computed range from, say, −1 to +1, or 0 to 2. This is the "lowest power ideal" dither, in that it does not introduce noise modulation (which would manifest as a constant noise floor), and completely eliminates the harmonic distortion from quantisation. If a *colored* dither is used instead at these intermediate processing stages, then frequency content may "bleed" into other frequency ranges that are more noticeable, which could become distractingly audible.

If the signal being dithered is to undergo no further processing — if it is being dithered to its final result for distribution — then a "colored" dither or noise shaping is appropriate. This can effectively lower the audible noise level, by putting most of that noise in a frequency range where it is less critical.

Digital Photography and Image Processing

An illustration of dithering. Red and blue are the only colors used but, as the red and blue squares are made smaller, the patch appears purple.

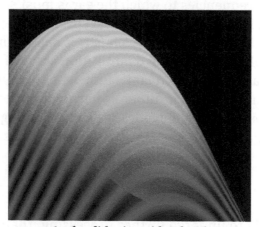

256 color dithering with IrfanView

Dithering is used in computer graphics to create the illusion of "color depth" in images with a limited color palette - a technique also known as color quantization. In a dithered image, colors that are not available in the palette are approximated by a diffusion of colored pixels from within the available palette. The human eye perceives the diffusion as a mixture of the colors within it. Dithered images, particularly those with relatively few colors, can often be distinguished by a characteristic graininess or speckled appearance.

By its nature, dithering introduces pattern into an image - the theory being that the image will be viewed from such a distance that the pattern is not discernible to the human eye. Unfortunately this is often not the case, and often the patterning is visible - for example, often with images found on the web. In these circumstances it has been shown that a blue noise dither pattern is the least unsightly and distracting. The error diffusion techniques were some of the first methods to generate blue noise dithering patterns. However, other techniques such as ordered dithering can also generate blue noise dithering without the tendency to degenerate into areas with artifacts.

Examples

Color dithering on a towel

Reducing the color depth of an image can often have significant visual side-effects. If the original image is a photograph, it is likely to have thousands, or even millions of distinct colors. The process of constraining the available colors to a specific *color palette* effectively throws away a certain amount of color information.

A number of factors can affect the resulting quality of a color-reduced image. Perhaps most significant is the color palette that will be used in the reduced image. For example, an original image may be reduced to the 216-color "web-safe" color palette. If the original pixel colors are simply translated into the closest available color from the palette, no dithering will occur. However, typically this approach will result in flat areas (contours) and a loss of detail, and may produce patches of color that are significantly different from the original. Shaded or gradient areas may appear as *color bands*, which may be distracting. The application of dithering can help to minimize such visual artifacts, and usually results in a better representation of the original. Dithering helps to reduce color banding and flatness.

One of the problems associated with using a fixed color palette is that many of the needed colors may not be available in the palette, and many of the available colors may not be needed; a fixed palette containing mostly shades of green would not be well-suited for images that do not contain many shades of green, for instance. The use of an optimized color palette can be of benefit in such cases. An optimized color palette is one in which the available colors are chosen based on how frequently they are used in the original source image. If the image is reduced based on an optimized palette the result is often much closer to the original.

The number of colors available in the palette is also a contributing factor. If, for example, the palette is limited to only 16 colors then the resulting image could suffer from additional loss of detail, resulting in even more pronounced problems with flatness and color banding. Once again, dithering can help to minimize such artifacts.

Original photo; note the smoothness in the detail.

Original image using the web-safe color palette with no dithering applied. Note the large flat areas and loss of detail.

Original image using the web-safe color palette with Floyd–Steinberg dithering. Note that even though the same palette is used, the application of dithering gives a better representation of the original.

Here, the original has been reduced to a 256-color optimized palette with Floyd–Steinberg dithering applied. The use of an optimized palette, rather than a fixed palette, allows the result to better represent the colors in the original image.

Depth is reduced to a 16-color optimized palette in this image, with no dithering. Colors appear muted, and color banding is pronounced.

This image also uses the 16-color optimized palette, but the use of dithering helps to reduce banding.

Applications

Much display hardware, including early computer video adapters and many modern LCDs used in mobile phones and inexpensive digital cameras, shows a much smaller color range than more advanced displays. One common application of dithering is to more accurately display graphics containing a greater range of colors than the hardware is capable of showing. For example, dithering might be used in order to display a photographic image containing millions of colors on video hardware that is only capable of showing 256 colors at a time. The 256 available colors would be used to generate a dithered approximation of the original image. Without dithering, the colors in the original image might simply be "rounded off" to the closest available color, resulting in a new image that is a poor representation of the original. Dithering takes advantage of the human eye's tendency to "mix" two colors in close proximity to one another.

Some LCDs may use temporal dithering to achieve a similar effect. By alternating each pixel's color value rapidly between two approximate colors in the panel's color space (also known as Frame Rate Control), a display panel which natively supports only 18-bit color (6 bits per channel) can represent a 24-bit "true" color image (8 bits per channel).

Dithering such as this, in which the computer's display hardware is the primary limitation on color depth, is commonly employed in software such as web browsers. Since a web browser may be retrieving graphical elements from an external source, it may be necessary for the browser to perform dithering on images with too many colors for the available display. It was due to problems with dithering that a color palette known as the "web-safe color palette" was identified, for use in choosing colors that would not be dithered on displays with only 256 colors available.

But even when the total number of available colors in the display hardware is high enough to "properly" render full color digital photographs (such as those using 15- and 16-bit RGB Hicolor 32,768/65,536 color modes), banding may still be evident to the eye, especially in large areas of smooth shade transitions (although the original image file has no banding at all). Dithering the 32 or 64 RGB levels will result in a pretty good "pseudo truecolor" display approximation, which the eye will not resolve as *grainy*. Furthermore, images displayed on 24-bit RGB hardware (8 bits per RGB primary) can be dithered to simulate somewhat higher bit depth, and/or to minimize the loss of hues available after a gamma correction. High-end still image processing software commonly uses these techniques for improved display.

Another useful application of dithering is for situations in which the graphic file format is the limiting factor. In particular, the commonly used GIF format is restricted to the use of 256 or fewer colors in many graphics editing programs. Images in other file formats, such as PNG, may also have such a restriction imposed on them for the sake of a reduction in file size. Images such as these have a fixed color palette defining all the colors that the image may use. For such situations, graphical editing software may be responsible for dithering images prior to saving them in such restrictive formats.

Dithering is analogous to the halftone technique used in printing. The recent widespread adoption of inkjet printers and their ability to print isolated dots has increased the use of dithering in printing. For this reason the term *dithering* is sometimes used interchangeably with the term *halftoning*, particularly in association with digital printing.

A typical desktop inkjet printer can print just 16 colors (the combination of dot or no dot from cyan, magenta, yellow and black print heads). Some of these ink combinations are not useful though, because when the black ink is used it typically obscures any of the other colors. To reproduce a large range of colors, dithering is used. In densely printed areas, where the color is dark the dithering is often not visible because the dots of ink merge producing a more uniform print. However, a close inspection of the light areas of a print where the dithering has placed dots much further apart reveals the tell-tale dots of dithering.

Algorithms

There are several algorithms designed to perform dithering. One of the earliest, and still one of the most popular, is the Floyd–Steinberg dithering algorithm, and was developed in 1975. One of the strengths of this algorithm is that it minimizes visual artifacts through an error-diffusion process; error-diffusion algorithms typically produce images that more closely represent the original than simpler dithering algorithms.

Dithering methods include:

- *Thresholding* (also average dithering): each pixel value is compared against a fixed threshold. This may be the simplest dithering algorithm there is, but it results in immense loss of detail and contouring.

- *Random dithering* was the first attempt (at least as early as 1951) to remedy the drawbacks of thresholding. Each pixel value is compared against a random threshold, resulting in a staticky image. Although this method doesn't generate patterned artifacts, the noise tends to swamp the detail of the image. It is analogous to the practice of mezzotinting.

- *Patterning* dithers using a fixed pattern. For each of the input values a fixed pattern is placed in the output image. The biggest disadvantage of this technique is that the output image is larger (by a factor of the fixed pattern size) than the input pattern.

- *Ordered dithering* dithers using a "dither matrix". For every pixel in the image the value of the pattern at the corresponding location is used as a threshold. Neighboring pixels do not affect each other, making this form of dithering suitable for use in animations. Different patterns can generate completely different dithering effects. Though simple to implement, this dithering algorithm is not easily changed to work with free-form, arbitrary palettes.

  - A *halftone dithering* matrix produces a look similar to that of halftone screening in newspapers. This is a form of clustered dithering, in that dots tend to cluster together. This can help hide the adverse effects of blurry pixels found on some older output devices. The primary use for this method is in offset printing and laser printers. In both these devices the ink or toner prefers to clump together and will not form the isolated dots generated by the other dithering methods.

  - A *Bayer matrix* produces a very distinctive cross-hatch pattern.

  - A matrix tuned for *blue noise*, such as those generated by the "void-and-cluster" method, produces a look closer to that of an error diffusion dither method.

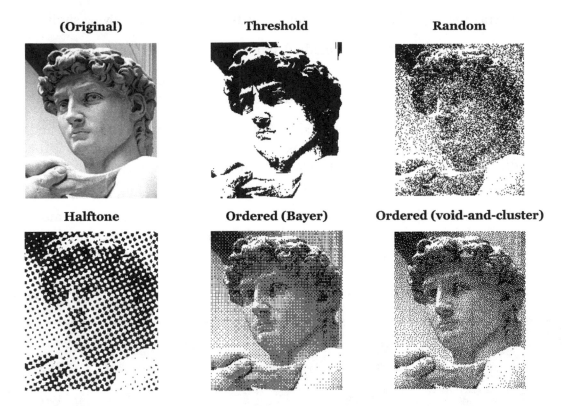

(Original)   **Threshold**   **Random**

Halftone   **Ordered (Bayer)**   **Ordered (void-and-cluster)**

- *Error-diffusion dithering* is a feedback process that diffuses the quantization error to neighboring pixels.

    o Floyd–Steinberg (FS) dithering only diffuses the error to neighboring pixels. This results in very fine-grained dithering.

    o Jarvis, Judice, and Ninke dithering diffuses the error also to pixels one step further away. The dithering is coarser, but has fewer visual artifacts. However, it is slower than Floyd–Steinberg dithering, because it distributes errors among 12 nearby pixels instead of 4 nearby pixels for Floyd–Steinberg.

    o Stucki dithering is based on the above, but is slightly faster. Its output tends to be clean and sharp.

    o Burkes dithering is a simplified form of Stucki dithering that is faster, but is less clean than Stucki dithering.

Floyd–Steinberg   **Jarvis, Judice & Ninke**   **Stucki**   **Burkes**

- o Sierra dithering is based on Jarvis dithering, but it's faster while giving similar results.

- o *Two-row Sierra* is the above method, but was modified by Sierra to improve its speed.

- o *Filter Lite* is an algorithm by Sierra that is much simpler and faster than Floyd–Steinberg, while still yielding similar results (and according to Sierra, better).

- o Atkinson dithering was developed by Apple programmer Bill Atkinson, and resembles Jarvis dithering and Sierra dithering, but it's faster. Another difference is that it doesn't diffuse the entire quantization error, but only three quarters. It tends to preserve detail well, but very light and dark areas may appear blown out.

- o Gradient-based error-diffusion dithering was developed recently to remove the structural artifact produced in the original FS algorithm by a modulated randomization, and to enhance the structures by a gradient-based diffusion modulation.

| Sierra | Two-row Sierra | Sierra Lite | Atkinson | Gradient-based |

Other Applications

Stimulated Brillouin Scattering (SBS) is a nonlinear optical effect that limits the launched optical power in fiber optic systems. This power limit can be increased by dithering the transmit optical center frequency, typically implemented by modulating the laser's bias input.

An artificial jitter (dither) can be used in electronics for reducing quantization errors in A/D-Elements. Another common application is to get through EMC tests by smearing out single frequency peaks.

Another type of temporal dithering has recently been introduced in financial markets, in order to reduce the incentive to engage in high-frequency trading. ParFX, a London foreign exchange market that began trading in 2013, imposes brief random delays on all incoming orders; other currency exchanges are reportedly experimenting with the technique. The use of such temporal buffering or dithering has been advocated more broadly in financial trading of equities, commodities, and derivatives.

Evaluation

Dense LU Factorization is a popular benchmark to evaluate the performance of parallel(super) computers. It is an important parallel kernel due to its use in scientific applications. Its performance is primarily computation bound. Its performance is excellent with respect to memory allocation and access, communication and scheduling. These lead to higher efficient systems.

Dense LU Factorization is used a mechanism to solve dense linear systems. A set of n linear equations in n variables is solved by performing LU Factorization and solving the triangular system which is obtained. The algorithms have different variations. To mention, we have Crout's algorithm which performs an in-place computation. Numerical stability is derived with partial pivoting. Most formulations of LU are blocked algorithms with underlying sequential operations delegated to a high performance linear algebra library.

In computer field major implementations use block-cyclic distributions of matrix blocks onto a two-dimensional process grid. The process grid dimensions derive a trade-off between communication and computation and are architecture- and implementation- sensitive. The critical panel factorization steps can be made less communication-bound by overlapping asynchronous collectives for pivoting with the computation of rank-k updates. By shifting the computation communication trade-off, a modified block-cyclic distribution can beneficially exploit more available parallelism on the critical path and reduce panel factorization's memory hierarchy contention on now-ubiquitous multicore architectures.

In any matrix dealing we consider row-major and column-major composition. In the column-major process grid, the performance is reduced as too many processors contend for the memory access. In the row-major process grid, the performance is not degraded, but it sacrifices node and network locality in the critical pivoting steps. To overcome these two problems, third method called striding is used. Maximum available parallelism is achieved by the length or height of the process grid. To start with, a taller grid is considered and later it is rotated to obtain the advantages of row major form.

Let us assume an nXn matrix which is decomposed into block size of b^2 which is distributed across the grid.

Algorithm

Dense LU Factorization Algorithm

The factorization process can be described as follows: For step 0 to n-1

A) Active panel blocks are those at/below diagonal block step

1) for column in 0::b: (on each active panel block)

   a) Each block identifies its maximum value below the diagonal in the current column within that block and contributes to a reduction among the active panel blocks.

   b) The resut of the reduction identifies the pivot row, which is swapped to the diagonal position and broadcast to all of the active panel blocks.

   c) Each active panel block performs a rank-1 update of the section after column with multipliers from column and the pivot row.

2) The sequence of pivot exchanges is broadcast to the blocks of U and the trailing sub-matrix,

   Which communicate to apply the same swaps as the active panel.

3) Active panel blocks send their contents, each a portion of L, to the blocks to their right.

4) U blocks to the right of the diagonal each perform a triangular solve, and send the result to the blocks below them.

5) Blocks in the trailing sub matrix each compute a trailing update as the product of the L and U blocks they have received.

B) Data Distribution

There are several aspects that are to be considered when distributing matrix blocks onto the available processors. The amount of computation that has to be performed on each block of data to achieve the final factorization differs based on the location of the block in the overall matrix. The accumulated wisdom in the community has shown that a two dimensional block-cyclic data distribution achieves satisfactory load balance while also presenting good communication behavior and stability.

For such a data distribution, the available processes (N), are first arranged into a two- dimensional process grid of dimensions PXQ such that N = P XQ. The aspect ratio of the process grid and how the process ranks are arranged within this grid depend on system architecture. The two dimensional block cyclic pattern can be obtained by tiling the process grid onto the matrix as shown in Figure.

The figure depicts a matrix decomposed into blocks. The bold lines are the boundaries of the process grid and the label in each block is the process rank to which it is mapped. Expressions for the traditional block-cyclic mapping of a block, whose coordinates in the blocked view of the input matrix is (x; y), onto a process grid of dimensions PXQ are as follows2:

$m_1 = x \bmod P$ (x in grid)

$n_1 = y \bmod Q$ (y in grid)

$frow(x; y; P;Q) = m_1Q + n_1$ --------------------------------(1)

$fcol(x; y; P;Q) = n_1P + m_1$ -----------------------------------(2)

Equation 1 yields the process rank for a row-major process grid, while equation 2 yields the process rank for a column-major process grid.

C) Granularity Spectrum

The factorization presents a challenging spectrum of computation and communication grain sizes. The trailing updates comprise the bulk of the computation in a dense LU solver. Each trailing update is an $O(b^3)$ matrix-matrix multiplication(i.e. a call to the dgemm() level-3 BLAS routine). The triangular solves (via dtrsm()) are of similar computational cost. Each trailing update or triangular solve takes tens of milliseconds for the block sizes common on today's architectures. Large messages drive the heavy computation kernels.In contrast, the active panel is communication intensive, with b small-message pivot reductions and broadcasts occurring in rapid succession, interspersed with smaller computations. Eachof the se fine-grained steps on the active panel nominally takehundreds of microseconds to single digit milliseconds.

D) Lookahead

Ideally, every processor would remain busy during the entirefactorization process. However, in each step, only a subset of processors own blocks that participate in the active panel.Thus, to avoid idling processors, work from multiple stepsmust be overlapped. The extent of the overlap (specifically,the number of steps that the active panel runs ahead of trailingupdates) in an implementation of dense LU is known as its lookahead depth.

Gaussian Elimination

In linear algebra, Gaussian elimination (also known as row reduction) is an algorithm for solving systems of linear equations. It is usually understood as a sequence of operations performed on the corresponding matrix of coefficients. This method can also be used to find the rank of a matrix, to calculate the determinant of a matrix, and to calculate the inverse of an invertible square matrix. The method is named after Carl Friedrich Gauss (1777–1855), although it was known to Chinese mathematicians as early as 179 CE.

To perform row reduction on a matrix, one uses a sequence of elementary row operations to modify the matrix until the lower left-hand corner of the matrix is filled with zeros, as much as possible. There are three types of elementary row operations: 1) Swapping two rows, 2) Multiplying a row by a non-zero number, 3) Adding a multiple of one row to another row. Using these operations, a matrix can always be transformed into an upper triangular matrix, and in fact one that is in row echelon form. Once all of the leading coefficients (the left-most non-zero entry in each row) are 1, and every column containing a leading coefficient has zeros elsewhere, the matrix is said to be in reduced row echelon form. This final form is unique; in other words, it is independent of the sequence of row operations used. For example, in the following sequence of row operations (where multiple elementary operations might be done at each step), the third and fourth matrices are the ones in row echelon form, and the final matrix is the unique reduced row echelon form.

$$\begin{bmatrix} 1 & 3 & 1 & 9 \\ 1 & 1 & -1 & 1 \\ 3 & 11 & 5 & 35 \end{bmatrix} \rightarrow \begin{bmatrix} 1 & 3 & 1 & 9 \\ 0 & -2 & -2 & -8 \\ 0 & 2 & 2 & 8 \end{bmatrix} \rightarrow \begin{bmatrix} 1 & 3 & 1 & 9 \\ 0 & -2 & -2 & -8 \\ 0 & 0 & 0 & 0 \end{bmatrix} \rightarrow \begin{bmatrix} 1 & 0 & -2 & -3 \\ 0 & 1 & 1 & 4 \\ 0 & 0 & 0 & 0 \end{bmatrix}$$

Using row operations to convert a matrix into reduced row echelon form is sometimes called Gauss–Jordan elimination. Some authors use the term Gaussian elimination to refer to the process until it has reached its upper triangular, or (non-reduced) row echelon form. For computational reasons, when solving systems of linear equations, it is sometimes preferable to stop row operations before the matrix is completely reduced.

Definitions and Example of Algorithm

The process of row reduction makes use of elementary row operations, and can be divided into two parts. The first part (sometimes called Forward Elimination) reduces a given system to *row echelon form*, from which one can tell whether there are no solutions, a unique solution, or infinitely many solutions. The second part (sometimes called back substitution) continues to use row operations until the solution is found; in other words, it puts the matrix into *reduced* row echelon form.

Another point of view, which turns out to be very useful to analyze the algorithm, is that row reduction produces a matrix decomposition of the original matrix. The elementary row operations may be viewed as the multiplication on the left of the original matrix by elementary matrices. Alternatively, a sequence of elementary operations that reduces a single row may be viewed as multiplication by a Frobenius matrix. Then the first part of the algorithm computes an LU decomposition, while the second part writes the original matrix as the product of a uniquely determined invertible matrix and a uniquely determined reduced row echelon matrix.

Row Operations

There are three types of elementary row operations which may be performed on the rows of a matrix:

Type 1: Swap the positions of two rows.

Type 2: Multiply a row by a nonzero scalar.

Type 3: Add to one row a scalar multiple of another.

If the matrix is associated to a system of linear equations, then these operations do not change the solution set. Therefore, if one's goal is to solve a system of linear equations, then using these row operations could make the problem easier.

Echelon Form

For each row in a matrix, if the row does not consist of only zeros, then the left-most non-zero entry is called the *leading coefficient* (or *pivot*) of that row. So if two leading coefficients are in the same column, then a row operation of type 3 could be used to make one of those coefficients zero. Then by using the row swapping operation, one can always order the rows so that for every non-zero row, the leading coefficient is to the right of the leading coefficient of the row above. If this is the case, then matrix is said to be in row echelon form. So the lower left part of the matrix contains only zeros, and all of the zero rows are below the non-zero rows. The word "echelon" is used here because one can roughly think of the rows being ranked by their size, with the largest being at the top and the smallest being at the bottom.

For example, the following matrix is in row echelon form, and its leading coefficients are shown in red.

$$\begin{bmatrix} 0 & 2 & 1 & -1 \\ 0 & 0 & 3 & 1 \\ 0 & 0 & 0 & 0 \end{bmatrix}$$

It is in echelon form because the zero row is at the bottom, and the leading coefficient of the second row (in the third column), is to the right of the leading coefficient of the first row (in the second column).

A matrix is said to be in reduced row echelon form if furthermore all of the leading coefficients are equal to 1 (which can be achieved by using the elementary row operation of type 2), and in every column containing a leading coefficient, all of the other entries in that column are zero (which can be achieved by using elementary row operations of type 3).

Example of the Algorithm

Suppose the goal is to find and describe the set of solutions to the following system of linear equations:

$$2x + y - z = 8 \qquad (L_1)$$
$$-3x - y + 2z = -11 \qquad (L_2)$$
$$-2x + y + 2z = -3 \qquad (L_3)$$

The table below is the row reduction process applied simultaneously to the system of equations, and its associated augmented matrix. In practice, one does not usually deal with the systems in terms of equations but instead makes use of the augmented matrix, which is more suitable for computer manipulations. The row reduction procedure may be summarized as follows: eliminate x from all equations below L_1, and then eliminate y from all equations below L_2. This will put the system into triangular form. Then, using back-substitution, each unknown can be solved for.

System of equations	Row operations	Augmented matrix
$2x + y - z = 8$ $-3x - y + 2z = -11$ $-2x + y + 2z = -3$		$\begin{bmatrix} 2 & 1 & -1 & 8 \\ -3 & -1 & 2 & -11 \\ -2 & 1 & 2 & -3 \end{bmatrix}$
$2x + y - z = 8$ $\frac{1}{2}y + \frac{1}{2}z = 1$ $2y + z = 5$	$L_2 + \frac{3}{2}L_1 \rightarrow L_2$ $L_3 + L_1 \rightarrow L_3$	$\begin{bmatrix} 2 & 1 & -1 & 8 \\ 0 & 1/2 & 1/2 & 1 \\ 0 & 2 & 1 & 5 \end{bmatrix}$
$2x + y - z = 8$ $\frac{1}{2}y + \frac{1}{2}z = 1$ $-z = 1$	$L_3 + -4L_2 \rightarrow L_3$	$\begin{bmatrix} 2 & 1 & -1 & 8 \\ 0 & 1/2 & 1/2 & 1 \\ 0 & 0 & -1 & 1 \end{bmatrix}$
The matrix is now in echelon form (also called triangular form)		
$2x + y = 7$ $\frac{1}{2}y = \frac{3}{2}$ $-z = 1$	$L_2 + \frac{1}{2}L_3 \rightarrow L_2$ $L_1 - L_3 \rightarrow L_1$	$\begin{bmatrix} 2 & 1 & 0 & 7 \\ 0 & 1/2 & 0 & 3/2 \\ 0 & 0 & -1 & 1 \end{bmatrix}$
$2x + y = 7$ $y = 3$ $z = -1$	$2L_2 \rightarrow L_2$ $-L_3 \rightarrow L_3$	$\begin{bmatrix} 2 & 1 & 0 & 7 \\ 0 & 1 & 0 & 3 \\ 0 & 0 & 1 & -1 \end{bmatrix}$
$x = 2$ $y = 3$ $z = -1$	$L_1 - L_2 \rightarrow L_1$ $\frac{1}{2}L_1 \rightarrow L_1$	$\begin{bmatrix} 1 & 0 & 0 & 2 \\ 0 & 1 & 0 & 3 \\ 0 & 0 & 1 & -1 \end{bmatrix}$

The second column describes which row operations have just been performed. So for the first step, the x is eliminated from L_2 by adding $\frac{3}{2}L_1$ to L_2. Next x is eliminated from L_3 by adding $L1$ to $L3$. These row operations are labelled in the table as

$$L_2 + \frac{3}{2}L_1 \to L_2$$
$$L_3 + L_1 \to L_3.$$

Once y is also eliminated from the third row, the result is a system of linear equations in triangular form, and so the first part of the algorithm is complete. From a computational point of view, it is faster to solve the variables in reverse order, a process known as back-substitution. One sees the solution is z = -1, y = 3, and x = 2. So there is a unique solution to the original system of equations.

Instead of stopping once the matrix is in echelon form, one could continue until the matrix is in *reduced* row echelon form, as it is done in the table. The process of row reducing until the matrix is reduced is sometimes referred to as Gauss-Jordan elimination, to distinguish it from stopping after reaching echelon form.

History

The method of Gaussian elimination appears in the Chinese mathematical text Chapter Eight *Rectangular Arrays* of *The Nine Chapters on the Mathematical Art*. Its use is illustrated in eighteen problems, with two to five equations. The first reference to the book by this title is dated to 179 CE, but parts of it were written as early as approximately 150 BCE. It was commented on by Liu Hui in the 3rd century.

The method in Europe stems from the notes of Isaac Newton. In 1670, he wrote that all the algebra books known to him lacked a lesson for solving simultaneous equations, which Newton then supplied. Cambridge University eventually published the notes as *Arithmetica Universalis* in 1707 long after Newton left academic life. The notes were widely imitated, which made (what is now called) Gaussian elimination a standard lesson in algebra textbooks by the end of the 18th century. Carl Friedrich Gauss in 1810 devised a notation for symmetric elimination that was adopted in the 19th century by professional hand computers to solve the normal equations of least-squares problems. The algorithm that is taught in high school was named for Gauss only in the 1950s as a result of confusion over the history of the subject.

Some authors use the term *Gaussian elimination* to refer only to the procedure until the matrix is in echelon form, and use the term Gauss-Jordan elimination to refer to the procedure which ends in reduced echelon form. The name is used because it is a variation of Gaussian elimination as described by Wilhelm Jordan in 1888. However, the method also appears in an article by Clasen published in the same year. Jordan and Clasen probably discovered Gauss–Jordan elimination independently.

Applications

The historically first application of the row reduction method is for solving systems of linear equations. Here are some other important applications of the algorithm.

Computing Determinants

To explain how Gaussian elimination allows the computation of the determinant of a square matrix, we have to recall how the elementary row operations change the determinant:

- Swapping two rows multiplies the determinant by -1

- Multiplying a row by a nonzero scalar multiplies the determinant by the same scalar

- Adding to one row a scalar multiple of another does not change the determinant.

If the Gaussian elimination applied to a square matrix A produces a row echelon matrix B, let d be the product of the scalars by which the determinant has been multiplied, using above rules. Then the determinant of A is the quotient by d of the product of the elements of the diagonal of B: $\det(A) = \prod \text{diag}(B) / d$.

Computationally, for a $n \times n$ matrix, this method needs only $O(n^3)$ arithmetic operations, while solving by elementary methods requires $O(2^n)$ or $O(n!)$ operations. Even on the fastest computers, the elementary methods are impractical for n above 20.

Finding the Inverse of a Matrix

A variant of Gaussian elimination called Gauss–Jordan elimination can be used for finding the inverse of a matrix, if it exists. If A is a n by n square matrix, then one can use row reduction to compute its inverse matrix, if it exists. First, the n by n identity matrix is augmented to the right of A, forming a n by $2n$ block matrix $[A \mid I]$. Now through application of elementary row operations, find the reduced echelon form of this n by $2n$ matrix. The matrix A is invertible if and only if the left block can be reduced to the identity matrix I; in this case the right block of the final matrix is A^{-1}. If the algorithm is unable to reduce the left block to I, then A is not invertible.

For example, consider the following matrix

$$A = \begin{bmatrix} 2 & -1 & 0 \\ -1 & 2 & -1 \\ 0 & -1 & 2 \end{bmatrix}.$$

To find the inverse of this matrix, one takes the following matrix augmented by the identity, and row reduces it as a 3 by 6 matrix:

$$[A \mid I] = \begin{bmatrix} 2 & -1 & 0 & | & 1 & 0 & 0 \\ -1 & 2 & -1 & | & 0 & 1 & 0 \\ 0 & -1 & 2 & | & 0 & 0 & 1 \end{bmatrix}.$$

By performing row operations, one can check that the reduced row echelon form of this augmented matrix is:

$$[I \mid B] = \begin{bmatrix} 1 & 0 & 0 & \frac{3}{4} & \frac{1}{2} & \frac{1}{4} \\ 0 & 1 & 0 & \frac{1}{2} & 1 & \frac{1}{2} \\ 0 & 0 & 1 & \frac{1}{4} & \frac{1}{2} & \frac{3}{4} \end{bmatrix}.$$

One can think of each row operation as the left product by an elementary matrix. Denoting by B the product of these elementary matrices, we showed, on the left, that $BA = I$, and therefore, $B = A^{-1}$. On the right, we kept a record of $BI = B$, which we know is the inverse desired. This procedure for finding the inverse works for square matrices of any size.

Computing Ranks and Bases

The Gaussian elimination algorithm can be applied to any $m \times n$ matrix A. In this way, for example, some 6×9 matrices can be transformed to a matrix that has a row echelon form like

$$T = \begin{bmatrix} a & * & * & * & * & * & * & * & * \\ 0 & 0 & b & * & * & * & * & * & * \\ 0 & 0 & 0 & c & * & * & * & * & * \\ 0 & 0 & 0 & 0 & 0 & 0 & d & * & * \\ 0 & 0 & 0 & 0 & 0 & 0 & 0 & 0 & e \\ 0 & 0 & 0 & 0 & 0 & 0 & 0 & 0 & 0 \end{bmatrix}$$

where the *s are arbitrary entries and a, b, c, d, e are nonzero entries. This echelon matrix T contains a wealth of information about A: the rank of A is 5 since there are 5 non-zero rows in T; the vector space spanned by the columns of A has a basis consisting of the first, third, fourth, seventh and ninth column of A (the columns of a, b, c, d, e in T), and the *s tell you how the other columns of A can be written as linear combinations of the basis columns. This is a consequence of the distributivity of the dot product in the expression of a linear map as a matrix.

All of this applies also to the reduced row echelon form, which is a particular row echelon form.

Computational Efficiency

The number of arithmetic operations required to perform row reduction is one way of measuring the algorithm's computational efficiency. For example, to solve a system of n equations for n unknowns by performing row operations on the matrix until it is in echelon form, and then solving for each unknown in reverse order, requires $n(n-1)/2$ divisions, $(2n^3 + 3n^2 - 5n)/6$ multiplications, and $(2n^3 + 3n^2 - 5n)/6$ subtractions, for a total of approximately $2n^3/3$ operations. Thus it has arithmetic complexity of $O(n^3)$. This arithmetic complexity is a good measure of the time needed for the whole computation when the time for each arithmetic operation is approximately constant. This is the case when the coefficients are represented by floating point numbers or when they belong to a finite field. If the coefficients are integers or rational numbers exactly represented, the intermediate entries can grow exponentially large, so the bit complexity is exponential. However, there is a variant of Gaussian elimination, called Bareiss algorithm that avoids this exponential growth of the intermediate entries, and, with the same arithmetic complexity of $O(n^3)$, has a bit complexity of $O(n^5)$.

This algorithm can be used on a computer for systems with thousands of equations and unknowns. However, the cost becomes prohibitive for systems with millions of equations. These large systems are generally solved using iterative methods. Specific methods exist for systems whose coefficients follow a regular pattern.

To put an n by n matrix into reduced echelon form by row operations, one needs n^3 arithmetic operations; which is approximately 50% more computation steps.

One possible problem is numerical instability, caused by the possibility of dividing by very small numbers. If, for example, the leading coefficient of one of the rows is very close to zero, then to row reduce the matrix one would need to divide by that number so the leading coefficient is 1. This means any error that existed for the number which was close to zero would be amplified. Gaussian elimination is numerically stable for diagonally dominant or positive-definite matrices. For general matrices, Gaussian elimination is usually considered to be stable, when using partial pivoting, even though there are examples of stable matrices for which it is unstable.

Generalizations

The Gaussian elimination can be performed over any field, not just the real numbers.

Gaussian elimination does not generalize in any simple way to higher order tensors (matrices are array representations of order 2 tensors); even computing the rank of a tensor of order greater than 2 is a difficult problem.

Pseudocode

As explained above, Gaussian elimination writes a given $m \times n$ matrix A uniquely as a product of an invertible $m \times m$ matrix S and a row-echelon matrix T. Here, S is the product of the matrices corresponding to the row operations performed.

The formal algorithm to compute T from A follows. We write $A[i, j]$ for the entry in row , column j in matrix A with 1 being the first index. The transformation is performed *in place*, meaning that the original matrix A is lost and successively replaced by T.

```
for k = 1 ... min(m,n):

  Find the k-th pivot:

  i_max  := argmax (i = k ... m, abs(A[i, k]))

  if A[i_max, k] = 0

    error "Matrix is singular!"

  swap rows(k, i_max)

  Do for all rows below pivot:

  for i = k + 1 ... m:

    f := A[i, k] / A[k, k]

    Do for all remaining elements in current row:
```

```
for j = k + 1 ... n:
  A[i, j]  := A[i, j] - A[k, j] * f
Fill lower triangular matrix with zeros:
A[i, k]  := 0
```

This algorithm differs slightly from the one discussed earlier, because before eliminating a variable, it first exchanges rows to move the entry with the largest absolute value to the pivot position. Such *partial pivoting* improves the numerical stability of the algorithm; some other variants are used.

Upon completion of this procedure the augmented matrix will be in row-echelon form and may be solved by back-substitution.

With modern computers, Gaussian elimination is not always the fastest algorithm to compute the row echelon form of matrix. There are computer libraries, like BLAS, that exploit the specifics of the computer hardware and of the structure of the matrix to choose the best algorithm automatically.

System of Linear Equations

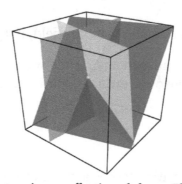

A linear system in three variables determines a collection of planes. The intersection point is the solution.

In mathematics, a system of linear equations (or linear system) is a collection of two or more linear equations involving the same set of variables. For example,

$$3x + 2y - z = 1$$
$$2x - 2y + 4z = -2$$
$$-x + \tfrac{1}{2}y - z = 0$$

is a system of three equations in the three variables x, y, z. A solution to a linear system is an assignment of values to the variables such that all the equations are simultaneously satisfied. A solution to the system above is given by

$$x = 1$$
$$y = -2$$
$$z = -2$$

since it makes all three equations valid. The word "*system*" indicates that the equations are to be considered collectively, rather than individually.

In mathematics, the theory of linear systems is the basis and a fundamental part of linear algebra, a subject which is used in most parts of modern mathematics. Computational algorithms for finding the solutions are an important part of numerical linear algebra, and play a prominent role in engineering, physics, chemistry, computer science, and economics. A system of non-linear equations can often be approximated by a linear system), a helpful technique when making a mathematical model or computer simulation of a relatively complex system.

Very often, the coefficients of the equations are real or complex numbers and the solutions are searched in the same set of numbers, but the theory and the algorithms apply for coefficients and solutions in any field. For solutions in an integral domain like the ring of the integers, or in other algebraic structures, other theories have been developed. Integer linear programming is a collection of methods for finding the "best" integer solution (when there are many). Gröbner basis theory provides algorithms when coefficients and unknowns are polynomials. Also tropical geometry is an example of linear algebra in a more exotic structure.

Elementary Example

The simplest kind of linear system involves two equations and two variables:

$$2x + 3y = 6$$
$$4x + 9y = 15.$$

One method for solving such a system is as follows. First, solve the top equation for x in terms of y:

$$x = 3 - \frac{3}{2}y.$$

Now substitute this expression for x into the bottom equation:

$$4\left(3 - \frac{3}{2}y\right) + 9y = 15.$$

This results in a single equation involving only the variable y. Solving gives $y = 1$, and substituting this back into the equation for x yields $x = 3/2$. This method generalizes to systems with additional variables.

General Form

A general system of m linear equations with n unknowns can be written as

$$a_{11}x_1 + a_{12}x_2 + \cdots + a_{1n}x_n = b_1$$
$$a_{21}x_1 + a_{22}x_2 + \cdots + a_{2n}x_n = b_2$$
$$\vdots \qquad \vdots \qquad \quad \vdots \qquad \vdots$$
$$a_{m1}x_1 + a_{m2}x_2 + \cdots + a_{mn}x_n = b_m.$$

Here $x_1, x_2, \ldots, x_n$ are the unknowns, $a_{11}, a_{12}, \ldots, a_{mn}$ are the coefficients of the system, and $b_1, b_2, \ldots, b_m$ are the constant terms.

Often the coefficients unknowns are real or complex numbers, but integers and rational numbers are also seen, as are polynomials and elements of an abstract algebraic structure.

Vector Equation

One extremely helpful view is that each unknown is a weight for a column vector in a linear combination.

$$x_1 \begin{bmatrix} a_{11} \\ a_{21} \\ \vdots \\ a_{m1} \end{bmatrix} + x_2 \begin{bmatrix} a_{12} \\ a_{22} \\ \vdots \\ a_{m2} \end{bmatrix} + \cdots + x_n \begin{bmatrix} a_{1n} \\ a_{2n} \\ \vdots \\ a_{mn} \end{bmatrix} = \begin{bmatrix} b_1 \\ b_2 \\ \vdots \\ b_m \end{bmatrix}$$

This allows all the language and theory of *vector spaces* (or more generally, *modules*) to be brought to bear. For example, the collection of all possible linear combinations of the vectors on the left-hand side is called their *span*, and the equations have a solution just when the right-hand vector is within that span. If every vector within that span has exactly one expression as a linear combination of the given left-hand vectors, then any solution is unique. In any event, the span has a *basis* of linearly independent vectors that do guarantee exactly one expression; and the number of vectors in that basis (its *dimension*) cannot be larger than m or n, but it can be smaller. This is important because if we have m independent vectors a solution is guaranteed regardless of the right-hand side, and otherwise not guaranteed.

Matrix Equation

The vector equation is equivalent to a matrix equation of the form

$$A\mathbf{x} = \mathbf{b}$$

where A is an $m \times n$ matrix, x is a column vector with n entries, and b is a column vector with m entries.

$$A = \begin{bmatrix} a_{11} & a_{12} & \cdots & a_{1n} \\ a_{21} & a_{22} & \cdots & a_{2n} \\ \vdots & \vdots & \ddots & \vdots \\ a_{m1} & a_{m2} & \cdots & a_{mn} \end{bmatrix}, \quad \mathbf{x} = \begin{bmatrix} x_1 \\ x_2 \\ \vdots \\ x_n \end{bmatrix}, \quad \mathbf{b} = \begin{bmatrix} b_1 \\ b_2 \\ \vdots \\ b_m \end{bmatrix}$$

The number of vectors in a basis for the span is now expressed as the *rank* of the matrix.

Solution Set

A solution of a linear system is an assignment of values to the variables $x_1, x_2, \ldots, x_n$ such that each of the equations is satisfied. The set of all possible solutions is called the solution set.

A linear system may behave in any one of three possible ways:

1. The system has *infinitely many solutions.*

2. The system has a single *unique solution.*

3. The system has *no solution.*

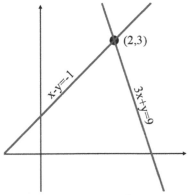

The solution set for the equations $x - y = -1$ and $3x + y = 9$ is the single point $(2, 3)$.

Geometric Interpretation

For a system involving two variables (x and y), each linear equation determines a line on the xy-plane. Because a solution to a linear system must satisfy all of the equations, the solution set is the intersection of these lines, and is hence either a line, a single point, or the empty set.

For three variables, each linear equation determines a plane in three-dimensional space, and the solution set is the intersection of these planes. Thus the solution set may be a plane, a line, a single point, or the empty set. For example, as three parallel planes do not have a common point, the solution set of their equations is empty; the solution set of the equations of three planes intersecting at a point is single point; if three planes pass through two points, their equations have at least two common solutions; in fact the solution set is infinite and consists in all the line passing through these points.

For n variables, each linear equation determines a hyperplane in n-dimensional space. The solution set is the intersection of these hyperplanes, which may be a flat of any dimension.

General Behavior

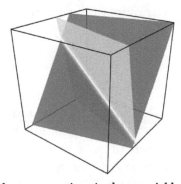

The solution set for two equations in three variables is usually a line.

In general, the behavior of a linear system is determined by the relationship between the number of equations and the number of unknowns:

- Usually, a system with fewer equations than unknowns has infinitely many solutions, but it may have no solution. Such a system is known as an underdetermined system.

- Usually, a system with the same number of equations and unknowns has a single unique solution.

- Usually, a system with more equations than unknowns has no solution. Such a system is also known as an overdetermined system.

In the first case, the dimension of the solution set is usually equal to $n - m$, where n is the number of variables and m is the number of equations.

The following pictures illustrate this trichotomy in the case of two variables:

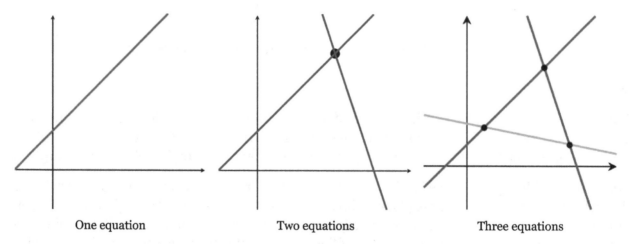

| One equation | Two equations | Three equations |

The first system has infinitely many solutions, namely all of the points on the blue line. The second system has a single unique solution, namely the intersection of the two lines. The third system has no solutions, since the three lines share no common point.

Keep in mind that the pictures above show only the most common case. It is possible for a system of two equations and two unknowns to have no solution (if the two lines are parallel), or for a system of three equations and two unknowns to be solvable (if the three lines intersect at a single point). In general, a system of linear equations may behave differently from expected if the equations are linearly dependent, or if two or more of the equations are inconsistent.

Properties

Independence

The equations of a linear system are independent if none of the equations can be derived algebraically from the others. When the equations are independent, each equation contains new information about the variables, and removing any of the equations increases the size of the solution set. For linear equations, logical independence is the same as linear independence.

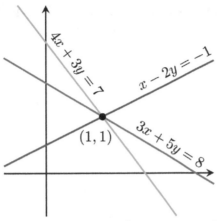

The equations $x - 2y = -1$, $3x + 5y = 8$, and $4x + 3y = 7$ are linearly dependent.

For example, the equations

$$3x + 2y = 6 \quad \text{and} \quad 6x + 4y = 12$$

are not independent — they are the same equation when scaled by a factor of two, and they would produce identical graphs. This is an example of equivalence in a system of linear equations.

For a more complicated example, the equations

$$x - 2y = -1$$
$$3x + 5y = 8$$
$$4x + 3y = 7$$

are not independent, because the third equation is the sum of the other two. Indeed, any one of these equations can be derived from the other two, and any one of the equations can be removed without affecting the solution set. The graphs of these equations are three lines that intersect at a single point.

Consistency

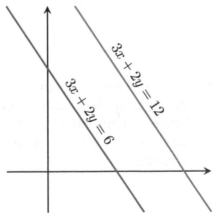

The equations $3x + 2y = 6$ and $3x + 2y = 12$ are inconsistent.

A linear system is inconsistent if it has no solution, and otherwise it is said to be consistent. When the system is inconsistent, it is possible to derive a contradiction from the equations, that may always be rewritten as the statement 0 = 1.

For example, the equations

$$3x + 2y = 6 \quad \text{and} \quad 3x + 2y = 12$$

are inconsistent. In fact, by subtracting the first equation from the second one and multiplying both sides of the result by 1/6, we get 0 = 1. The graphs of these equations on the xy-plane are a pair of parallel lines.

It is possible for three linear equations to be inconsistent, even though any two of them are consistent together. For example, the equations

$$x + y = 1$$
$$2x + y = 1$$
$$3x + 2y = 3$$

are inconsistent. Adding the first two equations together gives $3x + 2y = 2$, which can be subtracted from the third equation to yield 0 = 1. Note that any two of these equations have a common solution. The same phenomenon can occur for any number of equations.

In general, inconsistencies occur if the left-hand sides of the equations in a system are linearly dependent, and the constant terms do not satisfy the dependence relation. A system of equations whose left-hand sides are linearly independent is always consistent.

Putting it another way, according to the Rouché–Capelli theorem, any system of equations (overdetermined or otherwise) is inconsistent if the rank of the augmented matrix is greater than the rank of the coefficient matrix. If, on the other hand, the ranks of these two matrices are equal, the system must have at least one solution. The solution is unique if and only if the rank equals the number of variables. Otherwise the general solution has k free parameters where k is the difference between the number of variables and the rank; hence in such a case there are an infinitude of solutions. The rank of a system of equations can never be higher than [the number of variables] + 1, which means that a system with any number of equations can always be reduced to a system that has a number of independent equations that is at most equal to [the number of variables] + 1.

Equivalence

Two linear systems using the same set of variables are equivalent if each of the equations in the second system can be derived algebraically from the equations in the first system, and vice versa. Two systems are equivalent if either both are inconsistent or each equation of each of them is a linear combination of the equations of the other one. It follows that two linear systems are equivalent if and only if they have the same solution set.

Solving a Linear System

There are several algorithms for solving a system of linear equations.

Describing the Solution

When the solution set is finite, it is reduced to a single element. In this case, the unique solution is described by a sequence of equations whose left-hand sides are the names of the unknowns and right-hand sides are the corresponding values, for example $(x = 3, y = -2, z = 6)$. When an order on the unknowns has been fixed, for example the alphabetical order the solution may be described as a vector of values, like $(3, -2, 6)$ for the previous example.

It can be difficult to describe a set with infinite solutions. Typically, some of the variables are designated as free (or independent, or as parameters), meaning that they are allowed to take any value, while the remaining variables are dependent on the values of the free variables.

For example, consider the following system:

$$x + 3y - 2z = 5$$
$$3x + 5y + 6z = 7$$

The solution set to this system can be described by the following equations:

$$x = -7z - 1 \quad \text{and} \quad y = 3z + 2.$$

Here z is the free variable, while x and y are dependent on z. Any point in the solution set can be obtained by first choosing a value for z, and then computing the corresponding values for x and y.

Each free variable gives the solution space one degree of freedom, the number of which is equal to the dimension of the solution set. For example, the solution set for the above equation is a line, since a point in the solution set can be chosen by specifying the value of the parameter z. An infinite solution of higher order may describe a plane, or higher-dimensional set.

Different choices for the free variables may lead to different descriptions of the same solution set. For example, the solution to the above equations can alternatively be described as follows:

$$y = -\frac{3}{7}x + \frac{11}{7} \quad \text{and} \quad z = -\frac{1}{7}x - \frac{1}{7}.$$

Here x is the free variable, and y and z are dependent.

Elimination of Variables

The simplest method for solving a system of linear equations is to repeatedly eliminate variables. This method can be described as follows:

1. In the first equation, solve for one of the variables in terms of the others.

2. Substitute this expression into the remaining equations. This yields a system of equations with one fewer equation and one fewer unknown.

3. Repeat until the system is reduced to a single linear equation.

4. Solve this equation, and then back-substitute until the entire solution is found.

For example, consider the following system:

$$x + 3y - 2z = 5$$
$$3x + 5y + 6z = 7$$
$$2x + 4y + 3z = 8$$

Solving the first equation for x gives $x = 5 + 2z - 3y$, and plugging this into the second and third equation yields

$$-4y + 12z = -8$$
$$-2y + 7z = -2$$

Solving the first of these equations for y yields $y = 2 + 3z$, and plugging this into the second equation yields $z = 2$. We now have:

$$x = 5 + 2z - 3y$$
$$y = 2 + 3z$$
$$z = 2$$

Substituting $z = 2$ into the second equation gives $y = 8$, and substituting $z = 2$ and $y = 8$ into the first equation yields $x = -15$. Therefore, the solution set is the single point $(x, y, z) = (-15, 8, 2)$.

Row Reduction

In row reduction (also known as Gaussian elimination), the linear system is represented as an augmented matrix:

$$\begin{bmatrix} 1 & 3 & -2 & 5 \\ 3 & 5 & 6 & 7 \\ 2 & 4 & 3 & 8 \end{bmatrix}.$$

This matrix is then modified using elementary row operations until it reaches reduced row echelon form. There are three types of elementary row operations:

Type 1: Swap the positions of two rows.

Type 2: Multiply a row by a nonzero scalar.

Type 3: Add to one row a scalar multiple of another.

Because these operations are reversible, the augmented matrix produced always represents a linear system that is equivalent to the original.

There are several specific algorithms to row-reduce an augmented matrix, the simplest of which are Gaussian elimination and Gauss-Jordan elimination. The following computation shows Gauss-Jordan elimination applied to the matrix above:

$$\begin{bmatrix} 1 & 3 & -2 & 5 \\ 3 & 5 & 6 & 7 \\ 2 & 4 & 3 & 8 \end{bmatrix} \sim \begin{bmatrix} 1 & 3 & -2 & 5 \\ 0 & -4 & 12 & -8 \\ 2 & 4 & 3 & 8 \end{bmatrix} \sim \begin{bmatrix} 1 & 3 & -2 & 5 \\ 0 & -4 & 12 & -8 \\ 0 & -2 & 7 & -2 \end{bmatrix} \sim \begin{bmatrix} 1 & 3 & -2 & 5 \\ 0 & 1 & -3 & 2 \\ 0 & -2 & 7 & -2 \end{bmatrix}$$

$$\sim \begin{bmatrix} 1 & 3 & -2 & 5 \\ 0 & 1 & -3 & 2 \\ 0 & 0 & 1 & 2 \end{bmatrix} \sim \begin{bmatrix} 1 & 3 & -2 & 5 \\ 0 & 1 & 0 & 8 \\ 0 & 0 & 1 & 2 \end{bmatrix} \sim \begin{bmatrix} 1 & 3 & 0 & 9 \\ 0 & 1 & 0 & 8 \\ 0 & 0 & 1 & 2 \end{bmatrix} \sim \begin{bmatrix} 1 & 0 & 0 & -15 \\ 0 & 1 & 0 & 8 \\ 0 & 0 & 1 & 2 \end{bmatrix}.$$

The last matrix is in reduced row echelon form, and represents the system $x = -15$, $y = 8$, $z = 2$. A comparison with the example in the previous section on the algebraic elimination of variables shows that these two methods are in fact the same; the difference lies in how the computations are written down.

Cramer's Rule

Cramer's rule is an explicit formula for the solution of a system of linear equations, with each variable given by a quotient of two determinants. For example, the solution to the system

$$x + 3y - 2z = 5$$
$$3x + 5y + 6z = 7$$
$$2x + 4y + 3z = 8$$

is given by

$$x = \frac{\begin{vmatrix} 5 & 3 & -2 \\ 7 & 5 & 6 \\ 8 & 4 & 3 \end{vmatrix}}{\begin{vmatrix} 1 & 3 & -2 \\ 3 & 5 & 6 \\ 2 & 4 & 3 \end{vmatrix}}, \quad y = \frac{\begin{vmatrix} 1 & 5 & -2 \\ 3 & 7 & 6 \\ 2 & 8 & 3 \end{vmatrix}}{\begin{vmatrix} 1 & 3 & -2 \\ 3 & 5 & 6 \\ 2 & 4 & 3 \end{vmatrix}}, \quad z = \frac{\begin{vmatrix} 1 & 3 & 5 \\ 3 & 5 & 7 \\ 2 & 4 & 8 \end{vmatrix}}{\begin{vmatrix} 1 & 3 & -2 \\ 3 & 5 & 6 \\ 2 & 4 & 3 \end{vmatrix}}.$$

For each variable, the denominator is the determinant of the matrix of coefficients, while the numerator is the determinant of a matrix in which one column has been replaced by the vector of constant terms.

Though Cramer's rule is important theoretically, it has little practical value for large matrices, since the computation of large determinants is somewhat cumbersome. (Indeed, large determinants are most easily computed using row reduction.) Further, Cramer's rule has very poor numerical properties, making it unsuitable for solving even small systems reliably, unless the operations are performed in rational arithmetic with unbounded precision.

Matrix Solution

If the equation system is expressed in the matrix form $A\mathbf{x} = \mathbf{b}$, the entire solution set can also be expressed in matrix form. If the matrix A is square (has m rows and $n=m$ columns) and has full rank (all m rows are independent), then the system has a unique solution given by

$$\mathbf{x} = A^{-1}\mathbf{b}$$

where A^{-1} is the inverse of A. More generally, regardless of whether $m=n$ or not and regardless of the rank of A, all solutions (if any exist) are given using the Moore-Penrose pseudoinverse of A, denoted $A^{\dagger}$, as follows:

$$\mathbf{x} = A^{\dagger}\mathbf{b} + (I - A^{\dagger}A)\mathbf{w}$$

where $\mathbf{w}$ is a vector of free parameters that ranges over all possible $n\times 1$ vectors. A necessary and sufficient condition for any solution(s) to exist is that the potential solution obtained using $\mathbf{w} = \mathbf{0}$ satisfy $A\mathbf{x} = \mathbf{b}$ — that is, that $AA^{\dagger}\mathbf{b} = \mathbf{b}$. If this condition does not hold, the equation system is inconsistent and has no solution. If the condition holds, the system is consistent and at least one solution exists. For example, in the above-mentioned case in which A is square and of full rank, $A^{\dagger}$ simply equals A^{-1} and the general solution equation simplifies to $\mathbf{x} = A^{-1}\mathbf{b} + (I - A^{-1}A)\mathbf{w} = A^{-1}\mathbf{b} + (I - I)\mathbf{w} = A^{-1}\mathbf{b}$ as previously stated, where $\mathbf{w}$ has completely dropped out of the solution, leaving only a single solution. In other cases, though, $\mathbf{w}$ remains and hence an infinitude of potential values of the free parameter vector $\mathbf{w}$ give an infinitude of solutions of the equation.

Other Methods

While systems of three or four equations can be readily solved by hand, computers are often used for larger systems. The standard algorithm for solving a system of linear equations is based on Gaussian elimination with some modifications. Firstly, it is essential to avoid division by small numbers, which may lead to inaccurate results. This can be done by reordering the equations if necessary, a process known as *pivoting*. Secondly, the algorithm does not exactly do Gaussian elimination, but it computes the LU decomposition of the matrix A. This is mostly an organizational tool, but it is much quicker if one has to solve several systems with the same matrix A but different vectors b.

If the matrix A has some special structure, this can be exploited to obtain faster or more accurate algorithms. For instance, systems with a symmetric positive definite matrix can be solved twice as fast with the Cholesky decomposition. Levinson recursion is a fast method for Toeplitz matrices. Special methods exist also for matrices with many zero elements (so-called sparse matrices), which appear often in applications.

A completely different approach is often taken for very large systems, which would otherwise take too much time or memory. The idea is to start with an initial approximation to the solution (which does not have to be accurate at all), and to change this approximation in several steps to bring it closer to the true solution. Once the approximation is sufficiently accurate, this is taken to be the solution to the system. This leads to the class of iterative methods.

Homogeneous Systems

A system of linear equations is homogeneous if all of the constant terms are zero:

$$a_{11}x_1 + a_{12}x_2 + \cdots + a_{1n}x_n = 0$$
$$a_{21}x_1 + a_{22}x_2 + \cdots + a_{2n}x_n = 0$$
$$\vdots \qquad \vdots \qquad\qquad \vdots \qquad \vdots$$
$$a_{m1}x_1 + a_{m2}x_2 + \cdots + a_{mn}x_n = 0.$$

A homogeneous system is equivalent to a matrix equation of the form

$$A\mathbf{x} = \mathbf{0}$$

where A is an $m \times n$ matrix, x is a column vector with n entries, and 0 is the zero vector with m entries.

Solution Set

Every homogeneous system has at least one solution, known as the zero solution (or trivial solution), which is obtained by assigning the value of zero to each of the variables. If the system has a non-singular matrix ($\det(A) \neq 0$) then it is also the only solution. If the system has a singular matrix then there is a solution set with an infinite number of solutions. This solution set has the following additional properties:

1. If u and v are two vectors representing solutions to a homogeneous system, then the vector sum u + v is also a solution to the system.

2. If u is a vector representing a solution to a homogeneous system, and r is any scalar, then ru is also a solution to the system.

These are exactly the properties required for the solution set to be a linear subspace of R^n. In particular, the solution set to a homogeneous system is the same as the null space of the corresponding matrix A. Numerical solutions to a homogeneous system can be found with a singular value decomposition.

Relation to Nonhomogeneous Systems

There is a close relationship between the solutions to a linear system and the solutions to the corresponding homogeneous system:

$$A\mathbf{x} = \mathbf{b} \qquad \text{and} \qquad A\mathbf{x} = \mathbf{0}.$$

Specifically, if p is any specific solution to the linear system $Ax = b$, then the entire solution set can be described as

$$\{\mathbf{p} + \mathbf{v} : \mathbf{v} \text{ is any solution to } A\mathbf{x} = \mathbf{0}\}.$$

Geometrically, this says that the solution set for $Ax = b$ is a translation of the solution set for $Ax = 0$. Specifically, the flat for the first system can be obtained by translating the linear subspace for the homogeneous system by the vector p.

This reasoning only applies if the system $Ax = b$ has at least one solution. This occurs if and only if the vector b lies in the image of the linear transformation A.

References

- Xaingyu Y. Hu (2016). "Simple gradient-based error-diffusion method" (abstract). Journal of Electronic Imaging. 25 (4): 043029. doi:10.1117/1.JEI.25.4.043029

- Thomas J. Lynch (1985). Data Compression: Techniques and Applications. Lifetime Learning Publications. ISBN 978-0-534-03418-4

- Lipshitz, Stanley P; Vanderkooy, John; Wannamaker, Robert A. (November 1991). "Minimally Audible Noise Shaping". J. Audio Eng. Soc. 39 (11): 836–852. Retrieved 28 October 2009

- Grcar, Joseph F. (2011a), "How ordinary elimination became Gaussian elimination", Historia Mathematica, 38 (2): 163–218, arXiv:0907.2397 , doi:10.1016/j.hm.2010.06.003

- Deutsch, Diana (1999). The psychology of music. Gulf Professional Publishing. p. 153. ISBN 978-0-12-213565-1. Retrieved 24 May 2011

- Vanderkooy, John; Lipshitz, Stanley P (December 1987). "Dither in Digital Audio". J. Audio Eng. Soc. 35 (12): 966–975. Retrieved 28 October 2009

- Lawrence G. Roberts (February 1962). "Picture Coding Using Pseudo-Random Noise" (abstract). IEEE Transactions on Information Theory. 8 (2): 145–154. doi:10.1109/TIT.1962.1057702

- Atkinson, Kendall A. (1989), An Introduction to Numerical Analysis (2nd ed.), New York: John Wiley & Sons, ISBN 978-0-471-50023-0

- Ulichney, Robert A (1994). "Halftone Characterization in the Frequency Domain" (PDF). Archived (PDF) from the original on 2014-02-14. Retrieved 2013-08-12

- L. Schuchman (December 1964). "Dither Signals and Their Effect on Quantization Noise" (abstract). IEEE Trans. Commun. 12 (4): 162–165. doi:10.1109/TCOM.1964.1088973

- Farebrother, R.W. (1988), Linear Least Squares Computations, STATISTICS: Textbooks and Monographs, Marcel Dekker, ISBN 978-0-8247-7661-9

- Silva, Aristófanes Correia; Lucena, Paula Salgado; Figuerola, Wilfredo Blanco (13 December 2000). "Average Dithering". Image Based Artistic Dithering. Visgraf Lab. Retrieved 2007-09-10

- Lipson, Marc; Lipschutz, Seymour (2001), Schaum's outline of theory and problems of linear algebra, New York: McGraw-Hill, pp. 69–80, ISBN 978-0-07-136200-9

Sorting Algorithm: An Integrated Study

Sorting enables the processing of data in a precise order. Enumeration, odd-even sort and merge sort are discussed in this chapter. Through enumeration, the position of an element can be found by ordering a list. Another technique for sorting is odd-even sort, which compares adjacent odd/even indexed pair and if a pair is wrongly sequenced, it is switched. The following chapter elucidates the various tools and techniques that are related to sorting.

Enumeration

An enumeration is a complete, ordered listing of all the items in a collection. The term is commonly used in mathematics and computer science to refer to a listing of all of the elements of a set. The precise requirements for an enumeration (for example, whether the set must be finite, or whether the list is allowed to contain repetitions) depend on the discipline of study and the context of a given problem.

Some sets can be enumerated by means of a natural ordering (such as 1, 2, 3, 4, ... for the set of positive integers), but in other cases it may be necessary to impose a (perhaps arbitrary) ordering. In some contexts, such as enumerative combinatorics, the term *enumeration* is used more in the sense of *counting* – with emphasis on determination of the number of elements that a set contains, rather than the production of an explicit listing of those elements.

Enumeration in Combinatorics

In combinatorics, enumeration means counting, i.e., determining the exact number of elements of finite sets, usually grouped into infinite families, such as the family of sets each consisting of all permutations of some finite set. There are flourishing subareas in many branches of mathematics concerned with enumerating in this sense objects of special kinds. For instance, in *partition enumeration* and *graph enumeration* the objective is to count partitions or graphs that meet certain conditions.

Enumeration in Set Theory

In set theory, the notion of enumeration has a broader sense, and does not require the set being enumerated to be finite.

Enumeration as Listing

When an enumeration is used in an ordered list context, we impose some sort of ordering structure requirement on the index set. While we can make the requirements on the ordering quite lax in order to allow for great generality, the most natural and common prerequisite is that the index set be well-ordered. According to this characterization, an ordered enumeration is defined to be a surjection (an onto relationship) with a well-ordered domain. This definition is natural in the sense that a given well-ordering on the index set provides a unique way to list the next element given a partial enumeration.

Enumeration in Countable vs. Uncountable Context

The most common use of enumeration in set theory occurs in the context where infinite sets are separated into those that are countable and those that are not. In this case, an enumeration is merely an enumeration with domain ω, the ordinal of the natural numbers. This definition can also be stated as follows:

- As a surjective mapping from $\mathbb{N}$ (the natural numbers) to S (i.e., every element of S is the image of at least one natural number). This definition is especially suitable to questions of computability and elementary set theory.

We may also define it differently when working with finite sets. In this case an enumeration may be defined as follows:

- As a bijective mapping from S to an initial segment of the natural numbers. This definition is especially suitable to combinatorial questions and finite sets; then the initial segment is $\{1,2,...,n\}$ for some n which is the cardinality of S.

In the first definition it varies whether the mapping is also required to be injective (i.e., every element of S is the image of *exactly one* natural number), and/or allowed to be partial (i.e., the mapping is defined only for some natural numbers). In some applications (especially those concerned with computability of the set S), these differences are of little importance, because one is concerned only with the mere existence of some enumeration, and an enumeration according to a liberal definition will generally imply that enumerations satisfying stricter requirements also exist.

Enumeration of finite sets obviously requires that either non-injectivity or partiality is accepted, and in contexts where finite sets may appear one or both of these are inevitably present.

Examples

- The natural numbers are enumerable by the function f(x) = x. In this case $f : \mathbb{N} \to \mathbb{N}$ is simply the identity function.

- $\mathbb{Z}$, the set of integers is enumerable by

$$f(x) := \begin{cases} -(x+1)/2, & \text{if } x \text{ is odd} \\ x/2, & \text{if } x \text{ is even.} \end{cases}$$

$f : \mathbb{N} \to \mathbb{Z}$ is a bijection since every natural number corresponds to exactly one integer. The following table gives the first few values of this enumeration:

x	0	1	2	3	4	5	6	7	8
$f(x)$	0	−1	1	−2	2	−3	3	−4	4

- All (non empty) finite sets are enumerable. Let S be a finite set with $n > 0$ elements and let $K = \{1,2,...,n\}$. Select any element s in S and assign $f(n) = s$. Now set $S' = S - \{s\}$ (where $-$ denotes set difference). Select any element $s' \in S'$ and assign $f(n-1) = s'$. Continue this process until all elements of the set have been assigned a natural number. Then $f : K \to S$ is an enumeration of S.

- The real numbers have no countable enumeration as proved by Cantor's diagonal argument and Cantor's first uncountability proof.

Properties

- There exists an enumeration for a set (in this sense) if and only if the set is countable.

- If a set is enumerable it will have an uncountable infinity of different enumerations, except in the degenerate cases of the empty set or (depending on the precise definition) sets with one element. However, if one requires enumerations to be injective *and* allows only a limited form of partiality such that if $f(n)$ is defined then $f(m)$ must be defined for all $m < n$, then a finite set of N elements has exactly $N!$ enumerations.

- An enumeration e of a set S with domain $\mathbb{N}$ induces a well-order $\leq$ on that set defined by $s \leq t$ if and only if $\min e^{-1}(s) \leq \min e^{-1}(t)$. Although the order may have little to do with the underlying set, it is useful when some order of the set is necessary.

Ordinal Enumeration

In set theory, there is a more general notion of an enumeration than the characterization requiring the domain of the listing function to be an initial segment of the Natural numbers where the domain of the enumerating function can assume any ordinal. Under this definition, an enumeration of a set S is any surjection from an ordinal α onto S. The more restrictive version of enumeration mentioned before is the special case where α is a finite ordinal or the first limit ordinal ω. This more generalized version extends the aforementioned definition to encompass transfinite listings.

Under this definition, the first uncountable ordinal ω_1 can be enumerated by the identity function on ω_1 so that these two notions do not coincide. More generally, it is a theorem of ZF that any well-ordered set can be enumerated under this characterization so that it coincides up to relabeling with the generalized listing enumeration. If one also assumes the Axiom of Choice, then all sets can be enumerated so that it coincides up to relabeling with the most general form of enumerations.

Since set theorists work with infinite sets of arbitrarily large cardinalities, the default definition among this group of mathematicians of an enumeration of a set tends to be any arbitrary α-sequence exactly listing all of its elements. Indeed, in Jech's book, which is a common reference for set theorists, an enumeration is defined to be exactly this. Therefore, in order to avoid ambiguity, one may use the term finitely enumerable or denumerable to denote one of the corresponding types of distinguished countable enumerations.

Enumeration as Comparison of Cardinalities

Formally, the most inclusive definition of an enumeration of a set S is any surjection from an arbitrary index set *I* onto *S*. In this broad context, every set *S* can be trivially enumerated by the identity function from *S* onto itself. If one does *not* assume the axiom of choice or one of its variants, *S* need not have any well-ordering. Even if one does assume the axiom of choice, *S* need not have any natural well-ordering.

This general definition therefore lends itself to a counting notion where we are interested in "how many" rather than "in what order." In practice, this broad meaning of enumeration is often used to compare the relative sizes or cardinalities of different sets. If one works in Zermelo-Fraenkel set theory without the axiom of choice, one may want to impose the additional restriction that an enumeration must also be injective (without repetition) since in this theory, the existence of a surjection from *I* onto *S* need not imply the existence of an injection from *S* into *I*.

Enumeration in Computability Theory

In computability theory one often considers countable enumerations with the added requirement that the mapping from $\mathbb{N}$ (set of all natural numbers) to the enumerated set must be computable. The set being enumerated is then called recursively enumerable (or computably enumerable in more contemporary language), referring to the use of recursion theory in formalizations of what it means for the map to be computable.

In this sense, a subset of the natural numbers is computably enumerable if it is the range of a computable function. In this context, enumerable may be used to mean computably enumerable. However, these definitions characterize distinct classes since there are uncountably many subsets of the natural numbers that can be enumerated by an arbitrary function with domain ω and only countably many computable functions. A specific example of a set with an enumeration but not a computable enumeration is the complement of the halting set.

Furthermore, this characterization illustrates a place where the ordering of the listing is important. There exists a computable enumeration of the halting set, but not one that lists the elements in an increasing ordering. If there were one, then the halting set would be decidable, which is provably false. In general, being recursively enumerable is a weaker condition than being a decidable set.

Enumerative Combinatorics

Enumerative combinatorics is an area of combinatorics that deals with the number of ways that certain patterns can be formed. Two examples of this type of problem are counting combinations and counting permutations. More generally, given an infinite collection of finite sets S_i indexed by the natural numbers, enumerative combinatorics seeks to describe a *counting function* which counts the number of objects in S_n for each *n*. Although counting the number of elements in a set is a rather broad mathematical problem, many of the problems that arise in applications have a relatively simple combinatorial description. The twelvefold way provides a unified framework for counting permutations, combinations and partitions.

The simplest such functions are *closed formulas*, which can be expressed as a composition of elementary functions such as factorials, powers, and so on. For instance, as shown below, the number of different possible orderings of a deck of *n* cards is $f(n) = n!$. The problem of finding a closed formula is known as algebraic enumeration, and frequently involves deriving a recurrence relation or generating function and using this to arrive at the desired closed form.

Often, a complicated closed formula yields little insight into the behavior of the counting function as the number of counted objects grows. In these cases, a simple asymptotic approximation may be preferable. A function $g(n)$ is an asymptotic approximation to $f(n)$ if $f(n)/g(n) \to 1$ as $n \to \infty$. In this case, we write $f(n) \sim g(n)$.

Generating Functions

Generating functions are used to describe families of combinatorial objects. Let $\mathcal{F}$ denote the family of objects and let $F(x)$ be its generating function. Then:

$$F(x) = \sum_{n=0}^{\infty} f_n x^n$$

Where f_n denotes the number of combinatorial objects of size n. The number of combinatorial objects of size n is therefore given by the coefficient of x^n. Some common operation on families of combinatorial objects and its effect on the generating function will now be developed. The exponential generating function is also sometimes used. In this case it would have the form:

$$F(x) = \sum_{n=0}^{\infty} f_n \frac{x^n}{n!}$$

Once determined, the generating function yields the information given by the previous approaches. In addition, the various natural operations on generating functions such as addition, multiplication, differentiation, etc., have a combinatorial significance; this allows one to extend results from one combinatorial problem in order to solve others.

Union

Given two combinatorial families, $\mathcal{F}$ and $\mathcal{G}$ with generating functions $F(x)$ and $G(x)$ respectively, the disjoint union of the two families ($\mathcal{F} \cup \mathcal{G}$) has generating function $F(x) + G(x)$.

Pairs

For two combinatorial families as above the Cartesian product (pair) of the two families ($\mathcal{F} \times \mathcal{G}$) has generating function $F(x)G(x)$.

Sequences

A sequence generalizes the idea of the pair as defined above. Sequences are arbitrary Cartesian products of a combinatorial object with itself. Formally:

$$\text{Seq}(\mathcal{F}) = \epsilon \cup \mathcal{F} \cup \mathcal{F} \times \mathcal{F} \cup \mathcal{F} \times \mathcal{F} \times \mathcal{F} \cup \cdots$$

To put the above in words: An empty sequence or a sequence of one element or a sequence of two elements or a sequence of three elements, etc. The generating function would be:

$$1 + F(x) + [F(x)]^2 + [F(x)]^3 + \cdots = \frac{1}{1 - F(x)}$$

Combinatorial Structures

The above operations can now be used to enumerate common combinatorial objects including trees (binary and plane), Dyck paths and cycles. A combinatorial structure is composed of atoms. For example, with trees the atoms would be the nodes. The atoms which compose the object can either be labeled or unlabeled. Unlabeled atoms are indistinguishable from each other, while labelled atoms are distinct. Therefore, for a combinatorial object consisting of labeled atoms a new object can be formed by simply swapping two or more atoms.

Binary and Plane Trees

Binary and plane trees are examples of an unlabeled combinatorial structure. Trees consist of nodes linked by edges in such a way that there are no cycles. There is generally a node called the root, which has no parent node. In Plane trees each node can have an arbitrary number of children. In binary trees, a special case of plane trees, each node can have either two or no children. Let $\mathcal{P}$ denote the family of all plane trees. Then this family can be recursively defined as follows:

$$\mathcal{P} = \{\bullet\} \times \mathrm{Seq}(\mathcal{P})$$

In this case $\{\bullet\}$ represents the family of objects consisting of one node. This has generating function x. Let $P(x)$ denote the generating function $\mathcal{P}$. Putting the above description in words: A plane tree consists of a node to which is attached an arbitrary number of subtrees, each of which is also a plane tree. Using the operation on families of combinatorial structures developed earlier this translates to a recursive generating function:

$$P(x) = x \frac{1}{1 - P(x)}$$

After solving for $P(x)$:

$$P(x) = \frac{1 - \sqrt{1 - 4x}}{2}$$

An explicit formula for the number of plane trees of size n can now be determined by extracting the coefficient of x^n.

$$
\begin{aligned}
p_n &= [x^n]P(x) = [x^n]\frac{1 - \sqrt{1 - 4x}}{2} \\
&= [x^n]\frac{1}{2} - [x^n]\frac{1}{2}\sqrt{1 - 4x} \\
&= -\frac{1}{2}[x^n]\sum_{k=0}^{\infty}\binom{\frac{1}{2}}{k}(-4x)^k \\
&= -\frac{1}{2}\binom{\frac{1}{2}}{n}(-4)^n \\
&= \frac{1}{n}\binom{2n-2}{n-1}
\end{aligned}
$$

Note: The notation $[x^n] f(x)$ refers to the coefficient of x^n in $f(x)$. The series expansion of the square root is based on Newton's generalization of the binomial theorem. To get from the fourth to fifth line manipulations using the generalized binomial coefficient is needed.

The expression on the last line is equal to the $(n-1)^{th}$ Catalan number. Therefore $p_n = c_{n-1}$.

Enumeration Sort

First let us start our discussion with the definition of enumeration sort.

Definition 1. *Enumeration Sort: According to Knuth (1973), it is a method of finding the exact position of each element in a sorted list by comparing and finding the frequency of elements having smaller value. That is if p elements are smaller than a_q, then a_q occupies the (p+1)th position in the sorted list.*

Enumeration Sort Algorithm

Muller and Preparata (1975) proposed a non standard PRAM model to carry out enumeration sorting in log- arithmic time. The algorithm consumes $\theta(logn)$ to spawn n^2 processors and a constant time to sort.

Pseudo Code

```
Contract: EnumSort: List->List

Purpose: This algorithm is to sort a list of ele-
         ments in increasing order. Example:

    EnumSort([2,1,5,4,3])-> [1,2,3,4,5]

Procedure

        EnumSort(num

        List[0..n-1])

        begin

spawn n2 processors denoted by Pi,j where i,j ranges from 0 to n-1

        for all processors Pi,j where
              i,j

        ranges from 0 to n-1 do begin

        Initialize Position[i] to 0

        if numList[i]<numList[j] or numList[i]=numList [j]

        and i<j then Position[i] is set to 1

    endif

end
```

```
for all processors Pi, 0 where i ranges from 0 to n-1
  do begin

SortedList[(n-1)-Position[i]] is set to

          numList[i] end

end
```

Dry Run: Let us consider numList=[5,2,3]. Here n=3.

Table 1.1: Dry Run of the Enumeration Sort Algorithm-Finding the final Position of an

element	P00	P01	P02	P10	P11	P12
P20 P21	P22 Pos[0]=0		Pos[0]=0	Pos[0]=0	Pos[1]=1	Pos[1]=1
	Pos[1]=2		Pos[2]=1	Pos[2]=1	Pos[2]=1	

Table 1.2: Dry Run of the Enumeration Sort Algorithm-Determining the Sorted List

P00	P10	P20
Sorted[(3-1)-Pos[0]]	Sorted[(3-1)-Pos[1]]	Sorted[(3-1)-Pos[2]]
=Sorted[2]	=Sorted[0]	=Sorted[1]
=a[0]	=a[1]	=a[2]
=5	=2	=3

Table 1.3: Dry Run of the Enumeration Sort Algorithm-Final Sorted List

0	1	2
2	3	5

Odd–even Sort

In computing, an odd–even sort or odd–even transposition sort (also known as brick sort) is a relatively simple sorting algorithm, developed originally for use on parallel processors with local interconnections. It is a comparison sort related to bubble sort, with which it shares many characteristics. It functions by comparing all odd/even indexed pairs of adjacent elements in the list and, if a pair is in the wrong order (the first is larger than the second) the elements are switched. The next step repeats this for even/odd indexed pairs (of adjacent elements). Then it alternates between odd/even and even/odd steps until the list is sorted.

Sorting on Processor Arrays

On parallel processors, with one value per processor and only local left–right neighbor connections, the processors all concurrently do a compare–exchange operation with their neighbors, alternating between odd–even and even–odd pairings. This algorithm was originally presented, and shown to be efficient on such processors, by Habermann in 1972.

The algorithm extends efficiently to the case of multiple items per processor. In the Baudet–Stevenson odd–even merge-splitting algorithm, each processor sorts its own sublist at each step, using any efficient sort algorithm, and then performs a merge splitting, or transposition–merge, operation with its neighbor, with neighbor pairing alternating between odd–even and even–odd on each step.

Batcher's Odd–even Mergesort

A related but more efficient sort algorithm is the Batcher odd–even mergesort, using compare–exchange operations and perfect-shuffle operations. Batcher's method is efficient on parallel processors with long-range connections.

Algorithm

The single-processor algorithm, like bubblesort, is simple but not very efficient. Here a zero-based index is assumed:

```
function oddEvenSort(list) {

  function swap( list, i, j ){

    var temp = list[i];

    list[i] = list[j];

    list[j] = temp;

  }

  var sorted = false;

  while(!sorted)

  {

    sorted = true;

    for(var i = 1; i < list.length-1; i += 2)

    {

      if(list[i] > list[i+1])

      {

        swap(list, i, i+1);

        sorted = false;

      }

    }

    for(var i = 0; i < list.length-1; i += 2)

    {

      if(list[i] > list[i+1])
```

```
        {
            swap(list, i, i+1);
            sorted = false;
        }
      }
    }
}
```

This is an example of the algorithm in C++:

```cpp
 template <class T>
void OddEvenSort (T a[], int n)
{
    for (int i = 0 ; i < n ; i++)
    {
        if (i & 1) // 'i' is odd
        {
            for (int j = 2 ; j < n ; j += 2)
            {
                if (a[j] < a[j-1])
                    swap (a[j-1], a[j]) ;
            }
        }
        else
        {
            for (int j = 1 ; j < n ; j += 2)
            {
                if (a[j] < a[j-1])
                    swap (a[j-1], a[j]) ;
            }
        }
    }
}
```

This is an example of the algorithm in php:

```php
function oddEvenSorting(&$a) {
        $n = count($a);
        $sorted = false;
```

```
        while (!$sorted) {
                $sorted = true;
                for ($i = 1; $i < ($n - 1); $i += 2) {
                        if ($a[$i] > $a[$i + 1]) {
                                list($a[$i], $a[$i + 1]) = array($a[$i + 1], $a[$i]);
                                if ($sorted) $sorted = false;
                        }
                }


                for ($i = 0; $i < ($n - 1); $i += 2) {
                        if ($a[$i] > $a[$i + 1]) {
                                list($a[$i], $a[$i + 1]) = array($a[$i + 1], $a[$i]);
                                if ($sorted) $sorted = false;
                        }
                }
        }
}
```

This is an example of the algorithm in python:

```
def oddevenSort(x):
        sorted = False
        while not sorted:
                sorted = True
                for i in range(0, len(x)-1, 2):
                        if x[i] > x[i+1]:
                                x[i], x[i+1] = x[i+1], x[i]
                                sorted = False
                for i in range(1, len(x)-1, 2):
                        if x[i] > x[i+1]:
                                x[i], x[i+1] = x[i+1], x[i]
                                sorted = False
        return x
```

This is an example of the algorithm in MATLAB/OCTAVE:

```
function x = oddevenSort(x)
sorted = false;
n = length(x);
```

```
while ~sorted

    sorted = true;

    for ii=1:2:n-1

        if x(ii) > x(ii+1)

            [x(ii), x(ii+1)] = deal(x(ii+1), x(ii));

            sorted = false;

        end

    end

    for ii=2:2:n-1

        if x(ii) > x(ii+1)

            [x(ii), x(ii+1)] = deal(x(ii+1), x(ii));

            sorted = false;

        end

    end

end
```

Proof of Correctness

Claim: Let $a_1, \ldots, a_n$ be a sequence of data ordered by $<$. The odd-even sort algorithm correctly sorts this data in n passes. (A pass here is defined to be a full sequence of odd-even, or even-odd comparisons. The passes occur in order pass 1: odd-even, pass 2: even-odd, etc.)

Proof:

This proof is based loosely on one by Thomas Worsch.

Since the sorting algorithm only involves comparison-swap operations and is oblivious (the order of comparison-swap operations does not depend on the data), by Knuth's 0-1 sorting principle, it suffices to check correctness when each a_i is either 0 or 1. Assume that there are e 1's.

Observe that the rightmost 1 can be either in an even or odd position, so it might not be moved by the first odd-even pass. But after the first odd-even pass, the rightmost 1 will be in an even position. It follows that it will be moved to the right by all remaining passes. Since the rightmost one starts in position greater than or equal to e, it must be moved at most $n - e$ steps. It follows that it takes at most $n - e + 1$ passes to move the rightmost 1 to its correct position.

Now, consider the second rightmost 1. After two passes, the 1 to its right will have moved right by at least one step. It follows that, for all remaining passes, we can view the second rightmost 1 as the rightmost 1. The second rightmost 1 starts in position at least $e - 1$ at must be moved to position at most $n - 1$, so it must be moved at most $(n-1) - (e-1) = n - e$ steps. After at most 2 passes, the rightmost 1 will have already moved, so the entry to the right of the second rightmost 1 will be 0. Hence, for all passes after the first two, the second rightmost 1 will move to the right. It thus takes at most $n - e + 2$ passes to move the second rightmost 1 to its correct position.

Continuing in this manner, by induction it can be shown that the i-th rightmost 1 is moved to its correct position in at most $n-e+i+1$ passes. It follows that the e-th rightmost 1 is moved to its correct position in at most $n-e+(e-1)+1=n$ passes (consider: counting starts at value "0"). The list is thus correctly sorted in n passes. QED.

We remark that each pass takes O(n) steps, so this algorithm is O(n^2) complexity.

Odd Even Transposition Sort

Now let us start our discussion with the definition of odd even transposition sort.

Definition. *The odd even transposition algorithm sorts a given set of n numbers where n is even in n phases. Each phase requires n/2 compare and exchange operations. It oscillates between odd and even phases successively.*

Let $< b_1, b_2, .., b_n >$ be the sequence to be sorted. During the odd phase the elements with odd num- bered subscripts are compared their neighbors on the right and exchanged if necessary. That is the elements $(b_1, b_2), (b_3, b_4)..(b_{n-1}, b_n)$ are compared and exchanged, where n is odd.

During the even phase the elements with even numbered subscripts are compared with their neighbors on the right and exchanged if necessary. That is the elements $(b_2, b_3), (b_4, b_5)..(b_{n-2}, b_{n-1})$ are compared and exchanged, where n is even. After n phases the elements are sorted

Now we will discuss an algorithm for odd even transposition sort for one dimensional mesh processor array.

Algorithm for Odd Even Transposition Sort

Procedure Odd Even Transposition (1D Mesh Processor Array)

```
Begin
for i= 1 to n/2 do
begin
for all P_k k varies from 0 to n-1 do
begin
        if j < n-1 and j%2 not equal to 0 then
temp= successor(a)
successor(a)=maximum(a,t)
a = mini-
 mum(a,t)  en-
 dif
if  j%2  equal  to  0  then
 temp=successor(a)  succes-
```

```
sor(a)=maximum(a,t)  a=min-
imum(a,t)

e n -
  dif

end

end

end
```

Example

Let n=4 and a=<5,2,1,4>

According to the algorithm i varies from 1 to 2 The processors are P_0, P_1, P_2 and P_3. Let i=1 Since 0 is even, process P_0 will compare even vertices with its successor and exchange if necessary. That is a becomes <2,5,1,4>

P_1 will compare odd vertices with its successor and exchange if necessary. That is a becomes <2,1,5,4> P_2 will make a as <1,2,4,5> and P_3 will retain a.

Next i becomes 2 but no change in a.

Hence the final sequence is <1,2,4,5>.

Merge Sort

In computer science, merge sort (also commonly spelled mergesort) is an efficient, general-purpose, comparison-based sorting algorithm. Most implementations produce a stable sort, which means that the implementation preserves the input order of equal elements in the sorted output. Mergesort is a divide and conquer algorithm that was invented by John von Neumann in 1945. A detailed description and analysis of bottom-up mergesort appeared in a report by Goldstine and Neumann as early as 1948.

Algorithm

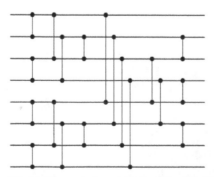

Visualization of the odd−even mergesort network with eight inputs

Conceptually, a merge sort works as follows:

1. Divide the unsorted list into n sublists, each containing 1 element (a list of 1 element is considered sorted).

2. Repeatedly merge sublists to produce new sorted sublists until there is only 1 sublist remaining. This will be the sorted list.

Top-down Implementation

Example C-like code using indices for top down merge sort algorithm that recursively splits the list (called *runs* in this example) into sublists until sublist size is 1, then merges those sublists to produce a sorted list. The copy back step is avoided with alternating the direction of the merge with each level of recursion.

```
// Array A[] has the items to sort; array B[] is a work array.
TopDownMergeSort(A[], B[], n)
{
    CopyArray(A, 0, n, B);          // duplicate array A[] into B[]
    TopDownSplitMerge(B, 0, n, A);   // sort data from B[] into A[]
}
// Sort the given run of array A[] using array B[] as a source.
// iBegin is inclusive; iEnd is exclusive (A[iEnd] is not in the set).
TopDownSplitMerge(B[], iBegin, iEnd, A[])
{
    if(iEnd - iBegin < 2)                    // if run size == 1
        return;                              //    consider it sorted
    // split the run longer than 1 item into halves
    iMiddle = (iEnd + iBegin) / 2;           // iMiddle = mid point
    // recursively sort both runs from array A[] into B[]
    TopDownSplitMerge(A, iBegin,  iMiddle, B);  // sort the left  run
    TopDownSplitMerge(A, iMiddle,    iEnd, B);  // sort the right run
    // merge the resulting runs from array B[] into A[]
    TopDownMerge(B, iBegin, iMiddle, iEnd, A);
}
//  Left source half is A[ iBegin:iMiddle-1].
// Right source half is A[iMiddle:iEnd-1   ].
// Result is           B[ iBegin:iEnd-1   ].
TopDownMerge(A[], iBegin, iMiddle, iEnd, B[])
{
```

```
        i = iBegin, j = iMiddle;

        // While there are elements in the left or right runs...

        for (k = iBegin; k < iEnd; k++) {

            // If left run head exists and is <= existing right run head.

            if (i < iMiddle && (j >= iEnd || A[i] <= A[j])) {

                B[k] = A[i];

                i = i + 1;

            } else {

                B[k] = A[j];

                j = j + 1;

            }

        }

}

CopyArray(A[], iBegin, iEnd, B[])

{

    for(k = iBegin; k < iEnd; k++)

        B[k] = A[k];

}
```

Bottom-up Implementation

Example C-like code using indices for bottom up merge sort algorithm which treats the list as an array of *n* sublists (called *runs* in this example) of size 1, and iteratively merges sub-lists back and forth between two buffers:

```
// array A[] has the items to sort; array B[] is a work array

void BottomUpMergeSort(A[], B[], n)

{

    // Each 1-element run in A is already "sorted".

    // Make successively longer sorted runs of length 2, 4, 8, 16... until whole array
is sorted.

    for (width = 1; width < n; width = 2 * width)

    {

        // Array A is full of runs of length width.

        for (i = 0; i < n; i = i + 2 * width)

        {

            // Merge two runs: A[i:i+width-1] and A[i+width:i+2*width-1] to B[]

            // or copy A[i:n-1] to B[] ( if(i+width >= n) )

            BottomUpMerge(A, i, min(i+width, n), min(i+2*width, n), B);
```

```
        }
        // Now work array B is full of runs of length 2*width.
        // Copy array B to array A for next iteration.
        // A more efficient implementation would swap the roles of A and B.
        CopyArray(B, A, n);
        // Now array A is full of runs of length 2*width.
    }
}
//  Left run is A[iLeft :iRight-1].
// Right run is A[iRight:iEnd-1  ].
BottomUpMerge(A[], iLeft, iRight, iEnd, B[])
{
    i = iLeft, j = iRight;
    // While there are elements in the left or right runs...
    for (k = iLeft; k < iEnd; k++) {
        // If left run head exists and is <= existing right run head.
        if (i < iRight && (j >= iEnd || A[i] <= A[j])) {
            B[k] = A[i];
            i = i + 1;
        } else {
            B[k] = A[j];
            j = j + 1;
        }
    }
}
void CopyArray(B[], A[], n)
{
    for(i = 0; i < n; i++)
        A[i] = B[i];
}
```

Top-down Implementation Using Lists

Pseudocode for top down merge sort algorithm which recursively divides the input list into smaller sublists until the sublists are trivially sorted, and then merges the sublists while returning up the call chain.

```
function merge_sort(list m)
    // Base case. A list of zero or one elements is sorted, by definition.
```

```
if length of m ≤ 1 then
    return m
// Recursive case. First, divide the list into equal-sized sublists
// consisting of the first half and second half of the list.
// This assumes lists start at index 0.
var left := empty list
var right := empty list
for each x with index i in m do
    if i < (length of m)/2 then
        add x to left
    else
        add x to right
// Recursively sort both sublists.
left := merge_sort(left)
right := merge_sort(right)
// Then merge the now-sorted sublists.
return merge(left, right)
```

In this example, the merge function merges the left and right sublists.

```
function merge(left, right)
    var result := empty list
    while left is not empty and right is not empty do
        if first(left) ≤ first(right) then
            append first(left) to result
            left := rest(left)
        else
            append first(right) to result
            right := rest(right)
    // Either left or right may have elements left; consume them.
    // (Only one of the following loops will actually be entered.)
    while left is not empty do
        append first(left) to result
        left := rest(left)
    while right is not empty do
        append first(right) to result
        right := rest(right)
    return result
```

Bottom-up Implementation Using Lists

Pseudocode for bottom up merge sort algorithm which uses a small fixed size array of references to nodes, where array[i] is either a reference to a list of size 2 ^{i} or 0. *node* is a reference or pointer to a node. The merge() function would be similar to the one shown in the top down merge lists example, it merges two already sorted lists, and handles empty lists. In this case, merge() would use *node* for its input parameters and return value.

```
function merge_sort(node head)

    // return if empty list

    if (head == nil)

        return nil

    var node array; initially all nil

    var node result

    var node next

    var int  i

    result = head

    // merge nodes into array

    while (result != nil)

        next = result.next;

        result.next = nil

        for(i = 0; (i < 32) && (array[i] != nil); i += 1)

            result = merge(array[i], result)

            array[i] = nil

        // do not go past end of array

        if (i == 32)

            i -= 1

        array[i] = result

        result = next

    // merge array into single list

    result = nil

    for (i = 0; i < 32; i += 1)

        result = merge(array[i], result)

    return result
```

Natural Merge Sort

A natural merge sort is similar to a bottom up merge sort except that any naturally occurring runs (sorted sequences) in the input are exploited. Both monotonic and bitonic (alternating up/down) runs may be exploited, with lists (or equivalently tapes or files) being convenient data structures (used as FIFO queues or LIFO stacks). In the bottom up merge sort, the starting point assumes each run is one item long. In practice, random input data will have many short runs that just happen to be sorted. In the typical case, the natural merge sort may not need as many passes because there are fewer runs to merge. In the best case, the input is already sorted (i.e., is one run), so the natural merge sort need only make one pass through the data. In many practical cases, long natural runs are present, and for that reason natural merge sort is exploited as the key component of Timsort. Example:

```
Start        : 3--4--2--1--7--5--8--9--0--6

Select runs : 3--4   2   1--7   5--8--9   0--6

Merge        : 2--3--4   1--5--7--8--9   0--6

Merge        : 1--2--3--4--5--7--8--9   0--6

Merge        : 0--1--2--3--4--5--6--7--8--9
```

Tournament replacement selection sorts are used to gather the initial runs for external sorting algorithms.

Analysis

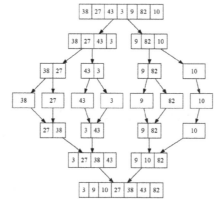

A recursive merge sort algorithm used to sort an array of 7 integer values. These are the steps a human would take to emulate merge sort (top-down).

In sorting n objects, merge sort has an average and worst-case performance of $O(n \log n)$. If the running time of merge sort for a list of length n is $T(n)$, then the recurrence $T(n) = 2T(n/2) + n$ follows from the definition of the algorithm (apply the algorithm to two lists of half the size of the original list, and add the n steps taken to merge the resulting two lists). The closed form follows from the master theorem.

In the worst case, the number of comparisons merge sort makes is equal to or slightly smaller than $(n \lceil \lg n \rceil - 2^{\lceil \lg n \rceil} + 1)$, which is between $(n \lg n - n + 1)$ and $(n \lg n + n + O(\lg n))$.

For large n and a randomly ordered input list, merge sort's expected (average) number of comparisons approaches $\alpha \cdot n$ fewer than the worst case where $\alpha = -1 + \sum_{k=0}^{\infty} \frac{1}{2^k + 1} \approx 0.2645$.

In the *worst* case, merge sort does about 39% fewer comparisons than quicksort does in the *aver-*

age case. In terms of moves, merge sort's worst case complexity is $O(n \log n)$—the same complexity as quicksort's best case, and merge sort's best case takes about half as many iterations as the worst case.

Merge sort is more efficient than quicksort for some types of lists if the data to be sorted can only be efficiently accessed sequentially, and is thus popular in languages such as Lisp, where sequentially accessed data structures are very common. Unlike some (efficient) implementations of quicksort, merge sort is a stable sort.

Merge sort's most common implementation does not sort in place; therefore, the memory size of the input must be allocated for the sorted output to be stored in.

Variants

Variants of merge sort are primarily concerned with reducing the space complexity and the cost of copying.

A simple alternative for reducing the space overhead to $n/2$ is to maintain *left* and *right* as a combined structure, copy only the *left* part of m into temporary space, and to direct the *merge* routine to place the merged output into m. With this version it is better to allocate the temporary space outside the *merge* routine, so that only one allocation is needed. The excessive copying mentioned previously is also mitigated, since the last pair of lines before the *return result* statement (function *merge* in the pseudo code above) become superfluous.

One drawback of merge sort, when implemented on arrays, is its $O(n)$ working memory requirement. Several in-place variants have been suggested:

- Katajainen *et al.* present an algorithm that requires a constant amount of working memory: enough storage space to hold one element of the input array, and additional space to hold $O(1)$ pointers into the input array. They achieve an $O(n \log n)$ time bound with small constants, but their algorithm is not stable.

- Several attempts have been made at producing an *in-place merge* algorithm that can be combined with a standard (top-down or bottom-up) merge sort to produce an in-place merge sort. In this case, the notion of "in-place" can be relaxed to mean "taking logarithmic stack space", because standard merge sort requires that amount of space for its own stack usage. It was shown by Geffert *et al.* that in-place, stable merging is possible in $O(n \log n)$ time using a constant amount of scratch space, but their algorithm is complicated and has high constant factors: merging arrays of length n and m can take $5n + 12m + o(m)$ moves. This high constant factor and complicated in-place algorithm was made simpler and easier to understand. Bing-Chao Huang and Michael A. Langston presented a straightforward linear time algorithm *practical in-place merge* to merge a sorted list using fixed amount of additional space. They both have used the work of Kronrod and others. It merges in linear time and constant extra space. The algorithm takes little more average time than standard merge sort algorithms, free to exploit O(n) temporary extra memory cells, by less than a factor of two. Though the algorithm is much faster in practical way but it is unstable also for some list. But using similar concept they have been able to solve this problem. Other in-place algorithms include SymMerge, which takes $O((n + m) \log (n + m))$ time in total. Plugging such an algorithm into merge sort increases its complexity to the non-linearithmic, but still quasilinear, $O(n (\log n)^2)$.

An alternative to reduce the copying into multiple lists is to associate a new field of information with each key (the elements in m are called keys). This field will be used to link the keys and any associated information together in a sorted list (a key and its related information is called a record). Then the merging of the sorted lists proceeds by changing the link values; no records need to be moved at all. A field which contains only a link will generally be smaller than an entire record so less space will also be used. This is a standard sorting technique, not restricted to merge sort.

Use with Tape Drives

Merge sort type algorithms allowed large data sets to be sorted on early computers that had small random access memories by modern standards. Records were stored on magnetic tape and processed on banks of magnetic tape drives, such as these IBM 729s.

An external merge sort is practical to run using disk or tape drives when the data to be sorted is too large to fit into memory. External sorting explains how merge sort is implemented with disk drives. A typical tape drive sort uses four tape drives. All I/O is sequential (except for rewinds at the end of each pass). A minimal implementation can get by with just 2 record buffers and a few program variables.

Naming the four tape drives as A, B, C, D, with the original data on A, and using only 2 record buffers, the algorithm is similar to Bottom-up implementation, using pairs of tape drives instead of arrays in memory. The basic algorithm can be described as follows:

1. Merge pairs of records from A; writing two-record sublists alternately to C and D.

2. Merge two-record sublists from C and D into four-record sublists; writing these alternately to A and B.

3. Merge four-record sublists from A and B into eight-record sublists; writing these alternately to C and D

4. Repeat until you have one list containing all the data, sorted—in $\log_2(n)$ passes.

Instead of starting with very short runs, usually a hybrid algorithm is used, where the initial pass will read many records into memory, do an internal sort to create a long run, and then distribute those long runs onto the output set. The step avoids many early passes. For example, an internal sort of 1024 records will save 9 passes. The internal sort is often large because it has such a benefit. In fact, there are techniques that can make the initial runs longer than the available internal memory.

A more sophisticated merge sort that optimizes tape (and disk) drive usage is the polyphase merge sort.

Optimizing Merge Sort

On modern computers, locality of reference can be of paramount importance in software optimization, because multilevel memory hierarchies are used. Cache-aware versions of the merge sort algorithm, whose operations have been specifically chosen to minimize the movement of pages in and out of a machine's memory cache, have been proposed. For example, the tiled merge sort algorithm stops partitioning subarrays when subarrays of size S are reached, where S is the number of data items fitting into a CPU's cache. Each of these subarrays is sorted with an in-place sorting algorithm such as insertion sort, to discourage memory swaps, and normal merge sort is then completed in the standard recursive fashion. This algorithm has demonstrated better performance on machines that benefit from cache optimization. (LaMarca & Ladner 1997)

Kronrod (1969) suggested an alternative version of merge sort that uses constant additional space. This algorithm was later refined. (Katajainen, Pasanen & Teuhola 1996)

Also, many applications of external sorting use a form of merge sorting where the input get split up to a higher number of sublists, ideally to a number for which merging them still makes the currently processed set of pages fit into main memory.

Parallel Merge Sort

Merge sort parallelizes well due to use of the divide-and-conquer method. Several parallel variants are discussed in the third edition of Cormen, Leiserson, Rivest, and Stein's *Introduction to Algorithms*. The first of these can be very easily expressed in a pseudocode with fork and join keywords:

```
// Sort elements lo through hi (exclusive) of array A.

algorithm mergesort(A, lo, hi) is

    if lo+1 < hi then  // Two or more elements.

        mid = ⌊(lo + hi) / 2⌋

        fork mergesort(A, lo, mid)

        mergesort(A, mid, hi)

        join

        merge(A, lo, mid, hi)
```

This algorithm is a trivial modification from the serial version, and its speedup is not impressive: when executed on an infinite number of processors, it runs in $\Theta(n)$ time, which is only a $\Theta(\log n)$ improvement on the serial version. A better result can be obtained by using a parallelized merge algorithm, which gives parallelism $\Theta(n / (\log n)^2)$, meaning that this type of parallel merge sort runs in

$$\Theta\left((n\log n)\cdot\frac{(\log n)^2}{n} \right) = \Theta((\log n)^3)$$

time if enough processors are available. Such a sort can perform well in practice when combined with a fast stable sequential sort, such as insertion sort, and a fast sequential merge as a base case for merging small arrays.

Merge sort was one of the first sorting algorithms where optimal speed up was achieved, with Richard Cole using a clever subsampling algorithm to ensure $O(1)$ merge. Other sophisticated parallel sorting algorithms can achieve the same or better time bounds with a lower constant. For example, in 1991 David Powers described a parallelized quicksort (and a related radix sort) that can operate in $O(\log n)$ time on a CRCW parallel random-access machine (PRAM) with n processors by performing partitioning implicitly. Powers further shows that a pipelined version of Batcher's Bitonic Mergesort at $O((\log n)^2)$ time on a butterfly sorting network is in practice actually faster than his $O(\log n)$ sorts on a PRAM, and he provides detailed discussion of the hidden overheads in comparison, radix and parallel sorting.

Comparison with Other Sort Algorithms

Although heapsort has the same time bounds as merge sort, it requires only $\Theta(1)$ auxiliary space instead of merge sort's $\Theta(n)$. On typical modern architectures, efficient quicksort implementations generally outperform mergesort for sorting RAM-based arrays. On the other hand, merge sort is a stable sort and is more efficient at handling slow-to-access sequential media. Merge sort is often the best choice for sorting a linked list: in this situation it is relatively easy to implement a merge sort in such a way that it requires only $\Theta(1)$ extra space, and the slow random-access performance of a linked list makes some other algorithms (such as quicksort) perform poorly, and others (such as heapsort) completely impossible.

As of Perl 5.8, merge sort is its default sorting algorithm (it was quicksort in previous versions of Perl). In Java, the Arrays.sort() methods use merge sort or a tuned quicksort depending on the datatypes and for implementation efficiency switch to insertion sort when fewer than seven array elements are being sorted. The linux kernel uses merge sort for its linked lists. Python uses Timsort, another tuned hybrid of merge sort and insertion sort, that has become the standard sort algorithm in Java SE 7, on the Android platform, and in GNU Octave.

References

- Katajainen, Jyrki; Pasanen, Tomi; Teuhola, Jukka (1996). "Practical in-place mergesort". Nordic Journal of Computing. 3. pp. 27–40. ISSN 1236-6064. Retrieved 2009-04-04

- Graham, R.L., Grötschel M., and Lovász L., eds. (1996). Handbook of Combinatorics, Volumes 1 and 2. Elsevier (North-Holland), Amsterdam, and MIT Press, Cambridge, Mass. ISBN 0-262-07169-X

- Joseph, George Gheverghese (1994) [1991]. The Crest of the Peacock: Non-European Roots of Mathematics (2nd ed.). London: Penguin Books. ISBN 0-14-012529-9

- Stanley, Richard P. (1997, 1999). Enumerative Combinatorics, Volumes 1 and 2. Cambridge University Press. ISBN 0-521-55309-1, ISBN 0-521-56069-1

- Wilf, Herbert S. (1994). Generatingfunctionology (2nd ed.). Boston, MA: Academic Press. ISBN 0-12-751956-4. Zbl 0831.05001

- S. Lakshmivarahan; S. K. Dhall & L. L. Miller (1984), Franz L. Alt and Marshall C. Yovits, eds., "Parallel Sorting Algorithms", Advances in computers, Academic Press, 23: 295–351, ISBN 978-0-12-012123-6

- Robert Sedgewick (2003). Algorithms in Java, Parts 1-4 (3rd ed.). Addison-Wesley Professional. pp. 454–464. ISBN 978-0-201-36120-9

- Allen Kent and James G. Williams (1993). Encyclopedia of Computer Science and Technology: Supplement 14. CRC Press. pp. 33–38. ISBN 978-0-8247-2282-1

- Cormen, Thomas H.; Leiserson, Charles E.; Rivest, Ronald L.; Stein, Clifford (2009) [1990]. Introduction to Algorithms (3rd ed.). MIT Press and McGraw-Hill. ISBN 0-262-03384-4

- Knuth, Donald (1998). "Section 5.2.4: Sorting by Merging". Sorting and Searching. The Art of Computer Programming. 3 (2nd ed.). Addison-Wesley. pp. 158–168. ISBN 0-201-89685-0

Search and Selection Algorithm: An Essential Aspect

Searching for something in a database is a basic function that a computer performs. People search the Internet for content everyday. A search algorithm performs the required function by finding data in a database. The process takes place in sorted, unsorted and random sequences. The section closely examines the key concepts of searching and selection by algorithm to provide an extensive understanding of the subject.

Search Algorithm

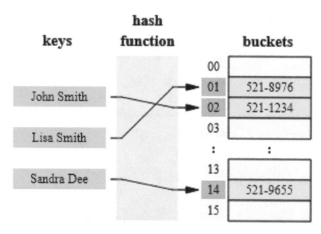

Visual representation of a hash table, a data structure that allows for fast retrieval of information.

In computer science, a search algorithm is an algorithm that retrieves information stored within some data structure. Data structures can include linked lists, arrays, search trees, hash tables, or various other storage methods. The appropriate search algorithm often depends on the data structure being searched. Searching also encompasses algorithms that query the data structure, such as the SQL SELECT command.

Search algorithms can be classified based on their mechanism of searching. Linear search algorithms check every record for the one associated with a target key in a linear fashion. Binary, or half interval searches, repeatedly target the center of the search structure and divide the search space in half. Comparison search algorithms improve on linear searching by successively eliminating records based on comparisons of the keys until the target record is found, and can be applied on data structures with a defined order. Digital search algorithms work based on the properties of digits in data structures that use numerical keys. Finally, hashing directly maps keys to records based on a hash function. Searches outside of a linear search require that the data be sorted in some way.

Search functions are also evaluated on the basis of their complexity, or maximum theoretical run time. Binary search functions, for example, have a maximum complexity of O(log(n)), or logarithmic time. This means that the maximum number of operations needed to find the search target is a logarithmic function of the size of the search space.

Classes

For Virtual Search Spaces

Algorithms for searching virtual spaces are used in constraint satisfaction problem, where the goal is to find a set of value assignments to certain variables that will satisfy specific mathematical equations and inequations / inequalities. They are also used when the goal is to find a variable assignment that will maximize or minimize a certain function of those variables. Algorithms for these problems include the basic brute-force search (also called "naïve" or "uninformed" search), and a variety of heuristics that try to exploit partial knowledge about structure of the space, such as linear relaxation, constraint generation, and constraint propagation.

An important subclass are the local search methods, that view the elements of the search space as the vertices of a graph, with edges defined by a set of heuristics applicable to the case; and scan the space by moving from item to item along the edges, for example according to the steepest descent or best-first criterion, or in a stochastic search. This category includes a great variety of general metaheuristic methods, such as simulated annealing, tabu search, A-teams, and genetic programming, that combine arbitrary heuristics in specific ways.

This class also includes various tree search algorithms, that view the elements as vertices of a tree, and traverse that tree in some special order. Examples of the latter include the exhaustive methods such as depth-first search and breadth-first search, as well as various heuristic-based search tree pruning methods such as backtracking and branch and bound. Unlike general metaheuristics, which at best work only in a probabilistic sense, many of these tree-search methods are guaranteed to find the exact or optimal solution, if given enough time. This is called "completeness".

Another important sub-class consists of algorithms for exploring the game tree of multiple-player games, such as chess or backgammon, whose nodes consist of all possible game situations that could result from the current situation. The goal in these problems is to find the move that provides the best chance of a win, taking into account all possible moves of the opponent(s). Similar problems occur when humans or machines have to make successive decisions whose outcomes are not entirely under one's control, such as in robot guidance or in marketing, financial, or military strategy planning. This kind of problem — combinatorial search — has been extensively studied in the context of artificial intelligence. Examples of algorithms for this class are the minimax algorithm, alpha–beta pruning, * Informational search and the A* algorithm.

For Sub-structures of a Given Structure

The name combinatorial search is generally used for algorithms that look for a specific sub-structure of a given discrete structure, such as a graph, a string, a finite group, and so on. The term combinatorial optimization is typically used when the goal is to find a sub-structure with a maximum (or minimum) value of some parameter. Since the sub-structure is usually represented in the computer by a set of integer variables with constraints, these problems can be viewed as special cases of constraint satisfaction or discrete optimization; but they are usually formulated and solved in a more abstract setting where the internal representation is not explicitly mentioned.

An important and extensively studied subclass are the graph algorithms, in particular graph traversal algorithms, for finding specific sub-structures in a given graph — such as subgraphs, paths, circuits, and so on. Examples include Dijkstra's algorithm, Kruskal's algorithm, the nearest neighbour algorithm, and Prim's algorithm.

Another important subclass of this category are the string searching algorithms, that search for patterns within strings. Two famous examples are the Boyer–Moore and Knuth–Morris–Pratt algorithms, and several algorithms based on the suffix tree data structure.

Search for the Maximum of a Function

In 1953, American statistician Jack Kiefer devised Fibonacci search which can be used to find the maximum of a unimodal function and has many other applications in computer science.

For Quantum Computers

There are also search methods designed for quantum computers, like Corley's algorithm, that are theoretically faster than linear or brute-force search even without the help of data structures or heuristics.

Searching in a Sorted Sequence in Parallel

Computer systems are often used to store large amounts of data from which individual records must be retrieved according to some search criterion. Thus the efficient storage of data to facilitate fast searching is an important issue. Everyday all search for something or other. Users generally browse the net for contents. This is a typical search handled by the search engine. In the case of organized data, we search for the data set. Searching may occur both in a sorted sequence or unsorted or random sequence.

The algorithm consists of a array where there are n elements. Let S be the array in which the data is stored. Let p be the number of processors used for searching. Generally $p<n$.

Algorithm Parallelsearch(S,n,y)

Input:- A sorted array $S=x_1, x_2, x_3 \dots x_n$ consisting of n elements.

A query element y.

Output:- y and its position in the corresponding sub array.
Decompose the array into P+1 equal parts.

Then a processor check if $y < x_k$ the last element in the sub array.

If $y<x_k$ the right sub arrays are ignored else the left sub array is ignored. Anyway at one point we choose the left sub array or the right sub array.

Thus we keep on reducing the elements for search since it is sorted. Finally we arrive at P from where we can directly search p.

The complexity of parallel searching algorithm is O(log(n+1)/log(p+1))

Example:-

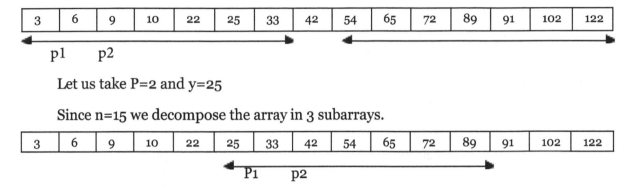

Let us take P=2 and y=25

Since n=15 we decompose the array in 3 subarrays.

3	6	9	10	22	25	33	42	54	65	72	89	91	102	122

P1   p2

Thus the element 25 is located by p1.

Searching on a Random Sequence in Parallel

In the information age, the huge amount of information and data available and exchanged, require a fast and efficient searching mechanisms for effective use of this information. Generally, to find an item in an unordered array of size n, it's used one of the following approaches: Scans all the values that require O (n) time. Using a sorting algorithm like Quicksort, Bubble sort, Binary Tree sort that varies in complexity from O (n log n) in the best case to O (n^2) in the worst case. Moreover, the memory usage for searching these items varies from O (1) to O (log n).

Using Heapsort that performs better than Quicksort or other sorting algorithms, it takes O (n log n) in the worst and best case, a searching mechanism is used subsequently to find the location of the searched item. Searching algorithms are techniques used to make the searching of an information in any field fast and more efficient. Searching problem is defined as follow: given an input x determines whether there exists a y such that f (x, y) is true.

Binary search is an algorithm for locating the position of an element x in a sorted list. It starts by dividing the array into subarrays L, R. Then, a comparison between the value of x and the values of the first elements in each subarray is done and to define in which subarray the searching process must start. This procedure (splitting and comparing) continues until finding the requested item (this procedure continue at most log n time). The idea on which the binary search algorithm based on is to reduce the searching space each time by a factor of two, the worst case performance of binary searching is log n for an input array of size n.

Parallel search or multithread search (SMP) is a way to increase search speed by using additional processors. Utilizing these additional processors is an interesting domain of research. SMP algorithms are classified by their scalability (that means the behavior of the algorithm as the number of processors become large) and their speed up. The speed up is defined as the ratio of the running time of the sequential execution to the running time of the parallel execution. It is mostly used as an indicator for a parallel program's performance.

Sequential Parallel Search Algorithm

Input:- An unsorted array S and the search element y.

Ouput:- The position of y

Selection Algorithm

In computer science, a selection algorithm is an algorithm for finding the kth smallest number in a list or array; such a number is called the kth *order statistic*. This includes the cases of finding the minimum, maximum, and median elements. There are $O(n)$ (worst-case linear time) selection algorithms, and sublinear performance is possible for structured data; in the extreme, $O(1)$ for an array of sorted data. Selection is a subproblem of more complex problems like the nearest neighbor and shortest path problems. Many selection algorithms are derived by generalizing a sorting algorithm, and conversely some sorting algorithms can be derived as repeated application of selection.

The simplest case of a selection algorithm is finding the minimum (or maximum) element by iterating through the list, keeping track of the running minimum – the minimum so far – (or maximum) and can be seen as related to the selection sort. Conversely, the hardest case of a selection algorithm is finding the median, and this necessarily takes $n/2$ storage. In fact, a specialized median-selection algorithm can be used to build a general selection algorithm, as in median of medians. The best-known selection algorithm is quickselect, which is related to quicksort; like quicksort, it has (asymptotically) optimal average performance, but poor worst-case performance, though it can be modified to give optimal worst-case performance as well.

Selection by Sorting

By sorting the list or array then selecting the desired element, selection can be reduced to sorting. This method is inefficient for selecting a single element, but is efficient when many selections need to be made from an array, in which case only one initial, expensive sort is needed, followed by many cheap selection operations – $O(1)$ for an array, though selection is $O(n)$ in a linked list, even if sorted, due to lack of random access. In general, sorting requires $O(n \log n)$ time, where n is the length of the list, although a lower bound is possible with non-comparative sorting algorithms like radix sort and counting sort.

Rather than sorting the whole list or array, one can instead use partial sorting to select the k smallest or k largest elements. The kth smallest (resp., kth largest element) is then the largest (resp., smallest element) of the partially sorted list – this then takes $O(1)$ to access in an array and $O(k)$ to access in a list. This is more efficient than full sorting, but less efficient than simply selecting, and takes $O(n + k \log k)$ time, due to the sorting of the k elements. Partial sorting algorithms can often be derived from (total) sorting algorithms. As with total sorting, partial sorting means that further selections (below the kth element) can be done in $O(1)$ time for an array and $O(k)$ time for a list. Further, if the partial sorting also partitions the original data into "sorted" and "unsorted", as with an in-place sort, the partial sort can be extended to a larger partial sort by only sorting the incremental portion, and if this is done, further selections above the kth element can also be done relatively cheaply.

Unordered Partial Sorting

If partial sorting is relaxed so that the k smallest elements are returned, but not in order, the factor of $O(k \log k)$ can be eliminated. An additional maximum selection (taking $O(k)$ time) is required, but since $k \leq n$, this still yields asymptotic complexity of $O(n)$. In fact, partition-based selection algorithms yield both the kth smallest element itself and the k smallest elements (with other elements not in order). This can be done in $O(n)$ time – average complexity of quickselect, and worst-case complexity of refined partition-based selection algorithms.

Conversely, given a selection algorithm, one can easily get an unordered partial sort (k smallest elements, not in order) in $O(n)$ time by iterating through the list and recording all elements less than the kth element. If this results in fewer than $k - 1$ elements, any remaining elements equal the kth element. Care must be taken, due to the possibility of equality of elements: one must not include all elements less than *or equal to* the kth element, as elements greater than the kth element may also be equal to it.

Thus unordered partial sorting (lowest k elements, but not ordered) and selection of the kth element are very similar problems. Not only do they have the same asymptotic complexity, $O(n)$, but a solution to either one can be converted into a solution to the other by a straightforward algorithm (finding a max of k elements, or filtering elements of a list below a cutoff of the value of the kth element).

Partial Selection Sort

A simple example of selection by partial sorting is to use the partial selection sort.

The obvious linear time algorithm to find the minimum (resp. maximum) – iterating over the list and keeping track of the minimum (resp. maximum) element so far – can be seen as a partial selection sort that selects the 1 smallest element. However, many other partial sorts also reduce to this algorithm for the case $k = 1$, such as a partial heap sort.

More generally, a partial selection sort yields a simple selection algorithm which takes $O(kn)$ time. This is asymptotically inefficient, but can be sufficiently efficient if k is small, and is easy to implement. Concretely, we simply find the minimum value and move it to the beginning, repeating on the remaining list until we have accumulated k elements, and then return the kth element. Here is partial selection sort-based algorithm:

```
function select(list[1..n], k)
    for i from 1 to k
        minIndex = i
        minValue = list[i]
        for j from i+1 to n
            if list[j] < minValue
                minIndex = j
                minValue = list[j]
```

```
    swap list[i] and list[minIndex]
return list[k]
```

Partition-based Selection

Linear performance can be achieved by a partition-based selection algorithm, most basically quick-select. Quickselect is a variant of quicksort – in both one chooses a pivot and then partitions the data by it, but while Quicksort recurses on both sides of the partition, Quickselect only recurses on one side, namely the side on which the desired kth element is. As with Quicksort, this has optimal average performance, in this case linear, but poor worst-case performance, in this case quadratic. This occurs for instance by taking the first element as the pivot and searching for the maximum element, if the data is already sorted. In practice this can be avoided by choosing a random element as pivot, which yields almost certain linear performance. Alternatively, a more careful deterministic pivot strategy can be used, such as median of medians. These are combined in the hybrid introselect algorithm (analogous to introsort), which starts with Quickselect but falls back to median of medians if progress is slow, resulting in both fast average performance and optimal worst-case performance. The average time complexity performance is $O(n)$.

The partition-based algorithms are generally done in place, which thus results in partially sorting the data. They can be done out of place, not changing the original data, at the cost of $O(n)$ additional space.

Median Selection as Pivot Strategy

A median-selection algorithm can be used to yield a general selection algorithm or sorting algorithm, by applying it as the pivot strategy in Quickselect or Quicksort; if the median-selection algorithm is asymptotically optimal (linear-time), the resulting selection or sorting algorithm is as well. In fact, an exact median is not necessary – an approximate median is sufficient. In the median of medians selection algorithm, the pivot strategy computes an approximate median and uses this as pivot, recursing on a smaller set to compute this pivot. In practice the overhead of pivot computation is significant, so these algorithms are generally not used, but this technique is of theoretical interest in relating selection and sorting algorithms.

In detail, given a median-selection algorithm, one can use it as a pivot strategy in Quickselect, obtaining a selection algorithm. If the median-selection algorithm is optimal, meaning $O(n)$, then the resulting general selection algorithm is also optimal, again meaning linear. This is because Quickselect is a decrease and conquer algorithm, and using the median at each pivot means that at each step the search set decreases by half in size, so the overall complexity is a geometric series times the complexity of each step, and thus simply a constant times the complexity of a single step, in fact $2=1/(1-(1/2))$ times (summing the series).

Similarly, given a median-selection algorithm or general selection algorithm applied to find the median, one can use it as a pivot strategy in Quicksort, obtaining a sorting algorithm. If the selection algorithm is optimal, meaning $O(n)$, then the resulting sorting algorithm is optimal, meaning $O(n \log n)$. The median is the best pivot for sorting, as it evenly divides the data, and thus guarantees optimal sorting, assuming the selection algorithm is optimal. A sorting analog to median of medians exists, using the pivot strategy (approximate median) in Quicksort, and similarly yields an optimal Quicksort.

Incremental Sorting by Selection

Converse to selection by sorting, one can incrementally sort by repeated selection. Abstractly, selection only yields a single element, the kth element. However, practical selection algorithms frequently involve partial sorting, or can be modified to do so. Selecting by partial sorting naturally does so, sorting the elements up to k, and selecting by partitioning also sorts some elements: the pivots are sorted to the correct positions, with the kth element being the final pivot, and the elements between the pivots have values between the pivot values. The difference between partition-based selection and partition-based sorting, as in quickselect versus quicksort, is that in selection one recurses on only one side of each pivot, sorting only the pivots (an average of $\log(n)$ pivots are used), rather than recursing on both sides of the pivot.

This can be used to speed up subsequent selections on the same data; in the extreme, a fully sorted array allows $O(1)$ selection. Further, compared with first doing a full sort, incrementally sorting by repeated selection amortizes the sorting cost over multiple selections.

For partially sorted data (up to k), so long as the partially sorted data and the index k up to which the data is sorted are recorded, subsequent selections of j less than or equal to k can simply select the jth element, as it is already sorted, while selections of j greater than k only need to sort the elements above the kth position.

For partitioned data, if the list of pivots is stored (for example, in a sorted list of the indices), then subsequent selections only need to select in the interval between two pivots (the nearest pivots below and above). The biggest gain is from the top-level pivots, which eliminate costly large partitions: a single pivot near the middle of the data cuts the time for future selections in half. The pivot list will grow over subsequent selections, as the data becomes more sorted, and can even be passed to a partition-based sort as the basis of a full sort.

Using Data Structures to Select in Sublinear Time

Given an unorganized list of data, linear time ($\Omega(n)$) is required to find the minimum element, because we have to examine every element (otherwise, we might miss it). If we organize the list, for example by keeping it sorted at all times, then selecting the kth largest element is trivial, but then insertion requires linear time, as do other operations such as combining two lists.

The strategy to find an order statistic in sublinear time is to store the data in an organized fashion using suitable data structures that facilitate the selection. Two such data structures are tree-based structures and frequency tables.

When only the minimum (or maximum) is needed, a good approach is to use a heap, which is able to find the minimum (or maximum) element in constant time, while all other operations, including insertion, are $O(\log n)$ or better. More generally, a self-balancing binary search tree can easily be augmented to make it possible to both insert an element and find the kth largest element in $O(\log n)$ time; this is called an *order statistic tree*. We simply store in each node a count of how many descendants it has, and use this to determine which path to follow. The information can be updated efficiently since adding a node only affects the counts of its $O(\log n)$ ancestors, and tree rotations only affect the counts of the nodes involved in the rotation.

Another simple strategy is based on some of the same concepts as the hash table. When we know the range of values beforehand, we can divide that range into h subintervals and assign these to h buckets. When we insert an element, we add it to the bucket corresponding to the interval it falls in. To find the minimum or maximum element, we scan from the beginning or end for the first nonempty bucket and find the minimum or maximum element in that bucket. In general, to find the kth element, we maintain a count of the number of elements in each bucket, then scan the buckets from left to right adding up counts until we find the bucket containing the desired element, then use the expected linear-time algorithm to find the correct element in that bucket.

If we choose h of size roughly sqrt(n), and the input is close to uniformly distributed, this scheme can perform selections in expected O(sqrt(n)) time. Unfortunately, this strategy is also sensitive to clustering of elements in a narrow interval, which may result in buckets with large numbers of elements (clustering can be eliminated through a good hash function, but finding the element with the kth largest hash value isn't very useful). Additionally, like hash tables this structure requires table resizings to maintain efficiency as elements are added and n becomes much larger than h^2. A useful case of this is finding an order statistic or extremum in a finite range of data. Using above table with bucket interval 1 and maintaining counts in each bucket is much superior to other methods. Such hash tables are like frequency tables used to classify the data in descriptive statistics.

Lower Bounds

In *The Art of Computer Programming*, Donald E. Knuth discussed a number of lower bounds for the number of comparisons required to locate the t smallest entries of an unorganized list of n items (using only comparisons). There is a trivial lower bound of $n - 1$ for the minimum or maximum entry. To see this, consider a tournament where each game represents one comparison. Since every player except the winner of the tournament must lose a game before we know the winner, we have a lower bound of $n - 1$ comparisons.

The story becomes more complex for other indexes. We define $W_t(n)$ as the minimum number of comparisons required to find the t smallest values. Knuth references a paper published by S. S. Kislitsyn, which shows an upper bound on this value:

$$W_t(n) \leq n - t + \sum_{n+1-t < j \leq n} \lceil \log_2 j \rceil \quad \text{for } n \geq t$$

This bound is achievable for $t=2$ but better, more complex bounds are known for larger t.

Space Complexity

The required space complexity of selection is easily seen to be $k + O(1)$ (or $n - k$ if $k > n/2$), and in-place algorithms can select with only O(1) additional storage. k storage is necessary as the following data illustrates: start with 1, 2, ..., k, then continue with $k + 1$, $k + 1$, ..., $k + 1$, and finally finish with j copies of 0, where j is from 0 to $k - 1$. In this case the kth smallest element is one of 1, 2, ..., k, depending on the number of 0s, but this can only be determined at the end. One must store the initial k elements until near the end, since one cannot reduce the number of possibilities below the lowest k values until there are fewer than k elements left. Note that selecting the minimum (or maximum) by tracking the running minimum is a special case of this, with $k = 1$.

This space complexity is achieved by doing a progressive partial sort – tracking a sorted list of the lowest k elements so far, such as by the partial insertion sort above. Note however that selection by partial sorting, while space-efficient, has superlinear time complexity, and that time-efficient partition-based selection algorithms require $O(n)$ space.

This space complexity bound helps explain the close connection between selecting the kth element and selecting the (unordered) lowest k elements, as it shows that selecting the kth element effectively requires selecting the lowest k elements as an intermediate step.

Space complexity is particularly an issue when k is a fixed fraction of n, particularly for computing the median, where $k = n/2$, and in on-line algorithms. The space complexity can be reduced at the cost of only obtaining an approximate answer, or correct answer with certain probability; these are discussed below.

Online Selection Algorithm

Online selection may refer narrowly to computing the kth smallest element of a stream, in which case partial sorting algorithms (with $k + O(1)$) space for the k smallest elements so far) can be used, but partition-based algorithms cannot be.

Alternatively, selection itself may be required to be online, that is, an element can only be selected from a sequential input at the instance of observation and each selection, respectively refusal, is irrevocable. The problem is to select, under these constraints, a specific element of the input sequence (as for example the largest or the smallest value) with largest probability. This problem can be tackled by the Odds algorithm, which yields the optimal under an independence condition; it is also optimal itself as an algorithm with the number of computations being linear in the length of input.

The simplest example is the secretary problem of choosing the maximum with high probability, in which case optimal strategy (on random data) is to track the running maximum of the first n/e elements and reject them, and then select the first element that is higher than this maximum.

Related Problems

One may generalize the selection problem to apply to ranges within a list, yielding the problem of range queries. The question of range median queries (computing the medians of multiple ranges) has been analyzed.

Language Support

Very few languages have built-in support for general selection, although many provide facilities for finding the smallest or largest element of a list. A notable exception is C++, which provides a templated nth_element method with a guarantee of expected linear time, and also partitions the data, requiring that the nth element be sorted into its correct place, elements before the nth element are less than it, and elements after the nth element are greater than it. It is implied but not required that it is based on Hoare's algorithm (or some variant) by its requirement of expected linear time and partitioning of data.

For Perl, the module Sort::Key::Top, available from CPAN, provides a set of functions to select the top n elements from a list using several orderings and custom key extraction procedures. Furthermore, the Statistics::CaseResampling module provides a function to calculate quantiles using quickselect.

Python's standard library (since 2.4) includes heapq.nsmallest() and nlargest(), returning sorted lists, in O($n \log k$) time.

Because language support for sorting is more ubiquitous, the simplistic approach of sorting followed by indexing is preferred in many environments despite its disadvantage in speed. Indeed, for lazy languages, this simplistic approach can even achieve the best complexity possible for the k smallest/greatest sorted (with maximum/minimum as a special case) if the sort is lazy enough.

Sequential Selection Algorithm

Selection algorithm is used to find the Kth smallest element in the data set. The selection algorithm takes two parameters: the selection element and an array or list. Let the array in which the data is to be selected be unsorted. Then linear search is used for selection. The array is searched from the first, comparing each element with the selection element until the desired selection element or sub list is found. The time complexity of this algorithm is O(kn) where k is the kth smallest or k^{th} largest element to be detected.

```
Algorithm sequential_select(a[n],k)

forifrom 1 to k mIndex
= i mValue = a[i]

for j from i+1 to n if
a[j] <mValue mIndex =
j mValue = a[j]

exchange a[i] and a[mIndex]

return a[k]
```

This locates the kth smallest element in a much easier way.

Partition Based Selection Algorithm

Selection is most complex if the data is not sorted. First we proceed by sorting the data. There are several sorting techniques like heap sort, quick sort, bubble sort and so on. The complexity of such algorithm ranges from O(nlogn) to O(n^2). We ignore the bubble sort and heap sort since they are not suitable in detecting the data. The quick sort plays a major role in selection.

In quick selection we have a routine called partition which places the key such a way that to the left of the key all elements are less and to the right of the key all elements are greater. Then it is sufficient at every step to migrate to either left half or right half. Thus the time taken for locating the selection element is O(logn). This will be comparable to the sequential selection method explained above when k is very large. Quick selection method is hence advantageous because in selection we follow only one half in contrast to quick sort method. The algorithms are written below.

```
        function partition(a[], lt, rt, pIn-
            dex) pValue := a[pIndex]

exchange a[pIndex] and a[rt] sIndex
 := lt

 for i from lt to rt-1

if a[i] <pValue

swap a[sIndex] and a[i] incrementsIn-
 dex

swap a[rt] and a[sIndex]

 returnsIndex

 function select(a[], lt, rt, k)

 loop

select pIndex between lt and rt pNewIndex
 := partition(a, lt, rt, pIndex) pDist :=
pNewIndex - lt + 1

if pDist = k

 return a[pNewIndex]

 else if k <pDist

rt := pNewIndex - 1

 else

k := k - pDist

lt := pNewIndex + 1
```

The quick selection algorithm depends upon the pivot that is chosen. If good pivots are there the algoirthm could run better. If bad pivots are consistently chosen the selection will take the worst case time. The sequential selection algorithm finds application in many computer areas like mining, prediction and so on.

Parallel Selection Algorithm

Parallel Selection algorithm is applicable for selecting the kth element in the very large array. The parallel selection uses n processors to select the desired data. Generally it is assumed that there is randomized distribution of data to n processors. The algorithm does not depend upon the number of data distributed to the processors, nor the values distributed. The input to the processor is from the array A and output is the element selected from array A with the rank i.

The selection algorithm for rank k assumes that input data A of size n are distributed uniformly across the p processors, such that each processor holds n/p elements. The output, namely the element from X with rank k, is returned on each processor. The randomized selection algorithm locates the element of rank k by pruning the set of candidate elements using the iterative procedure as explained below:

Two splitter elements (s_1,s_2) are chosen that partition the input into three groups, $A_0, A_1,$ and $A_2,$ such that each element in A_0 is less than s_1, each element in A_1 lies between s_1 and s_2 and each in A_2 is greater than s_2. The desire is to have the middle group A_1 much smaller than the outer two groups with the condition that the selection index lies within this middle group. The process is repeated iteratively on the group holding the selection index until the size of the group is small enough, whereby the remaining elements are gathered onto a single processor and the problem is solved sequentially. The key to this approach is choosing splitters s_1 and s_2 that minimize the size of the middle group while maximizing the probability of the condition that the selection index lies within this group. Splitters are chosen from a random sample of the input, by finding a pair of elements of certain rank in the sample. The algorithm is written below.

Fast Randomized Algorithm for Processor P_i Input

```
n - Total number of elements

p - Total number of processors, labeled from 0 to p - 1

A_i - List of elements on processor P_i, where |A_i | = n/p

C-A constant

ξ- log_n of the sample size

τ- Selection coefficient

s- selection coefficient  multiplier

ŋ- Min/Max constant

rank-desired rank among the elements

begin

Set ni = n/p

    While (n > C) and (|n - rank| > ŋ)

            Collect a sample S_i  from A_i by picking ni  elements at
            random on P_i .

            S = Gather(S_i, p).

            Set z = TRUE and select τ

            While (z ≡ TRUE)
```

On P0

Select s1, s2 from S with the appropriate ranks

Broadcast s1 and s2.

Partition A_i into < s1 and [s1, s2], and > s2, to give counts less,

middle,

(and high). Only save the elements that lie in the middle partition.

C_{less} = Combine(less,+);

C_{mid} = Combine(middle,+);

If (rank $\in$ (C_{less}, C_{less} + C_{mid}])

$n = C_{mid}$;

n_i = middle;

rank = rank − C_{less} ;

z = FALSE

Else

On P0: τ =s . τ

Endif

Endwhile

Endwhile

If (|n − rank|<= ŋ) then

If rank<= ŋ then the "minimum" approach is used, otherwise, the "maximum"

approach in parentheses, as follows is used.

Sequentially sort our ni elements in nondecreasing (nonincreasing) order using a modified insertion sort with output size $|A_i|$ = min(rank, n_i)

($|A_i|$ = min(n−rank+1, n_i)). An element that is greater (less) than the Li minimum (maximum) elements is discarded.

Gather the p sorted subsequences onto P0.

```
    Using a p-way tournament tree of losers constructed from the p
    sorted subsequences, (rank) (n - rank + 1) elements are extracted,
    to find the element q with selection index rank

Else

    A = Gather(A_i).

On P0

    Perform sequential selection to find element q of rank in L;

Endif

    result = Broadcast(q).
```

The parallel selection algorithm finds its application in image processing for computer vision and remote sensing, computational aerodynamics and data mining of large databases. The algorithm can be implemented in shared memory system and cluster systems.

References

- Blum, M.; Floyd, R. W.; Pratt, V. R.; Rivest, R. L.; Tarjan, R. E. (August 1973). "Time bounds for selection" (PDF). Journal of Computer and System Sciences. 7 (4): 448–461. doi:10.1016/S0022-0000(73)80033-9

- Donald Knuth. The Art of Computer Programming, Volume 3: Sorting and Searching, Third Edition. Addison-Wesley, 1997. ISBN 0-201-89685-0. Section 5.3.3: Minimum-Comparison Selection, pp. 207–219

- Floyd, R. W.; Rivest, R. L. (March 1975). "Expected time bounds for selection". Communications of the ACM. 18 (3): 165–172. doi:10.1145/360680.360691

- Kiwiel, K. C. (2005). "On Floyd and Rivest's SELECT algorithm". Theoretical Computer Science. 347: 214–238. doi:10.1016/j.tcs.2005.06.032

- Thomas H. Cormen, Charles E. Leiserson, Ronald L. Rivest, and Clifford Stein. Introduction to Algorithms, Second Edition. MIT Press and McGraw-Hill, 2001. ISBN 0-262-03293-7. Chapter 9: Medians and Order Statistics, pp. 183–196. Section 14.1: Dynamic order statistics, pp. 302–308

Permissions

We would like to thank the editorial team for lending their expertise to make the book truly unique. They have played a crucial role in the development of this book. Without their invaluable contributions this book wouldn't have been possible. They have made vital efforts to compile up to date information on the varied aspects of this subject to make this book a valuable addition to the collection of many professionals and students.

This book was conceptualized with the vision of imparting up-to-date and integrated information in this field. To ensure the same, a matchless editorial board was set up. Every individual on the board went through rigorous rounds of assessment to prove their worth. After which they invested a large part of their time researching and compiling the most relevant data for our readers.

The editorial board has been involved in producing this book since its inception. They have spent rigorous hours researching and exploring the diverse topics which have resulted in the successful publishing of this book. They have passed on their knowledge of decades through this book. To expedite this challenging task, the publisher supported the team at every step. A small team of assistant editors was also appointed to further simplify the editing procedure and attain best results for the readers.

Apart from the editorial board, the designing team has also invested a significant amount of their time in understanding the subject and creating the most relevant covers. They scrutinized every image to scout for the most suitable representation of the subject and create an appropriate cover for the book.

The publishing team has been an ardent support to the editorial, designing and production team. Their endless efforts to recruit the best for this project, has resulted in the accomplishment of this book. They are a veteran in the field of academics and their pool of knowledge is as vast as their experience in printing. Their expertise and guidance has proved useful at every step. Their uncompromising quality standards have made this book an exceptional effort. Their encouragement from time to time has been an inspiration for everyone.

The publisher and the editorial board hope that this book will prove to be a valuable piece of knowledge for students, practitioners and scholars across the globe.

Index

A

Asymptotic Notations, 90

B

Binary Trees, 68, 182
Block Diagonal Matrices, 129
Block Matrix Inversion, 129
Block Toeplitz Matrices, 130
Block Tridiagonal Matrices,
130

C

Color Palette, 148-151
Computability Theory, 57, 180
Computational Efficiency, 162
Computer Language, 24
Connection Architecture, 96
Conservative Synchronization, 142
Cryptographic Algorithms, 34

D

Daisy Chain, 118, 122
Data Parallelism, 12-13, 41-46
Diagonal Blocks, 129, 131
Digital Audio, 143-144
Digital Photography, 148
Digital Processing, 144
Direct Sum, 129, 131
Discrete Event Simulation, 133, 140-141
Discrete States, 35
Distributed Algorithms, 4, 29-30, 56
Distributed Bus, 119
Distributed Star, 120
Dither, 133, 143-148, 152, 154, 176
DNS Delegation, 7
Dominant Balance, 80
Dynamic Programming, 32-33, 57, 90

E

Echelon Form, 157-164, 172
Enumeration Sort, 183-184
Enumerative Combinatorics, 177, 180, 200
Euclid Algorithms, 27

E

Expressing Algorithms, 18
Expressive Power, 74
Extended Star, 120

F

Fully Connected Network, 121, 124

G

Gaussian Elimination, 157, 160-163, 172, 174, 176
Generative Recursion, 60-61
Granularity Spectrum, 156

H

Hash Partitioning, 136
Heterogeneous Computing, 106
Hybrid Algorithm, 55-56, 70, 73, 198
Hybrid Models, 15, 77
Hypercube Network, 124

I

Image Processing, 29, 148, 151
Indirect Recursion, 60, 70
Inelegant Program, 24
Infinite Asymptotics, 84
Infinitesimal Asymptotics, 84-85
Instruction Pipelining, 103, 107

K

Knuth Definition, 93

L

Linear Bus, 119
Linear Mapping, 131
Linear Programming, 31, 165
Load Balancing, 4, 6-8, 11-14, 45, 134-135

M

Master-Slave Model, 14
Matrix Multiplication, 13, 42-43, 114, 117, 125, 128, 131, 156
Mechanical Contrivances, 35
Mesh Network, 11, 114
Multiple Recursion, 59-60, 73
Multiprocessor System, 42, 46

N

Network Topology, 117-120, 124

O

Optimistic Synchronization, 142

Ordinal Enumeration, 179

P

Parallel Algorithm, 3-4, 12-13, 15, 77, 97, 114

Parallel Query, 133-134

Parallel Relational Operators, 136

Parallel Systems, 1-2, 97, 140

Parallelizability, 3

Partially Connected Network, 122

Performance Metrics, 97

Pipeline Bubble, 112

Predictability, 111

Processor Array, 100, 113, 189

Producer-Consumer Model, 14

Programming Environments, 45-46

Q

Quantum Algorithm, 30

Quantum Entanglement, 30

Quantum Superposition, 30

R

Randomized Algorithm, 31, 214

Range Index Partitioning, 136

Recursive Functions, 57, 60-61, 65, 74-75

Recursive Programs, 61, 74

Round Robin Partitioning, 136

S

Search Engine, 40, 204

Self-Modifying Programs, 110

Semaphores, 49, 51, 53-54

Shared Disk Architecture, 134-135

Shared Memory Architectures, 134

Shared Nothing Architectures, 134-135

Shortcut Rule, 76

Shortest Path Bridging, 7, 11, 98-99, 124, 132

Stack Space, 74

Structural Recursion, 60-61, 67

Supercomputers, 102-103, 105, 113

T

Task Graph Model, 13, 77

Task Parallelism, 13, 41, 44-47

Time Warp Algorithm, 142

U

Uninterruptible Instructions, 110

Uniprocessor Systems, 1

V

Vector Instructions, 102, 105

W

Waveform Analysis, 144

Weight-Driven Clock, 35

Work Pool Model, 13-14, 77

Wraparound Connection, 114

Wrapper Function, 70-72